Animoji	65
Wireless Charging	67
Pricing	68
Lock Screen and Home Screen	**70**
iPhone Power Button Changes	**73**
Home Screen	**76**
The Dock	76
Screenshots	**79**
Screenshot Editing	81
Cropping	*81*
The Toolbar	*82*
Undo and Redo	83
Additional Tools	83
Text Function	84
Signature	84
Magnifier	85
Sharing and Finishing	*87*
Screenshot Tips	87
Final Thoughts on Instant Markup	87
Drag and Drop	**89**
Multitasking on the iPad	91
Grouping Applications	93
Multitasking Plus Drag and Drop	95
Drag and Drop on the iPhone & iPod Touch	96
Final Thoughts on Drag and Drop	97

iCloud Drive App	**99**
Files App	**100**
Recents	101
Browse	102
Recently Deleted	*103*
Favorites	*104*
Tags	*104*
Creating a new tag.	105
Rearranging Items	*105*
Moving Files	*107*
Process 1: Traditional Method	107
Process 2: Drag and Drop	107
Files app and the Keyboard	108
Closing Thoughts on Files.app	108
Control Center	**110**
The New Look	111
Customizing Control Center	111
System Functions	113
Control Center System Functions	*114*
Music in Control Center	116
Screen Mirroring	116
Apple TV Remote	117
Volume Adjustment and Brightness	119
Camera in Control Center	120
Home in Control Center	121

iOS 11, tvOS 11, and watchOS 4 for Users and Developers — 15

Revision History — 15
Preface — 16
Other Works — 18
iBooks — 18
ePub — 18
Introduction — 19
Looking Back at the iPhone — 19
iOS 10.1 to iOS 10.3 — 25
iOS 10.1 — 26
Transit — 27
iOS 10.2 — 28
TV app — 29
iOS 10.3 — 30
Apple File System — 31
iOS 11 — 33
Incompatible Devices — 33
32-bit App Support — 34
Listing of 32-Bit apps — 35
Compatible Devices — 37
iPhones — 37
iPad — 37
iPad Pro — 37
iPods — 37

New Devices	**38**
New Macs	38
New iPads	39
2nd Generation iPad Pro	*40*
ProMotion	*42*
HomePod	42
Fall Event	45
Apple Watch	*46*
Hardware Changes	47
Bands	48
Apple Watch Colors	50
Apple TV	50
iPhones	53
iPhone 8 and 8 Plus	*53*
Processor	54
Screen	55
Battery	56
Pricing	*56*
iPhone X	56
Colors	*57*
Internals	*58*
Home Button	*59*
Biometrics	*59*
TrueDepth Camera	*60*
The Screen	*62*
Camera	*64*

Timers	122
Accessibility in Control Center	123
Notes	125
New Features	128
Screen Recording	*128*
Do Not Disturb While Driving	*130*
Customizing Do Not Disturb While Driving	132
Final Thoughts on Control Center	133
App Groups on iPad	**135**
Siri	**137**
Siri Data	137
Siri's Voice	138
Translations	138
Additional Siri Capabilities	140
New Design Elements	**142**
App Store Under iOS 10	**144**
App Store On iOS 11	**146**
Today	146
Games	148
Apps	149
Updates	149
Search	152
App Pages	152
Purchasing Content	154

Final Thoughts on the App Store Redesign 155

Messages — 157
Display of iMessage Apps — 157
Management of iMessage Apps — 159
Enhanced Interactions — 160
Person to Person Apple Pay — 160
Apple Pay Cash — 160
Business Chat — 162
Additional Screen Effects — 162
Final Thoughts on Messages — 164

Apple Pay Changes — 165

Camera — 166
Filters — 166
QR Codes — 169

Notes — 171
Tables — 171
Text Choices — 173
Pinned Notes — 174
Scanning Documents — 175
Quick Handwriting — 177
Optical Character Recognition — 178
Final Thoughts on Notes — 179

Music — 180
Sharing Music — 181

Setting Up Your Profile	182
Your Profile Page	185
Adding or Removing Playlists	186
Method 1:	186
Method 2:	187
Items to Note	188
Finding Friends	188
Sharing Your Profile	189
Final Thoughts on Sharing	190
Curated Playlists	190
My Chill Mix	191
MusicKit	192
Accounts and Passwords	**193**
Autofill for Username and Passwords	193
Keyboard Improvements	**196**
Photos	**198**
Facial Recognition	198
Live Photos	199
Media File Formats	201
High Efficiency Image Format	202
High Efficiency Video Codec	203
Impact on Users	203
Final Thoughts on Photos	204
Weather	**205**
Home	**208**

Entering or Leaving	209
Other Home app Changes	210
Safari	**212**
Intelligent Tracking Prevention	212
Action Taken	*213*
Autoplay	214
Video Player Changes	214
Insecure Connections	215
Reader Mode Enhancements	217
Final Thoughts on Safari	218
Calculator	**220**
Other System Refinements	**221**
Settings	221
iCloud Settings	221
Family Sharing of iCloud Storage	*222*
Cellular	225
Notifications	225
General Settings	228
Accessibility	*228*
Verbosity	*228*
Braille	*230*
Audio	*230*
Display Accommodations	*230*
Subtitles and Captioning	*231*
Final Thoughts on Accessibility Changes	*231*

Device Storage	232
Background App Refresh	234
Restrictions	234
Dictionary	235
Shutdown	235
Siri and Search	235
Touch ID and Passcode	236
iTunes and App Store	236
Mail	237
Notes	237
News	237
Photos and Camera	237
Social Media Accounts	237
Final Thoughts on Settings Changes	238
Swift Playgrounds	**239**
Quick Setup	**240**
Augmented Reality	**241**
Machine Learning	**243**
Final Thoughts on iOS 11 for Users	**244**
watchOS	**246**
watchOS 1 to watchOS 3	246
watchOS 4	248
User Interface	*248*
Watch Faces	*249*

Kaleidoscope	249
Toy Story	250
Siri	251
The Dock	*252*
Dock Modes	253
Workouts	*254*
New Workout Type	254
Other Workout Interface Changes	255
Enhanced Swimming	255
Do Not Disturb	256
Gym Equipment	256
Coaching	256
Goals	256
Final Thoughts on Workouts	258
Music	*259*
New Music Design	259
Now Playing Complication	260
Other watchOS Enhancements	*262*
Apple Pay Cash	262
News app	262
File System	262
Final Thoughts on watchOS	*263*

tvOS 264

Right-to-Left Language Support 264

App Sizes 264

Dark Mode Changes 265

Home Screen 265

Final Thoughts on tvOS 11   266

iOS 11, tvOS 11, and watchOS 4 Developer Changes   267

Swift 3.2   267

Swift 4   269

Private Extensions to a class   269

Functions with Classes and Protocols   270

Rewritten Strings functions   272

Substring   273

Unicode   274

Xcode 9   275

Source Control   275

Other Source Control Features   *278*

Source Control Navigator   *278*

Branching   *280*

Tags   *281*

Remotes   *282*

Final Thoughts on GitHub Integration   282

Xcode Server   283

Other Xcode 9 Changes   286

Downloading Profiles   286

Simulator Changes   287

Code Editor Window   289

Markdown Support   *289*

Refactoring Swift   *290*

Assets	*292*
P3 Color Gamut	*292*
Colors	*293*
Color Sets	*295*
Using a Named Color	*297*
P3 Colors on the Web	*297*
Developing on iOS	**298**
Setting up Wireless Development	298
Final Thought on Xcode Changes	301
APFS Changes	**302**
Unicode Variants	302
Normalization Schemes	303
AirPlay 2	**305**
MusicKit	**307**
ARKit	**310**
Metal 2	**312**
CoreML	**316**
Converting Models	317
Drag and Drop	**319**
Drag Interaction	*320*
Dropping Items	321
Performing the Actual Drop	322
Final Thoughts on Drag and Drop	323
Networking Changes	**324**

Network Stack Changes 325
New Network Extensions 327
Final Thoughts on Networking Changes 328

Final Thoughts on iOS 11 for Developers 329

watchOS 4 for Developers 331

Groups 331
Water Lock 331
Autorotate 333
Paging Views 333
Setting a Page Index 334
Other watchOS Changes 334
SceneKit and SpriteKit 335
Workouts 335
CoreBluetooth 335
Final Thoughts on watchOS 4 for Developers 335

tvOS 11 for Developers 337

On Demand Resources 337
Right to Left Language Support 338
Safe Areas 338
Opting Out of Safe Area Insets 339
Notifications on tvOS 11 340
Wireless Development 341
Final Thoughts on tvOS 11 for Developers 343

Final Thoughts on iOS 11, tvOS 11, and watchOS 4 344

iOS 11, tvOS 11, and watchOS 4 for Users and Developers

Revision History

1.0	9/19/2017	Initial Release
1.0.1	9/24/2017	Fixed typographical issues

Preface

iOS is now entering double digits in terms of age. In that time it has evolved significantly in the intervening decade. The largest improvements have come not only in hardware or software. On a personal level, the last decade has been a whirlwind tour of a variety of things. For specifics, contact me on twitter or via email.

I wrote my first e-book in 2012, five years ago. That was for OS X 10.8 Mountain Lion Client as well as Server. It was all combined into one book. The impetus for writing it was not only the need of a creative outlet, but also the fact that I enjoyed using Apple's platforms. The OS X 10.8 Mountain Lion book was also a chance to use the new, at that time, iBooks Author application to create a book.

Since 2012, I have written e-books for each new version macOS as well as iOS, with the exception of iOS 7, which was only due to a time crunch. It was not my first reviews of new OS X versions, I actually wrote a review for Mac OS X 10.7 Lion Server for a website that I used to contribute to.

Each new e-book seems to get a bit longer, which in some respects make sense given that each new operating system builds upon its predecessors. My smallest e-book is just over 20,000 words at 20,352 words. That was the OS X 10.9 Mavericks book.

If you add up the total word count in all of my books, excluding this one and my macOS High Sierra for Users, Administrators, and Developers book. The total word count comes to 242,889. That's almost a quarter million words. Now, if you add the macOS High Sierra for Users, Administrators, and Developers, you get to 279,187 words. There are just shy of 35,300 words in that book.

This book, dwarfs all of my other books, by a wide margin. There are 73,663 words in this book. Without any images, and before any formatting for e-pub, this book is 150 pages, again without any formatting. This means it will only be longer once it is actually formatted. This means that the book you are reading is more than twice as long as compared to my iOS 10 e-book, which was the previous winner for length of an e-book.

iOS 11 is one of the largest updates that iOS has seen to date. So it would make complete sense that this book would be the largest. A breakdown of the User section, compared to the developer section for my iOS books is 2.32 to 1, where the user sections are more than twice as large as the developer sections.

I generally breakdown my iOS books into two sections, Users and Developers, hence the title of the books. As Apple has added new platforms, like watchOS and tvOS, I have attempted to incorporate those into the e-books as well. In the past I did not do so well in including watchOS and tvOS developer information. As a matter of fact, in my iOS 10 book, there was nothing directly for tvOS and watchOS. This has been rectified with this book, although it is nowhere near the same size as the behemoth the iOS Developer section. Despite this there are two sections one dedicated to tvOS and one dedicated to watchOS.

This year I did something a bit different when it came to writing my books. I kept track of the amount of time that was spent on each of my two books this year. For this book, there were a total of 98 hours and 45 minutes of writing and editing. This does not count the time to put in the images and gathering those nor does it include formatting of the books. The was another 38 hours and 30 minutes. This brings the grand total for information gathering, writing, editing, and formatting to 171 hours and 45 minutes.

If you gain any value from the book, tell your friends, family, and share on social media and also purchase any of my e-books, or the paperbacks. If I forgot anything, which truth be told I most likely did, or if there are any corrections let me know.

Wayne Dixon
books@waynedixon.com
http://www.twitter.com/waynedixon

Other Works

iBooks

iOS 8 for Users and Developers
iOS 9 for Users and Developers
iOS 10 for Users and Developers
iOS 11, tvOS 11, and watchOS 4 for Users and Developers

OS X 10.8 Mountain Lion and Mountain Lion Server Review
OS X 10.9 Mavericks Client and Server Review
OS X 10.10 Yosemite for Users, Administrators, and Developers
OS X 10.11 El Capitan for Users, Administrators, and Developers
macOS Sierra for Users, Administrators, and Developers
macOS High Sierra for Users, Administrators, and Developers

ePub

iOS 6: A History and Review
iOS 8 for Users and Developers
iOS 9 for Users and Developers
iOS 10 for Users and Developers
iOS 11, tvOS 11, and watchOS 4 for Users and Developers

OS X 10.9 Mavericks Client and Server Review
OS X 10.10 Yosemite for Users, Administrators, and Developers
OS X 10.11 El Capitan for Users, Administrators, and Developers
macOS Sierra for Users, Administrators, and Developers
macOS High Sierra for Users, Administrators, and Developers

Introduction

2017 marks the tenth anniversary of iOS. It was way back in January of 2007 when the iPhone was first unveiled to the world by Steve Jobs.

Looking Back at the iPhone

The iPhone has now made it to a decade. There is a famous quote from then Microsoft CEO Steve Ballmer, that states "There's no chance that the iPhone is going to get any significant market share." There is a second quote, from 2006 with Palm's CEO Ed Colligan, "We've learned and struggled for a few years here figuring out how to make a decent phone ... PC guys are not going to just figure this out, They're not going to just walk in." As you might have been able to guess, both of these predictions ended up being wrong.

When iOS was first shown the public in January of 2007, nobody could really image just how far it would come in just a decade. iOS has grown to encompass more than just the iPhone. It has come to encompass iPhones, iPod Touches, and iPads. There are two other systems that are cousins of iOS, they are tvOS and watchOS. It is well known by now that the original multitouch device that Apple was developing was a tablet. The tablet, in the form of the iPad, would be unveiled in January of 2010 and released in April of the same year.

The year 2007 was a seminal year for me, in many respects, but particularly in regards to technology. 2007 was the year that I joined Twitter, switched to the Mac, and got my first smart phone, the original iPhone.

Twitter is my preferred social network. It is the one that I get the most benefit from. I am on a few social networks, but Twitter is my go to. In March of 2007, I bought my first 20-inch iMac. I made that decision after I had installed Windows Vista on a PC that would have the video drivers crash every five minutes. That is not hyperbole. They would actually crash after five minutes. One thing

for Vista, it did not crash the computer, just restarted the desktop window manager, but for all intents and purposes it crashed..

That iMac would be the start of my foray into being super productive with technology. Along with my first smart phone, I also bought my first laptop, all in 2007. 2007 was a somewhat expensive year for me.

I was not there on day one to get a phone. Instead, I was there on day two. June 30th, 2007. The original iPhone that I bought was the 4GB Model. I got up early to drive to the nearest Apple Store to wait until they opened. I remember the first time I really sat and used the iPhone, I knew that it would be a turning point, even with its limited functionality, by today's standards, the original iPhone was very limited. However, it has come a long way in the last decade. The original iPhone had a 3.5-inch screen, a 2G Data connection, and no camera. But man, that was a great device for the time. Even though the first iPhone was very limited in its capabilities, it was still a great device to hold, and a marvel of technological engineering.

The original iPhone was touted as being "A Widescreen iPod with touch controls, a Revolutionary mobile phone, and a Breakthrough Internet Communications device." Given the status of the phones at the time, it truly was a revolutionary device. While the original iPhone was truly revolutionary, and years ahead of the competition. It did not really become widely accepted until the following year, 2008.

iPhone OS 2.0 in 2008 included the most requested feature, third party applications. The ability for third-parties to create applications that would actually run on an iPhone was probably the tipping point for all modern computing. If it were not for the App Store, arriving when it did, it is possible that many of the technologies and features that we rely on today, may not have arrived until later than they have. The first iOS Twitter client, Tweetie, brought a new feature that would eventually be integrated into iOS itself, "Pull to Refresh". Given the platform, pull to refresh is very intuitive and fits naturally into the entire ecosystem.

iOS has grown to include a whole slew of features, a list that cannot be comprehensive, but does include: Multitasking, background audio, background app refresh, push notifications, split view, handwriting recognition, and syncing between devices, and so much more.

None of this would be possible without the push for more ubiquitous mobile internet. The original iPhone was $499 for a 4GB model, which was subsidized on the new AT&T network, which was formerly Cingular. Because data usage was expected to be low, and as a way to entice customers, AT&T offered Unlimited internet access on their new iPhones. In 2010, AT&T stopped offering their "Unlimited" plans to new customers. However, existing customers could keep their plans. At the end of 2015, AT&T indicated that they would be bringing back their Unlimited Plans. Technology does have its way of cycling back around.

The iPhone 3G, released in 2008, introduced a whole new speed bump, with faster 3G data connectivity and a 2.0 megapixel camera on the back. The iPhone 3GS, was all about speed, as it the internals got a significant boost. The iPhone 4 is probably one of the most iconic iPhones, with its all glass back and aluminum sides. Despite the sleek design, it may turn out to be the most controversial.

First, a prototype was lost in a bar and it had the infamous "Antenna-gate" issue. If you placed your hand around the antennas, the signal would degrade enough so that a phone call could be dropped. The iPhone 4 was also the model that first expanded beyond AT&T and the GSM standard. Verizon was added as a second carrier. This brought not only a redesign antenna system to the Verizon iPhone, but also CDMA to the iPhone. The iPhone 4 was also the first phone to come in another color besides black. It came in a white option, although much later due to manufacturing issues.

The iPhone 4 was a phone that some could consider the first of the modern iPhones. This is because the iPhone 4 is the first iPhone to use an entirely custom Apple-designed system on a chip. By using a custom designed chip, Apple could closely integrate the hardware and software, which would ultimately provide a user experience that could not be rivaled, and still has not been so to date. The second reason is that it was the first iPhone with a flat back. The original iPhone, the iPhone 3G, and iPhone 3GS all had rounded backs.

The third reason iPhone 4 brought a new "Retina" screen to the iPhone. This was double the pixel density of previous models. To date, all of the iPhones after the iPhone 4 have all had flat backs. They may have had different materials, but they have been flat backed.

The iPhone 4s adopted the antenna redesign but also ushered in a new era, with the Siri voice assistant. Siri, while limited at its launch, has grown to be of significant use to a number of users.

The iPhone 5 brought its own features to the iPhone line. It was the first phone to go beyond the standard 3.5-inch size. It was a 4-inch model. It was the same width, just a different height. The iPhone 5 brought with it a new type of connector, lightning. Since the original iPod in 2001, the portable consumers products that Apple produced included the 30-pin dock connector. This was the start of the transition, which is still in use today.

The iPhone 5s, brought with it a new internal processor, as has each iPhone revision. This one, however, was a bit different. It was the first 64-bit ARM processor that was used by Apple, and one of the first 64-bit ARM-based processors on the market. At the time, it caught everyone by surprise because it was widely considered impractical to use a 64-bit processor, when 32-bit was sufficient. The primary benefit of a 64-bit processor was the ability to go above 4 gigabytes of memory. iPhones, until then had run at most 1 gigabyte of RAM, and that was only the iPhone 5 that had 1 gigabyte. The iPhone 4 and 4S had 512 megabytes, The iPhone 3GS had 512 megabytes, the iPhone 3G only 256 megabytes, and the original iPhone with 128 megabytes. It was not until the iPhone 6s, in 2015 that an iPhone got more than 1 gigabyte of memory.

The 64-bit processor has allowed Apple to create faster hardware as well as set itself up for the future. The iPhone 6 released in 2014, went beyond what had been done to bring a whole new size to the iPhone. Gone were the days of the 4-inch phone, and welcome to the 4.7-inch and 5.5-inch phones. This was the first time that Apple had created two sizes of phones for a new Phone release. The iPhone 6 Plus was the first iPhone to have a 1080p screen. This means that you could watch a Blu-ray quality movie on your iPhone. The iPhone 6s and 6s Plus increased the memory to 2 gigabytes and added a new color option, Rose Gold.

The iPhone 7 and iPhone 7 Plus brought even better cameras, in particular with the iPhone 7 Plus where the new dual-lens camera system allows for Portrait photos with a Bokeh depth effect to be taken. The iPhone 7 Plus also has 3 gigabytes of memory. This memory and speed all allow for super fast usage as well as being able to have as little lag as possible.

Just as with hardware, software does not stand still once it is released. There are bug fixes as well as security updates for every new version of iOS. Let us begin by looking at some of the changes that have occurred between the last released version of iOS, iOS 10, and the current release.

iOS 10.1 to iOS 10.3

When Apple releases a version of iOS or macOS, they do not stop after the initial release. They add new versions to fix bugs and add features. Typically Apple releases three or four minor versions after their initial release of an iOS version. With iOS 10, Apple has released three subsequent updates. Every update contains security fixes, but there are usually a couple of new features beyond those. Let us look at the new features in each of these versions.

iOS 10.1

Apple added a couple new features to iOS 10.1. The biggest draw for the iPhone is its camera. This has not always been the case. In particular, iPhone, iPhone 3G, and iPhone 3GS were all mediocre cameras when they were released. While the iPhone 4's camera indicated that Apple was taking photography a bit more seriously, it was the iPhone 4s that really made the iPhone a replacement for a traditional point and shoot camera.

At their September 2016 event, Apple unveiled their new iPhones, the iPhone 7 and iPhone 7 Plus. There was one major feature of the iPhone 7 Plus that was not ready in time for the initial launch of iOS 10. That feature is Portrait Mode.

Portrait Mode uses the dual cameras on the iPhone 7 Plus to be able to create a bokeh-like effect. The bokeh effect provides a blurred background while focusing on the object in the foreground. Portrait Mode is designed for faces, however it will work on other objects as well.

A couple of examples are below.

iOS 10.1 added a feature that would identify people's faces within the Photos app. One of the problems with this is that the information is not synchronized between devices. The reason this is the case is that one of Apple's core tenets: customer privacy. With iOS 10.1, Apple loosened this restriction, a little bit. The people's names are now synchronized to iCloud. This means that should you need to restore, the people will be correctly identified.

Transit

When the iPhone was originally released, it included Google Maps for being able to use location services and be able to locate where you are located. With iOS 6, Apple introduced a new mapping application, Apple Maps. With Apple Maps. Apple has added transit directions. iOS 10.1 added transit information for Tokyo, Osaka, and Nagoya. This information train, subway, ferry, and even national and local bus lines.

iOS 10.2

iOS 10.2 also added some new features. The first big user-facing feature is an all new set of Emoji. The Emoji included new faces, food, animals, sports and professions. This is the case with iOS 10.2.

Emoji have not been without its share of controversy. For instance, in iOS 10.2, Apple changed the gun emoji to be a water pistol instead. The decision to change this was because the gun emoji was being used towards others. Given the issues with guns in the U.S., and across the world, Apple made the decision to change the emoji. While this was controversial, it was not the emoji that caused the biggest uproar.

Emoji allows individuals to express certain things in pictures instead of words. The primary Emoji, that I encounter, that are used to express a certain sentiment are the following:

The one that created the most controversy was actually the Peach. In iOS 10, the Peach looked like it did under iOS 9. With iOS 10.2, beta 1, Apple changed the Peach to look more like, well, a Peach. This change did not go over well with Apple community. This is due to the Peach emoji not always being used to indicate a Peach, but often as something else. However, even with the controversy the new Emoji were not the only feature of iOS 10.2.

One of the major enhancements to iOS 10 was the features of Messages. In iOS 10, Messages added a couple of new features. One of these was some full-screen effects. These effects allow for being able to give even more texture to your messaging conversations. The full-screen effects that were shipped with iOS 10 included: Balloons, Confetti, Lasers, Fireworks, an Shooting Stars. iOS 10.2 added two more: Love and Celebration.

The "Love" effect will produce a large heart. This heart will be somewhat transparent and reflect some of the previous items in the large heart.

The Celebration effect will shower down some large yellow glitter from the upper right corner of the screen. The glitter will take some time, but it will slowly fall to the ground.

TV app

The biggest addition to iOS 10.2 was the TV app. TV was debuted by Apple at their September event. The TV app allows Apple to suggest TV shows and Movies that you might want to watch next. This is done by analyzing your library, connecting applications and uses your viewing history to suggest what you may want to watch next. Along with this, it also will provide you with the next episode of a series that you have been watching previously. Alongside this, you can also browse your purchased TV Shows and movies from right within the App.

The TV app is not just for the Apple TV, but also for iOS devices, like the iPhone and iPad. The TV app replaced the "Videos" app on iOS devices.

iOS 10.3

iOS 10.3 has also added a couple of new features. Have you been using an application and then all of sudden, out of the blue, you get a popup asking to rate or review. If you tap on "No" or "Not Now", many applications will respect this and not ask again; at least for a while. However, there are many applications that will not respect this and constantly ask. To combat this, Apple has made a change with iOS 10.3. With iOS 10.3 Apple has introduced a new Reviews API.

The Reviews API is a new method for allowing developers to request ratings. With this new framework, Apple allows developer to request a rating, up to three times per year.

A user should not see a ratings request no more than three times in a twelve-month period. Developers cannot specify exactly when the popup will appear, but can simply request it. Even with it being less likely that users will be shown a request for a review, users do have the ability to turn off the request for ratings entirely. When this is done, developers will not have any indication that the users are not actually seeing the popups.

Alongside this, developers now have the ability to respond to ratings given by users. This is not a threaded conversation, since a developer will be able to respond once to a rating/review, and the reviewer will be able to respond to the developer's response, just once. This is intended to allow a developer to respond directly to their customers, without making it a support system. This will also help in allowing other see what the developer is thinking, particularly if there is an issue. This is possible since all replies are public.

Apple File System

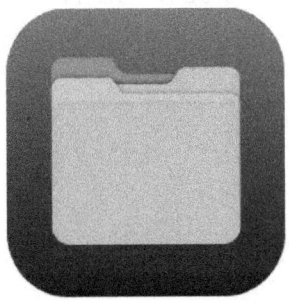

The biggest change in iOS 10.3 was probably not even noticed by most users. When a user updated to iOS 10.3, the underlying file structure was updated to the Apple File System, or APFS. There are many benefits to APFS, but the biggest is that iOS devices may gain a significant amount of space back.

APFS is a modern file system that is designed with solid-state drives in mind, which is in all iOS devices. Even with solid-state drives being the primary focus, due their future-looking nature, it can still handle spinning hard drives, as ones found in Macs. APFS has some new features that will be beneficial in the future. These features include, Clones, Snapshots, Encryption, and Data Integrity.

There is one issue that arose for some applications with the upgrade to APFS. The issue was with the way some applications handled file names. Some of these items could not be read, or would cause the application to crash. Most of the affected applications were updated and the issue was rectified. A more permanent fix will come in a future iOS version, likely iOS 12.

One thing that you may not be aware regarding APFS was that Apple was doing test runs for conversion beginning with iOS 10. The actual conversion was never performed, but there was a test. This test was done to be able to report back to Apple regarding any possible issues. These tests allowed the conversion to APFS to successfully run on millions of devices, most of these without any knowledge of the user.

Now that the features of iOS 10.1 through 10.3 have been discussed, we can move onto all of the new features of iOS 11, which are extensive.

iOS 11

Every version of iOS will bring a set of new features, iOS 11 does this in spades, particularly for the iPad, which, to some, had seemed to be neglected by Apple. This has very much been rectified with iOS 11.

The focus of iOS 11 has been the iPad. Some of the new features include, Drag and Drop, enhanced split view, application groups, Files.app, and ProMotion. There have also been a bunch of other changes that will help not only iPad users, but also iPhone and iPod touch users as well.

Before we dive into all of the new features, let us look at the compatible devices, this is vitally important since it will be determine if your current device will be able to run iOS 11.

Incompatible Devices

Each new release of iOS brings the possibility that some older devices will not longer be capable of running the latest operating system. The reason why these devices may not be compatible can include: not enough memory, chipsets in these devices, or even just general performance concerns with the latest operating system.

The introduction of iOS 11 does mean the end for some older devices. In particular, the iPhone 5, the iPhone 5c, and the iPad 4th Generation. These devices all have lightning connectors, they are not the first devices that have a lightning connector to no longer be compatible with iOS, that honor belongs to the iPod touch, 5th Generation. However, this group of devices are all 32-bit devices. These are the last of the 32-bit iOS devices that Apple created. The removal of these devices actually has another side-effect, removal of 32-bit App support.

32-bit App Support

When the original iPhone was released in 2010, the processor was 32-bit only. The iOS line remained 32-bit only until 2013, when the iPhone 5s came with the 64-bit A7 chip. Until iOS 10, applications that were 32-bit only, namely those created before 2013, were still able to be run on iOS. With iOS 11, this is no longer the case, all 32-bit app support has been removed.

What does this mean? It's quite simple, you will not be able to run older applications and games on your device. When you attempt to run a 32-bit application you will be presented the following popup:

"First Aid" Needs to be Updated. The developer of this app needs to update it to work with iOS 11". Prior to publication they did update their app to work on iOS 11. There are two buttons, "Learn More" and "OK". Clicking on Learn More will bring up the application in the App Store. There is a caveat to this, the Learn More link will only work if the app is still available in the App Store. If it is not available, the link will not do anything. If the app is still in the App Store, you can contact the developer and inquire if they will be updating the application. Clicking on "OK" will close the dialog. There is an easy way to be able to find which applications will no longer be available under iOS 11.

Listing of 32-Bit apps

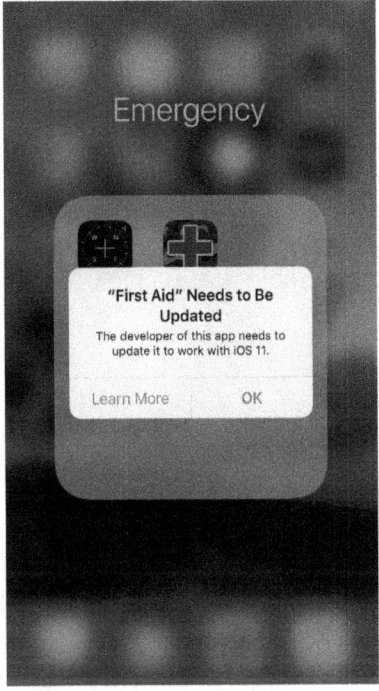

To list all of the 32-bit applications that are on your device, simply perform the following:

1. Open the Settings app
2. Tap on "General"
3. Tap on "About"
4. Tap on "Applications".

This will list out all of the 32-bit applications on your iOS devices. This can be done in iOS 10 as well as on iOS 11. If you cannot tap on "Applications", then your iOS device does not have any 32-bit applications installed on it.

When you upgrade from iOS 10 to iOS 11, the 32-bit apps will remain installed. However, if you are restoring from a backup, the applications will not actually install.

The removal of 32-bit applications does two things for Apple. First, it allows Apple to have smaller operating system sizes. This is because the 32-bit frameworks do not need to be installed on your device. Secondly, this allows the older applications that are currently in the App Store to be removed. This would be due to the fact that the apps are no longer being updated or maintained, which does not provide a good user experience. The last benefit of removing 32-bit applications and their operating system support will mean that development on future versions of iOS will be even easier. Even with the removal of 32-bit applications and devices, there are still some devices that are compatible. Let us look at these.

Compatible Devices

Despite the iPhone 5, iPhone 5c and 4th Generation iPad no longer being compatible, there are still a number of devices that are compatible. The devices that are compatible include:

iPhones
iPhone 5s
iPhone SE
iPhone 6
iPhone 6 Plus
iPhone 6s
iPhone 6s Plus
iPhone 7
iPhone 7 Plus
iPhone 8
iPhone 8 Plus
iPhone X

iPad
iPad Air
iPad Mini 2
iPad Air 2
iPad Mini 3
iPad Mini 4
9.7-inch 5th Generation iPad (2017)

iPad Pro
12.9-inch 1st Generation iPad Pro
9.7-inch iPad Pro
10.5-inch iPad Pro
12.9-inch 2nd Generation iPad Pro

iPods
6th Generation iPod Touch

All of these devices have at least the 64-bit A7 chip, and 1GB of RAM. This should allow for a nice iOS 11 experience on all of these devices.

New Devices

Apple can release products at any point throughout the year and people will absolutely report on it. This was not always the case though. Apple would have to use large events like MacWorld Expo to be able to garner a large enough audience. As Apple has grown beyond computers into consumer electronics, this has changed. The biggest announcement was, of course, the original iPhone back in January of 2007 at the MacWorld Expo. The iPhone shaped the way phones and technology in general, is handled be looked at, and likely will, for many years to come.

Apple has used its World Wide Developer Conference (WWDC), to unveil new products. The last time that they did this was actually 2013 when they released a refreshed MacBook Air, and unveiled the 2013 Mac Pro. Apple's WWDC presentations were sans hardware from 2014 to 2016. This shift was likely made for a couple of reasons. The first is to allow for plenty of hardware to announce at their Fall events. Starting in 2012, Apple began unveiling their flagship product, the iPhone, at their September event, instead of at WWDC where it had been unveiled since 2008. The second reason is that the products may not have been ready at that time, despite all of Apple's best efforts.

In 2017 though Apple went back to the tradition of unveiling new hardware at WWDC. They went back to this with gusto. One of the reasons to unveil new hardware at WWDC is because some of the changes in the hardware will directly affect developers, as is the case with this WWDC. Before we delve into the new iOS hardware, let us take a quick look at the new Macs that were unveiled.

New Macs

As the focus of this book is iOS, we will focus on that. But all of Apple's Macs were refreshed with the latest processors. The 27-inch 5K Retina iMac was refreshed to allow developers the ability to use external graphics cards, which can facilitate the development of Virtual Reality games. This included a demonstration of an iMac running at Star Wars interactive demo.

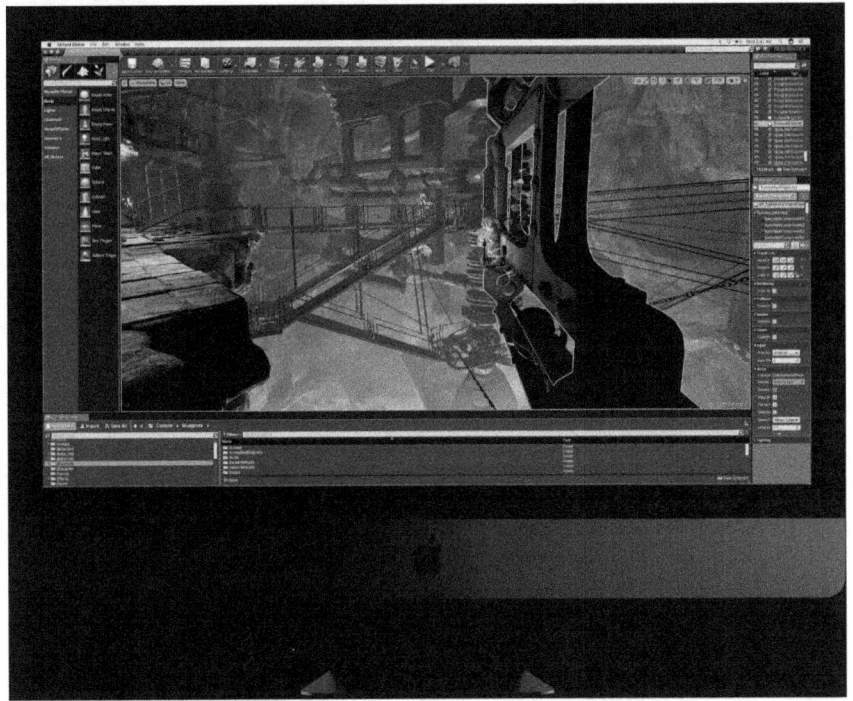

The biggest item on the Mac-side was the introduction of the all new iMac Pro. The iMac Pro is a Space Gray powerhouse. The iMac Pro sports workstation class hardware with 8, 10, or 18-core Intel Xeon, 32GB, 64GB, or 128GB Error Correcting RAM, a 1TB, 2TB, or even 4TB solid state drive, a 10 gigabit per second network card, four thunderbolt 3 ports, and is capable of supporting two 5K monitors, four 4K UHD (3840 by 2160) monitors, or four 4K (4096 by 2304) monitors. The monitors are powered by Radeon Vega 56, or Radeon Vega 64, with 8GB or 16GB of video memory, respectively. All of this enclosed within the 27-inch iMac form-factor. This all comes with a "professional" price that starts at $4,999. The refreshed Macs, and iMac Pro were not the only hardware announced. New iPads were also announced as well.

New iPads

It can be said that Apple's iPad strategy was quite convoluted. Take for instance, the ordering of iPads

    2010: iPad
    2011: iPad 2
    2012: The new iPad (3rd Generation)
    2012: The new iPad (4th Generation)
    2012:: iPad Mini
    2013: iPad Air
    2013: iPad Mini 2
    2014: iPad Air 2
    2014: iPad mini 3
    2015: iPad Pro (12.9-inch)
    2015: iPad Mini 4
    2016: iPad Pro (9.7-inch)
    2017: iPad (5th Generation)

The confusion started in 2012 when the iPad was called "The New iPad". Yes, it was a big jump from the original iPad and even the iPad 2. However, it was difficult to be able to accurately tell someone which iPad to purchase. If they wanted True-Tone, they had to get the 9.7-inch iPad Pro. But if they wanted size, or fast-charging via USB-C, they would have to get the 12.9-inch iPad Pro, but that was a compromise. It was not easy to tell someone what the "best" iPad was. This has been fixed

2nd Generation iPad Pro

The iPad Pro line up is now very simple. There are two sizes, the 10.5-inch iPad Pro and 12.9-inch iPad Pro. The difference between the two is only in terms of size of the screen. Everything else is the same. They both have:

- Apple A10X Fusion Processor'
- 4GB of Memory
- ProMotion display
- P3 Wide Color Gamut
- True Tone Display
- A10X Fusion Chip
- 12-megapixel camera with an $f/1.8$ aperture

- Digital zoom up to 5x
- Optical image stabilization
- Six-element lens
- Quad-LED True Tone flash
- Panorama (up to 63 megapixels)
- ProMotion technology
- Wide color display (P3)
- True Tone display
- Fast Charging via USB-C

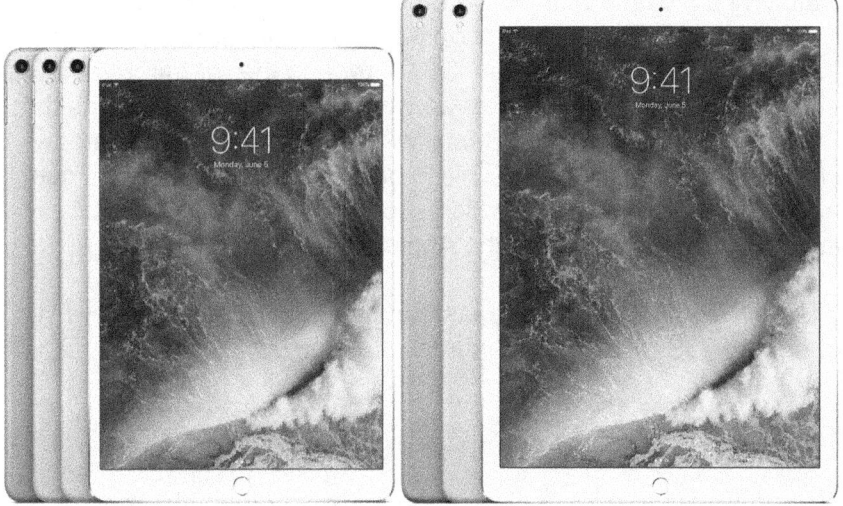

There is one subtle difference between the two iPad Pro sizes, the 12.9-inch does not come in Rose Gold. It only comes in Silver, Gold, and Space Gray. Both of these iPads are available in 64GB, 256GB, or 512GB Models. There is also an embedded Apple SIM in these models, in addition to the external SIM.

The 9.7-inch iPad Pro is now gone. This change in the line-up now makes it easier to differentiate the iPad lines. You have the iPad Mini 4, the iPad, and the iPad Pro. If someone were to ask "what is the best iPad", it is now easy to say the iPad Pro, and they only have to determine which size that they want. There is one specific feature of the new iPad Pro models that should be called out, ProMotion.

ProMotion

ProMotion is a new feature of the iPad Pros that allows the screen to refresh at 120Hz. The 120Hz refresh rate will allow animations to look even smoother than before. You may be thinking, "it does not look that different, does it?" You have to see it in action to really notice the difference.

Besides the increased refresh rate, ProMotion is able to also scale down the refresh rate when necessary. For instance, if you are watching a movie that is at 24-frames per second, ProMotion can reduce the refresh rate to not only give you the movie at 24 frames per second, but when it does reduce the refresh rate, it will also save some battery power as well. ProMotion also means that those who utilize an Apple Pencil will see improvement with how smoothly it can be tracked. This is because the Apple Pencil can now be queried at 240Hz, which should allow for significant improvements when using the Apple Pencil.

The new iPads were not the last new product released. There is one more iOS-based device that was released.

HomePod

One of the technology areas where there is competition between companies is when it comes to voice assistants. There are many competing products. Amazon has its Alexa product, Google has its Home product, and Samsung has Bixby. Apple also has its own voice-based assistant with Siri. Apple purchased Siri in 2010 and unveiled its integration with iOS in October of 2011. Even though Siri did not a large amount of functionality at the time, it has grown to include a lot more in the intervening years.

While a voice-based assistant works well on a phone, where it can really become useful is in the home. Amazon and Google both have products. Amazon with its Echo line, and Google has it's Google Home products. Apple's answer is the HomePod.

The HomePod is an audio-only cylindrical speaker. The HomePod is a mere 6.8 inches high by 5.6 inches wide. This means that it is just about as tall as an Airport Extreme and about 1.5 times a wide as one. So it s not a very large product. Despite its diminutive size, it is packed with a lot of technology. Inside the HomePod are seven tweeters, each with their own amplifier as well as a single woofer. All of this is encased in a mesh fabric and comes in two colors, White and Black. You can choose whichever one best fits the environment that it will be in.

The HomePod is designed to be able to produce the best sound it can. It does this by analyzing the room that it is in and will send audio in the direction that will produce the best sound.

Powering all of this analysis, and audio equipment, is an Apple A8 processor. This is the same processor that is in the 4th Generation Apple TV, the 6th Generation iPod Touch, and iPhone 6 and iPhone 6 Plus. The fact that the HomePod is running an A8 Processor means two things. The first is that the HomePod is running a version of iOS. One of the features of iOS is Siri. In order to hear what you have to say, the HomePod has an array of six microphones as well. The microphones should be able to hear you, when you do not think that it can, and even if you are across the room and even if it is playing music.

If you were to ask Apple what their top focal points are, one of those would most certainly be Music. This is one of the core features of the HomePod. This is the primary focus of the HomePod. The HomePod is designed to work with Apple Music to be able to play any song that you can think of. There are some who like to go in-depth with their knowledge of music. Siri can help you with this by providing you information about the current track, artist, or album. For instance, you can ask the HomePod, "What year was this released?", or "Who is playing guitar?" The HomePod should be able to find the answer for you.

If you have more than one HomePod, they can work in concert with each other to be able to play your music throughout your entire house all in sync. Alongside this is a shared playlist. This will be handy if you are hosting a party and you want your guests to be able to add additional tracks to the playlist. Similarly, if you have two HomePods within the same room, they will coordinate their playback to be able to produce an even better sound. This is

possible through a new protocol named AirPlay 2. There is more information about AirPlay 2 later in the book.

There are some touch controls on the top of the HomePod, however they are limited in what they will do. The available functions are: Play, Pause, Skip Back, and Sip Forward. It is not a full touch screen, but a basic LED touch panel.

Even though its primary focus is on audio, it does do some other functions as well. One of the interaction points with Siri is the Home app. The Home app allows you to configure and manage any of your "smart home" items, like light bulbs, shades, fans, and many other items. Since the HomePod is designed to be a stationary object, it can act as a HomeKit hub. This means that you will be able to tell Siri to "turn off the lights", or "Set the scene to movie time" and Siri will do just as you ask, provided you have a scene named "Movie Time".

Siri is designed to be a home assistant. This results in being able to ask the HomePod to start a timer, inquire about the weather, or even get conversions between measurements. For instance, you can say "How many ounces are in a cup", or "How many teaspoons in a tablespoon", or another similar question and the

HomePod will respond with the answer. Being able to do this, all without needing to pull out your phone, will be a big help, particularly if your hands are full.

The HomePod is a new product from Apple and will definitely amp up the competition between voice-assistant vendors. Only time will be able to tell just how useful the HomePod will be. However, as a start, the ability to play music, set timers, and ask questions along with the multi-room playback is a great start. It is available starting in December of 2017 for $349.

Fall Event

Apple has held their annual Fall Event. The biggest aspect to any Fall event is the unveiling of new iPhones. This event does indeed include new iPhones. Apple's fall event is the one that receives the most attention from not just technology media, but, more importantly, from those outside of the technology sphere. With that fact in mind Apple chose to hold this year's event at the new Steve Jobs Theater on the new Apple Park campus. To me, it seems quite befitting to have the first event at the new Steve Jobs Theater be the unveiling of iPhones. This is because back in

January of 2007, Steve Jobs stood on stage at the MacWorld Expo in San Francisco and unveiled the first iPhone, one that would revolutionize not just only the mobile phone industry, but also the technology sphere in general. The mobile phone revolution has ushered in one of the greatest technology shifts of the last few centuries. While Today's iPhone announcements may, to some, seem evolutionary, rather than revolutionary, the march of progress continues.

Apple Watch

The Apple Watch is one of Apple's newer product lines. When it was introduced three years ago at the September 2014 event, Apple positioned the Apple Watch as a smaller version of the iPhone. While this was a good premise to start a product, ultimately the market has steered the Apple Watch to primarily become a fitness and notification mechanism. While Apple has continued to improve the software, most notably with watchOS 3, and now with WatchOS 4, the hardware, besides internal changes, has remained unchanged. The hardware that was present on the original Apple Watch is the same that was on the Apple Watch Series 2. One of the downsides to the Apple Watch, up to now, has been the need for many to bring their iPhones with them when they go and exercise. The Apple Watch Series 2 obviated this, in someways, by providing a GPS radio in the watch. This is beneficial to those who wanted to plot a route for their outdoor workouts, but it did not completely reduce the need for bringing an iPhone along.

Hardware Changes

The new Apple Watch Series 3 has made a big leap forward, in this regard. The Apple Watch Series 3 now includes an LTE radio. The inclusion of an LTE radio opens up many more opportunities for fitness. The biggest, and most obvious, is that the Series 3 you can now leave your iPhone at home. To complement this new capability, watchOS 4 includes a new feature that will allow you to automatically sync some of your favorite music to the Apple Watch. This is quite useful if you want to exercise and only bring your bluetooth headphones and your Apple Watch. Combining this with the new watchOS 4 feature that allows you to pair your Apple Watch with gym equipment, and the other new feature to quickly add a new exercise to your current session directly on the watch, one can quickly see that it becomes even easier to switch your current exercise, or music, without needing to fumble with your watch.

There are both upsides and downsides to the inclusion of LTE on the Apple Watch. The upside is that Apple has worked with the carriers to be able to receive phone calls on your Apple Watch. This is not only a convenient feature when around the house, but it will be super helpful should you need to call emergency services. The addition of LTE also means that you will be able to receive iMessages, phone calls, and perform many of the same tasks you would on an iPhone, but with your Apple Watch. Starting in October, you will even be able to stream your Apple Music right from you watch, over LTE.

The processor in the Apple Watch Series 3 has been upgrade to a faster dual-core model, named the S3. Along with this there is a new Apple Wireless chip, the W2. The W2 make some enhancements over the W1, but what those are is not known.

There is an additional hardware change. The Apple Watch Series 3 includes a new barometric altimeter. The barometric altimeter will allow you to more accurately track flights walked up as well as differences in elevation when you are exercising outdoors.

The Apple Watch Series 3, with Cellular has 16GB of storage available on it, this is up from 8GB on the non-cellular models and the older Apple Watches. The last tweak is that the back of the Apple Watch Series 3, with cellular is ceramic and no longer composite. This is due to the nature of radio and the need to be able to send signals through the back of the watch. The advance in processing power has allowed Apple to let Siri actually respond with voice instead of just text.

The last change regarding cellular is the location of the wireless radio for cellular. It is actually embedded within the screen which leaves even more room for the other internals that are needed. Let us turn to some accessories for the Apple Watch, most notably the bands.

Bands

One of the ways that individuals customize their Apple Watch is through bands. Apple has unveiled a new style of band, the Sport Loop. The Sport Loop combines the best of the Sport band with the best of the Milanese Loop. The Sport Loop functions like the Milanese in that you can precisely position it how you need. At the same time though, it is able to breathe like the sport band so that you can use it while exercising.

There are eight colors for the Sport Loop. These colors are:

- Flash
- Spicy Orange
- Electric Pink
- Midnight Blue
- Black Sport
- Seashell
- Dark Olive
- Pink Sand

Just like traditional sport bands, these cost $49. The Sport Loop is not the only update, there are two new Hermès bands as well. One for the 38mm, the Hermès Bordeaux Swift Leather Double Tour, and the corresponding Single Tour version available for both the 38mm and 42mm. The Double Tour is $489, and the Single Tour is $339. There are still more bands available.
There is a whole new line of Nylon Colors. The available colors for Nylon are:

- Dark Olive Woven Nylon
- Midnight Blue Woven Nylon
- White Woven Nylon
- Spicy Orange Woven Nylon
- Berry Woven Nylon
- Black Woven Nylon
- White Woven Nylon
- Midnight Blue Woven Nylon
- Black Woven Nylon

There is a single new Nike Sport Band, the Pure Platinum/Black band. It is available for $49. The last new set of bands available are the Leather ones, with buckles. The new options are:

- Cosmos Blue Classic Buckle
- Pink Fuchsia Classic Buckle
- Dark Aubergine Classic Buckle
- Ruby (PRODUCT)RED Classic Buckle

- Cosmos Blue Leather Loop (42mm only)
- Charcoal Gray Leather Loop (42mm only)

Just like the other bands, these are available for order today and delivery of September 22nd. These bands cost $149 each.

Apple Watch Colors

Outside of the addition of LTE, there have been a couple of other hardware changes. The Apple Watch initially came in two colors, Silver and Space Gray. There were three different possible materials choices for the case; aluminum, stainless steel, and also solid gold, but that was for the high-end "edition" model. The Apple Watch Series 2 expanded the colors to include Rose Gold and Gold for the aluminum in addition to a new white ceramic as the "Apple Watch Edition" model. This year there are a couple new colors. There is a new "Blush Gold" aluminum color and a new "Gray" for the ceramic edition of the Apple Watch. While these may be modest changes, these will definitely help attract more users, and provide a few more options in the product line.
The Apple Watch Series 3 comes in the same color choices. For the Sport model the options are Silver, Space Gray, and Gold. Pricing for the 38MM aluminum starts at $329. The Cellular option is $70 more at $399. The 42MM is $359 for the non-cellular model and $429 for the cellular model. The Apple Watch Edition is only available in a cellular model. The 38MM is $1299, and the 42MM is $1349.

The Stainless Steel and Hermes models are available in the same colors as before. The Stainless Steel model only comes in two colors, Silver and Space Gray, and just like the Apple Watch Edition, the Stainless Steel model is only available in a cellular configuration. The 38mm is available for $599, and the 42mm is $649. The Hermes is only available in Stainless Steel and only comes in cellular models.

Apple TV

The Apple TV began life in 2007 as a modified version of a Mac Mini. This was replaced with a small "puck" like device in the 2nd and 3rd Generation Apple TVs. In 2015, Apple unveiled their all new 4th Generation Apple TV. This Apple TV changed the paradigm for the Apple TV to one that was based upon applications and not based upon whom Apple was willing to partner with. The Apple TV has seen a modicum of success in the last two years. Today, Apple announced an all new Apple TV 4K. The changes that have been brought with the Apple TV 4K bring capabilities to the Apple TV that allow it to take advantage of today's television technology.

The most notable upgrade to the Apple TV 4K is the fact that it can do 4K. 4K television have been around for almost a decade and it is very likely that any TV that you purchase will be a 4K Television. 4K offers twice the number of vertical pixels, 2160, as well as twice the number of horizontal pixels, 3840 pixels over traditional HD TVs, which have a resolution of 1920 pixels wide by 1080 Pixels high. This means that there are four times the number of pixels on the same size screen. This should allow for better clarity and smoother action scenes.

The second, and possibly more noticeable feature, is the addition of High Dynamic Range, or HDR. You may already be familiar with HDR if you use your iPhone to take pictures. HDR on an iPhone will take three pictures and take the best features of each and combine them into a single picture. Ultimately, this results in better colors and more contrast within a picture. The same general thing occurs with HDR on TVs. HDR on a TV will allow for even blacker blacks and even brighter whites. This means that all of the colors on a screen will be even brighter and clearer, which will see the picture even more life-like.

The internals of the Apple TV 4K have been significantly improved. It now sports an A10X Fusion processor in it. This is the same as the 10.5-inch iPad Pro and 2nd Generation 12.9-inch iPad Pro. The Apple TV 4K also has Bluetooth 5.0 for connectivity to the latest peripherals. Alongside this comes HDMI 2.0a and Gigabit Ethernet. This is up from Bluetooth 4.2, HDMI 1.4, and 10/100 ethernet. The wireless has also been improved to support the 5GHz band

Apple would not introduce a 4K Apple TV without having some 4K content to go with it. iTunes now has 4K content within the store. 4K movies will cost the same as HD movies. So around $20 for new releases. Rentals will cost the same around $6 for new releases. With having four times as many pixels being shown within a 4K movie, you might think that the size of the file would be significantly higher. In reality, they are not. With the new High Efficiency Video Codec (HEVC) in tvOS 11, and iOS 11, 4K movies will be able to be better compressed all while maintaining their quality. This means that 4K movies should come in around 4GB for a 90 minute movie. This is approximately the same size as a 1080p movie that is not encoded with HEVC.

If you already have HD Movies, they will automatically be upgraded to 4K versions. This is a great perk for those who already have large iTunes collections.

The addition of 4K and HDR to the Apple TV will make it a worthy upgrade for anyone who has an Apple TV and a 4K TV. The Apple TV 4K is available for $179 for the 32GB model and $199 for the

64GB model. The 32GB 4th Generation Apple TV is still around for $149.

iPhones

With the iPhone being the biggest consumer item for Apple, making up 60% of all of Apple's profits, and with selling millions of phones every quarter, it is hard to keep a lid on all of the changes that are to come with a new iPhone. This year presents a big change for iPhones. The biggest being that there are three different models being introduced. From 2007 through 2013, there was only one model introduced. It may have come in some colors, but there was only one size. From 2007 to 2011, this was a 3.5-inch sized iPhone. For 2012 and 2013, this was 4-inch screen. Since 2014, there have been two sizes, 4.7-inch and 5.5-inch screens, starting with the iPhone 6 and iPhone 6 Plus. These two sizes continue with the 8 and 8 Plus. Let us look at the new iPhone 8 and iPhone 8 Plus.

iPhone 8 and 8 Plus

The iPhone 8 and iPhone 8 Plus continue on the tradition of their predecessors. The general form factor of the phone has remained unchanged since the introduction of the iPhone 6 and iPhone 6 Plus in 2014. There have been some interior structural changes, like with the iPhone 6s and iPhone 6 Plus becoming a bit more rigid to combat any inadvertent bending. Many people may complain that the outside of the iPhone has remained unchanged for four releases now, however this does come with some benefits. For instance, it means that Apple has gotten really good at making the exterior cases for the phone. Along side this, many of your peripherals will continue to work with a new phone, just like they did on the old phone. However, that is not always the case.

The biggest change with the iPhone 7 and iPhone 7 Plus models were that the headphone jack was removed. The removal of the headphone jack allowed Apple to make the iPhone something that it was not previously capable of being; water resistant. One of the quickest ways to kill any electronic device is to expose it to water.

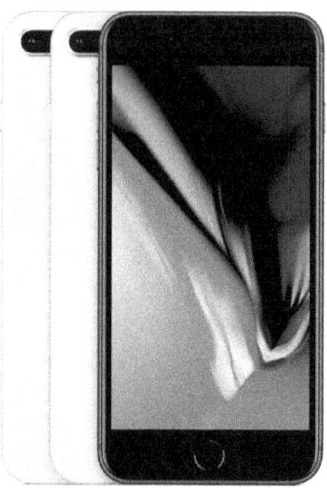

The change to the water resistant case, which required removal of the headphone jack, has lead to fewer iPhones being destroyed by being put into water; whether willingly or unwillingly.

Processor

One change that occurs every year is the interior components. The new iPhone 8 and iPhone 8 Plus contains the new A11 Bionic processor along with its M11 motion co-processor. The A11 Bionic This brings even better battery efficiency and processing to the phone. The A11 Bionic is a six core processor that consists of four high efficiency cores that are up to 70 percent faster than A10 Fusion. It also has two high performance cores that are up to 25 percent faster than the A10 Fusion. To go with the processor, Apple has included a new Apple-designed graphics processor as

well. This will get 30% faster performance over the graphics in the A10 Fusion.
There is an all new item incorporated with the A11 Bionic, a neural engine. The neural engine will allow even faster processing of Augmented Reality and Machine Learning than the A10 Fusion. The neural engine is designed not only for Augmented Reality and Machine Learning, but can be used for many other things like processing of items within photos and much much more. The new items within the iPhone 8 and iPhone 8 Plus do not end there. Let us look now turn to the screen.

Screen

The screen on the iPhone 8 and iPhone 8 Plus are significantly better with an all new technology that Apple is calling Retina HD displays. Retina HD displays incorporate True Tone technology to adjust the screen to the right brightness, contrast, and color based upon the surroundings. The iPhone 8 and iPhone 8 Plus also incorporate the Wide Color Gamut, which will be able to show the best colors possible.
With the glass back on the iPhone 8 and iPhone 8 Plus, Apple has matched the aluminum band around the iPhone 8 and iPhone 8 Plus to be the exact same color as the back. Besides matching aesthetically, this also allows for more rigidity within the iPhone.
Camera
The biggest usage of any iPhone is the camera. The camera in the iPhone 8 and iPhone 8 Plus have been vastly improved. They now both feature Quad-LED True Tone flash with Slow Sync. They are also capable of recording 4K video at 60 frames per second, which will make your 4K video even more life-like. The cameras have otherwise remained largely the same.
The iPhone 8 Plus has seen a bit of an improvement on its own. It now has a new feature, Portrait Lighting. Similar to the way that Portrait photos were brought to the iPhone 7 Plus last year, Portrait Lighting is in beta, but it allows you to perform some interesting effects with a Portrait photo. Portrait Lighting will take the information from the surrounding light and apply a lighting effect to the photo. The biggest benefit is that you can do this retroactively and you can also change the lighting effect afterwards.

Battery

One of the things you can always expect is that battery life on the iPhone will remain fairly consistent. The iPhone 8 and iPhone 8 Plus are no exception. They get the same battery life as their predecessors.

The iPhone 8 has a new set of materials on the outside. The front and back are now both glass. The glass is surrounded by a band of aluminum. The glass back allows for an all new feature to iPhones, wireless charging.

The wireless charging that is included with the iPhone 8 and iPhone 8 Plus is the Qi, pronounced "she", standard. This means that if you have a Qi-compliant charging pad, it will work with the iPhone 8 and iPhone 8 Plus. The inclusion of wireless charging will allow users to simply place their iPhone on a charging pad and it should begin charging. This means that you will not have to plug in your iPhone just to have it charge. This is convenient, not only for home, but also if you travel. This is because you can bring a charging mat that will allow your iPhone, Apple Watch Series 3, and even AirPods charge wirelessly.
There is a new product coming in 2018 called "AirPower". AirPower is a mat designed by Apple that will allow you to charge all of your Apple devices at once.

Pricing

The iPhone 8 and iPhone 8 Plus come in two configurations. 64GB and 256GB and come in three colors; Silver, Space Gray, and Gold. The prices have gone up slightly to $699 and $799, respectively, for the 64GB models. The 256GB models are $849 and $949 respectively.

iPhone X

Apple announced the iPhone 8 and iPhone 8 Plus. There is just "one more thing" that Apple announced, a third new phone. That model is the future of smartphones, and is the iPhone X. The iPhone X is an all new design for the iPhone. Before we dive into the features of the iPhone X, let us talk about colors, which many

may think are not important, but are often used to help personalize an iPhone.

Colors

The original iPhone in 2007 came in just one color, aluminum. The iPhone 3G introduced a second color, white. These two colors remained the only options until 2013 when Gold was introduced with the iPhone 5s. Unless you were willing to purchase a Space Gray, or Black, iPhone, all other faces on the iPhone line are white. This changes with the iPhone X. Now, all fronts of the iPhone X are black. This means that for those who only wanted a black bezel to their iPhones can now get something besides Black or Space Gray.

The back of the iPhone is where people really select their colors. iPhones since the iPhone 6s, meaning the 6s and 7, have had four options. Silver, Gold, Rose Gold, and Space Gray. The iPhone X has a slightly different set of colors as options. There are only two options available, Silver and Space Gray. There is no option for the front face, as it barely there. The selection of Silver and Space Gray should come as no surprise, as these are likely the most popular colors purchased. It is not easy to determine

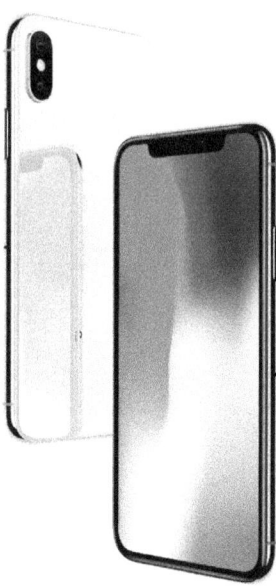

which model will be the most popular, and with such a revolutionary phone, it may be prudent to stick with just a couple of colors to gauge interest before expanding the color choice. Let us dive into the internals of the iPhone X.

Internals

One change that occurs with each new iPhone is the interior components. The new iPhone X contains the new A11 Bionic processor along with its M11 motion co-processor. The A11 Bionic This brings even better battery efficiency and processing to the phone. The A11 Bionic is a six core processor that consists of four high efficiency cores that are up to 70 percent faster than A10 Fusion. It also has two high performance cores that are up to 25 percent faster than the A10 Fusion. To go with the processor, Apple has included a new Apple-designed graphics processor as well. This will get 30% faster performance over the graphics in the A10 Fusion.

There is an all new item incorporated with the A11 Bionic, a neural engine. The neural engine will allow even faster processing of Augmented Reality and Machine Learning than the A10 Fusion. The neural engine is designed not only for Augmented Reality and Machine Learning, but can be used for many other things like processing of items within photos and much much more. The neural engine will work very well with a new feature, one that replaces the home button.

Home Button

The new iPhone X an edge to edge screen. The thing that is most conspicuously missing is the home button. The home button no longer has a place on the iPhone X. With the home button gone, there have been some other changes. One of the primary functions of the home button is to get you back to the home screen. This is still accessible, however there is a new way of doing so. The home screen is now accessed by swiping up from the bottom of the screen. Doing this will actually bring up the app switcher, which is very similar to the function within the iPad. To actually get to the home screen just tap on an empty area of the app switcher and the home screen will appear. Again, this is exactly how it works on an iPad under iOS 11. The second primary function of the home button to both unlock the phone as well as to use Apple Pay, and finally to force a refresh should something cause your iPhone to freeze. How are these to be done with the iPhone X? There are new methods for accomplishing all of these tasks.

Biometrics

Apple Pay is a core part of Apple's strategy for iOS and macOS and it makes up a good part of their services revenue. To that end, Apple would not remove Apple Pay from its products; particularly when they announced the Person-to-Person Apple Pay within iMessage on iOS 11. Without a home button with integrated Touch ID to place your finger on to authenticate Touch ID, you can now use the new Face ID technology.

At the top of the iPhone X there is a notch that contains a number of sensors. These include the front camera as well as the new infrared sensors for the new Face ID. Face ID is the replacement for TouchID on the iPhone X. If you have used Touch ID, and a vast majority of users have, you are accustomed to placing your finger on the Touch ID sensor. Face ID is similar, but instead of your finger, the new infrared sensors scan your face to determine that it is indeed you. The setup for Face ID is similar to Touch ID. When you setup Face ID, you move the camera around your face a bit. This is done to be able to get different angles of your face. This is exactly like setting up Touch ID where you place your finger in different spots to make sure that Touch ID works as often as possible.

Face ID will only unlock your iPhone X if you are actively looking at it. This means that the iPhone X will not unlock if you are looking away, or have your eyes closed. Unlike a fingerprint, people's faces do not stay the same over time. Hair styles change, men grow mustaches or beards, and people wear hats, add glasses, or many other alterations. As time progresses, Face ID will learn about all of these changes and continue to unlock your phone, just like it did when you initially set up Face ID. What powers all of Face ID is powered by the all new TrueDepth Camera sensor.

TrueDepth Camera

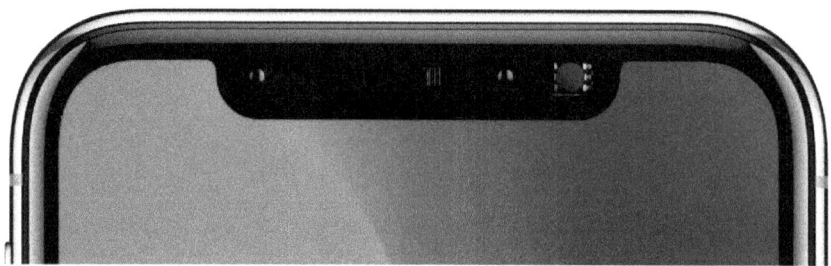

There is an area at the at the top of the screen of the iPhone X. This notch houses a number of the camera sensors for the iPhone. It also requires some accommodations within iOS. The adjustments that are needed revolve around the status bar. The status bar has been a staple of iOS since the beginning. iOS has always shown the time, carrier information, wireless status, and battery. This is still the case with the iPhone X, but the information is now displayed around the notch. On the left is the cellular and wireless information. While on the right is the time, Do not Disturb, Bluetooth, battery, and the current time.

One of the features introduced under iOS 9, is the "back" button to go back to where you were. This is still present. When you follow a deep link that allows you to go back to the previous app, this information will be shown on the left, however instead of being in the left of the status bar, it will be directly below the items on the left side of the status bar. This should actually make it easier for users to go back to the previous app. There is a lot sensors packed within the TrueDepth Camera, let us turn to that now.

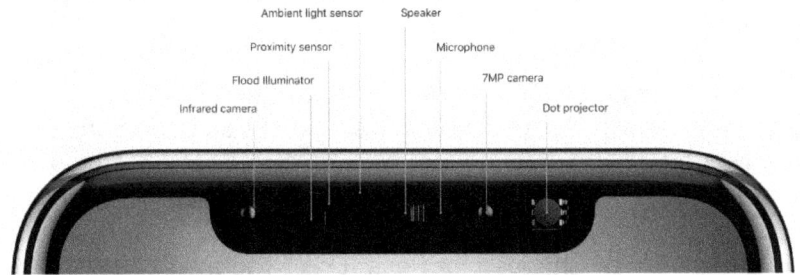

There are eight different sensors in the top. These are:

- Infrared Camera
- Flood Illuminator
- Proximity Sensor
- Ambient Light Sensor
- Speaker
- Microphone
- Front Camera
- Dot Projector

The Infrared Camera, Flood illuminator, and Dot Projector are all parts that work together to be sure that it is truly your face that is being shown on the screen. These three sensors, combined with the Neural Engine of the A11 Bionic, is able to quickly and seamlessly detect that you are who are you. The Dot Projector will project and detect 30,000 different invisible dots to be able to look at each feature of your face. The there are three items that occur nearly simultaneously. These items are:

1. Your Face is detected with the flood illuminator.
2. The infrared camera takes an infrared picture.
3. The Dot projector detects 30,000 invisible dots.

The infrared image and dot project are mathematically calculated using the Neural Engine within the A11 Bionic, and a calculation occurs. This is done through specialized hardware and machine learning algorithms that are within the neural engine. The neural engine is capable of handling 600 billion operations per second on a dual-core processor. All of this results in nearly instantaneous calculations. This new calculation is compared to the stored calculation within the secure enclave and if it matches, your phone is unlocked.

Security with Face ID is important, just as it is with Touch ID. Face ID will not allow pictures of you to be able to be used to unlock your iPhone X. Apple states that with Touch ID, the likelihood of someone being able to randomly come up and unlock your iPhone with their fingerprint is 1 in 50,000. With Face ID, this is reduced to 1 in a million. The chances for Face ID are reduced if someone closely related to you tries to unlock your iPhone X with Face ID. That is Face ID in a nutshell, let us move to the thing that you look at the most, the screen.

The Screen

The new iPhone X has a completely new edge-to-edge screen. This screen Optical Light Emitting Diode, or OLED, screen. OLED is a bit different from the traditional Liquid Crystal Display, or LCD, screens that have appeared on the previous iPhone models. There are two big benefits with OLED. The first is that OLED allows for darker blacks and brighter whites. This ultimately means that the picture that is shown will be even better than on LCDs. The second benefit is that OLED uses less electricity, which improves battery life. And who does not like better battery life?

To complement the new OLED screen, the iPhone X incorporates True Tone. True Tone is the same technology that is within the 10.5-inch iPad Pro and second generation 12.9-inch iPad Pro. True Tone utilizes a light sensor to be able to automatically adjust the colors on the screen. Combining True Tone with the OLED screen means that the display should be able to produce even better colors; particularly within sunlight.

The edge-to-edge form-factor means more than just less bezel space. It also means that the iPhone X has a distinct resolution. The resolution of the iPhone X is 2436 pixels tall by 1125 pixels wide. This is not a screen resolution that has been on an iPhone before. The biggest change occurred in 2014 with the release of the iPhone 6 and iPhone 6 Plus when developing on the iPhone required supporting two more screen sizes. This was in addition to the already known, at the time, 320 pixels by 480 pixels, the retina size of this, 640 pixels by 960 pixels. The first significant change was with the iPhone 5 and its screen resolution of 640 pixels by 1136 pixels. It was was only a difference of 176 pixels in height, and usually meant that you were able to show more items vertically.

The iPhone 6 and iPhone 6 Plus introduced the two new screen sizes of 750 pixels wide by 1334 pixels high. The iPhone 6 Plus introduced a screen resolution of 1080 pixels wide by 1920 pixels high. The way that developers can make sure that they work with any screen size is through the use of size classes. The addition of this new screen resolution shows that Apple is not afraid to branch out and create a screen resolution that does not fit what developers, as well as users, have become accustomed to. If you are a developer, it is becoming increasingly difficult to not use size classes within your applications. Any applications that do not conform to size class will quickly become apparent to users of the iPhone X.

One of the complaints, by some, is that the Plus-sized phones are not comfortable in the hand. The screen resolution of the iPhone X is, of course, due to the physical screen size; which is 5.15 inches. With the edge-to-edge nature of the screen, all of this fits within approximately the same size as the 4.7-inch iPhone 8. This screen size is not as large as the screen on the iPhone 8 Plus, which is 5.5-inches. Even with the physical screen being smaller, the screen resolution is still larger than the Plus-sized phones. This is a nice size between the two, which should help appease some of those who find the Plus-sized phone to be too large and having a larger area is just an added bonus.

Camera

The biggest digital camera on the market right now is the iPhone. The iPhone, along with other mobile phones, has replaced the use of traditional cameras for many people, including myself. This trend is why Apple has paid significant attention to the camera in recent releases of the iPhone. The camera in the iPhone X has some new capabilities that were not available previously. The camera is now capable of recording 1080p HD at 240 frames per second, 4K at 24 frames per second , and even 4K at 60 frames per second. The 1080p at 240fps, and 4K at 60fps are double what the previous iPhones were capable of handling. The new 4K at 24 fps is possible through the use of HEVC. HEVC is capable of handling many different frame rates. The use of 24 frames per second is standard within the movie world and will allow you to take film style video.

The addition of new video filming options will absolutely help drive even more video and photos being shot on iPhone, which is an ad campaign that they have been running, and this should allow even better submissions.

The new Front Camera, within the TrueDepth Camera system, is upgraded over the FaceTime HD camera on the iPhone 8 and iPhone 8 Plus. The front camera is also capable of taking Portrait Mode photos. Combining this with Portrait Lighting on the front camera, means that you can take some fantastic selfies. The front facing camera is great for selfies, but there is a new feature specifically on the iPhone X, that can be used with the front camera.

The first is Portrait Mode on the front facing camera. It is nice to be able to take Portrait photos with the rear facing camera, but being able to get a portrait mode selfie will allow you to up your selfie game against others. Another adjacent feature is Portrait Lighting. Portrait Lighting will let you adjust not only the lighting on your face, but also the lighting of the background. The best part is that this can be done after the fact. So if you take a selfie but think it could be a bit better with some more light, you can make the adjustments afterwards to get an even better picture.

There are some other enhancements with the rear-facing camera. You can now record video in 4K at 60 frames per second, this is double the speed on the iPhone 7 and 7 Plus. The telephoto lens on the iPhone X now includes optical image stabilization, which was not present on any previous iPhone, but is present on the iPhone 8 Plus.

The last new feature with the front camera is one that may be quite popular with kids.

Animoji

Take, for instance, the use of the eggplant, 🍆 emoji. It can be used to indicate that you want to eat some eggplant; however it can also be used as a phallic symbol. Similarly, you can send someone a peach, 🍑, emoji. Again, to signify that you want to eat a peach, or tell someone that you think they are a peach, or even that you are peachy keen. It also has been used as replacement for one backside. The last example that I will use is the infamous poop emoji, 💩. If you are of a certain age, you may

also refer to him as "Mr. Hanky". Just like the 🍌 and 🍑, 💩 can also be used in a variety of situations. One situation would allow you to indicate that you are not feeling well. Whereas another would be that you might be indicating to someone that they are being a pile of poop. All of these examples above are just a few of the various ways that emoji can be used to signal meaning. These are all just static two dimensional representations.

Apple has expounded upon this concept by including a new feature for iMessage called Animoji. Animoji take the concept of a static emoji but it utilizes your face as well as your voice, to determine which emoji might represent your current expression. Besides just choosing an emoji, which is a feat in itself, the emoji that it chooses is three dimensional and animated. Some of the emoji that are represented by Animoji are the 🐵👑🐱🐶, and yes even 💩. There are more, but these are just some of the one that are available.

Wireless Charging

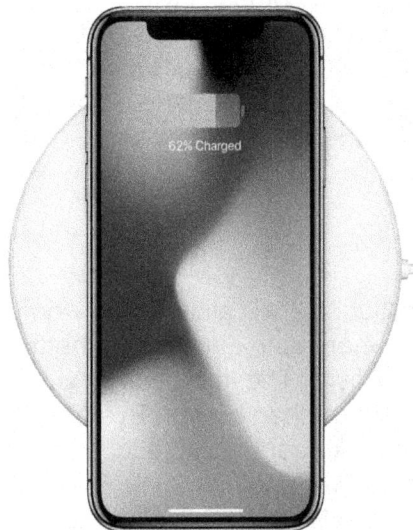

The back of the iPhone X is glass. This allows for a new feature, wireless charging. The standard that Apple is using on the iPhone X is the Qi, pronounced "she", standard. This means that if you have a Qi-compliant charging pad, it will work with the iPhone X. The inclusion of wireless charging will allow users to simply place their iPhone on a charging pad and it should begin charging. This means that you will not have to plug in your iPhone just to have it charge. This is convenient, not only for home, but also if you travel. This is because you can bring a charging mat that will allow your iPhone, Apple Watch Series 3, and even AirPods charge wirelessly.

There is a new product coming in 2018 called "AirPower". AirPower is a mat designed by Apple that will allow you to charge all of your Apple devices at once. This is great not just for travelers, but also as a place to be able to set all of your items and know where they are located.

Pricing

The iPhone X is the future of the smart phone, and with that it commands a futuristic price. The iPhone X comes in two configurations, 64GB and 256GB and as mentioned above, it comes in two colors, Silver and Space Gray. The 64GB model is $999 and the 256GB model is $1149. Apple Care on the iPhone X has also gone up to $199. This brings the total to somewhere between $1200 and $1349.

Final Thoughts

The new LTE-enabled Apple Watch Series 3 will allow those who exercise to leave their phones somewhere safe and no use them and without having to sacrifice connectivity. The improved processor will make things even smoother than before. Even though the Apple Watch Serires 2 is no longer available for sale, the Series 1 is still available at a new lower price, of $249. The inclusion of cellular as a standard on the Hermes, Stainless Steel, and Ceramic Edition will provide even more benefit for users who purchase those versions.

The new Apple TV 4K is a great upgrade to bring the Apple TV up to date to be able to take advantage of the latest technologies, like 4K and High Dynamic Range. Keeping the old 4th Generation Apple TV around at a lower price point will allow more options for Apple TVs and will allow those who do not have a 4K TV to be able to take advantage of the capabilities of the Apple TV. The automatic upgrade of previously purchased content to 4K is a definite plus that will benefit everyone, not just those who have 4K now, but will end up buying a 4K TV in the future. The biggest benefit is that the pricing of the 4K movies will be the same price as HD movies, which is great for consumers and will ultimately benefit the movie companies as well.

The new iPhone 8 and iPhone 8 Plus bring some solid enhancements to the already future-looking iPhone lineup. The iPhone 8 and iPhone 8 Plus add a couple of additional phones to the lineup and are ARKit compatible. The all new glass back will definitely allow the adoption of the Qi wireless charging standard to become the de facto standard. The iPhone 8 and iPhone 8 Plus are solid upgrades over the iPhone 7 and iPhone 7 Plus. The Retina HD with True Tone display will allow for better viewing all around. If you are in the market for an iPhone, the iPhone 8 and iPhone 8 Plus are solid upgrades. Just be sure to get your wallets ready for pre-orders of all of these starting on Friday.

The all new iPhone X, much like with the introduction of the MacBook in early 2015, is showing us the direction it is going to take not just the iPhone X, but phones in the future. The bezel-less display has some great upgrades, in particular the fact that a larger 5.8-inch screen fits into a form factor just slightly larger than the 4.7-inch screen. The new TrueDepth camera allows Face ID to exist. The addition of a neural engine within the A11 processor allows the computation that is necessary to make Face ID open quickly and seamlessly. The inclusion of wireless charging is a great step towards a completely wireless future. Even though it may seem trivial, the inclusion of the new Animoji will add a new dynamic to interactions amongst individuals. The new Animoji feature will be a great demo to show off just what the iPhone X is capable of doing. Even though the iPhone X is pricey at $999 for the 64GB model, it is the future, which means that the technology within the iPhone X will eventually trickle down to the lower end phones.

Now that we have covered the new devices, let us look at all of the new features of iOS 11. We will start with some new design elements, starting with the Lock Screen.

Lock Screen and Home Screen

The first thing you see when you wake your iPhone or iPad up is the lock screen. The Lock Screen on iOS was primarily designed as a place for you to be able to see notifications. While it still serves this purpose today, there is a bit more functionality. There are two more screens that coincide with the lock screen. The first is to the left, and this is the widget screen. Widgets were introduced in iOS 7. Notification Widgets allow quick access to information. This could be in the form of sports scores, weather updates, news, or even battery level for any connected device. If you swipe to the right of the Lock screen you will get quick access to the Camera. These two functions remain the same.

There have been a couple of slight changes to the Notifications Widgets in iOS 11. For the 12.9-inch iPad Pro, under iOS 10, the widgets were able to be in two columns. Under iOS 11, there is now only one column. While this may be a downside for some, it will create a more consistent experience for everyone across all iPads.

The Lock Screen itself has changed. It now combines both Notification Center and the traditional Lock Screen. This new interface is called the "Cover Sheet". It is given the name of Cover Sheet because it is accessible at all times, just like Notification Center was under previous versions of iOS.

The first change to the Cover Sheet in the "Now Playing" screen. There is now a semi-transparent overlay on your lock screen. You can scrub through the current item, pause, go forward and go backwards. You can also adjust where the audio is being output. To do this, tap on the AirPlay icon in the upper right corner of the now playing screen. Here you can adjust the volume, or select the output location. If you tap on any of the output locations, the audio will being playing to that location. Once you are finished, tap on the "Done" button and you will be brought back to the Now Playing overlay.

Underneath the Now playing there is some text, "Earlier Today". This is an indicator that you have notifications that came in earlier,

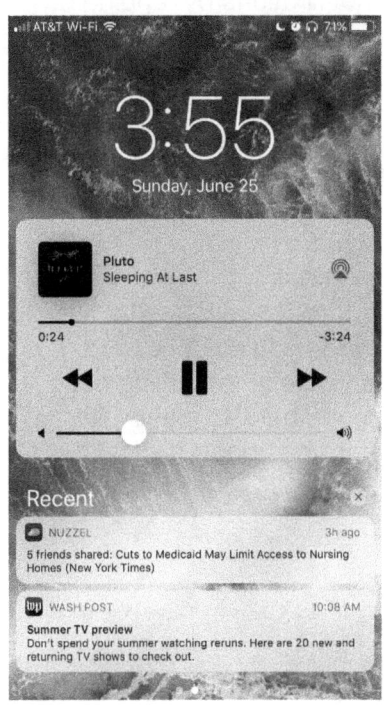

but have not been acted upon. You can simply swipe up to see the list of notifications. If you have been using iOS for a while, your natural inclination would be to swipe to the right to dismiss a notification. This action does continue work in iOS 11.

There is an alternative method, if you choose to use it. You can force press on the notification to be able to act upon it. Once you have force pressed, you can either dismiss the notification by tapping the "X" in the upper right, or by swiping down. Alternatively, if you want to act up on the notification later, you can just tap outside the notification and it will remain in your notification list.

iOS 10 added a feature called "rich notifications". These are notifications that allow you to perform some action. If a notification does have an action attached to it, you can swipe from the right to the left to be able to view the actions. By default there are two options, "view" and "clear".

You can also still dismiss all previous notifications by tapping on the "X" when you initially swipe up. This will remove all notifications for that group. Notifications are grouped by days. You will either need to tap on each individual X for each group to remove them, or you can force press on the X to clear all notifications. There are times that you do not wish to unlock your screen, but instead just perform a quick action. This can be done with Control Center, which has been changed in iOS 11. These changes will be covered a bit later in the book.

Many times, despite any best efforts, when you pull out your iPhone you often do not remember the purpose for pulling out your iPhone and end up putting the iPhone back to sleep. This is done by pressing the power button. There has been a slight change to the Power Button within iOS 11.

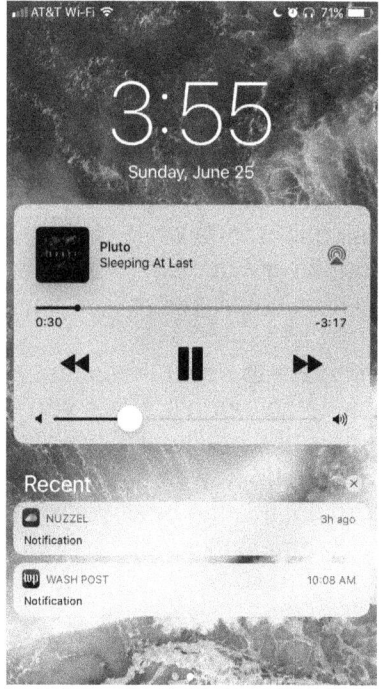

iPhone Power Button Changes

Almost every single handheld electronic device has a power button. This is used not only to turn off the device, but in the case of an iPhone, iPad, or iPod Touch, the Power Button is important in case the iOS device freezes.

With iOS 11, the Power Button has a new usage. If you click the Power Button, on an iPhone, five times in rapid succession, a new screen will appear. One that is similar to the one below.

On this screen you have a few options. These are the same ones that appear on the Apple Watch when you hold down the power button. The options that appear are:

- Power Off the iPhone
- View the Medical ID information
- Initiate Emergency SOS

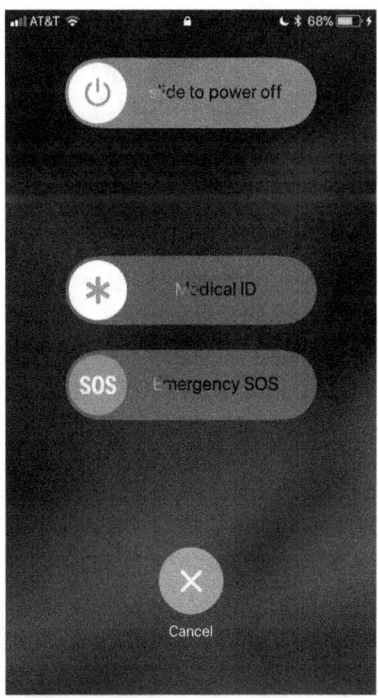

Security and Safety are something that Apple takes seriously. Apple has added many new security features since the iPhone initial release in June of 2007. Some of these include encrypting of data, an indicator for when your location is being used, and the most important is the addition of Touch ID with the iPhone 5s.

There is one last change that occurs when you click the power button five times, Touch ID is disabled. This has two different possible reasons. The first is that this means that if you are in fact injured, others can still access the emergency information but will not be able to unlock your phone by placing your finger on the sensor. This provides better security, in case you ever are injured.

The second use case for this, is one that has become problematic in the last few years. If you are involved in an automobile accident, it is possible that a police officer may want to take your phone and investigate if you were using your device immediately before the accident. Similarly, if you are traveling into a country, you may be required to give up your phone so its contents can be saved and investigated at a later date.

While a ruling by the United States Supreme Court has not been made, there have been conflicting rulings around whether someone can be compelled to use a fingerprint to unlock a device. It has been ruled that the Fifth Amendment of the United States Constitution protects users from divulging a passcode or password. The disabling of Touch ID, until a passcode is entered, can be used to protect your information, if someone tries to compel you to unlock your iPhone with your fingerprint.

The clicking of the power button five times to disable Touch ID is much more convenient than turning off Touch ID within settings, and then having to re-configure it later. It is also much easer than turning off and turning back on an iPhone, which can take some time. The clicking of the power button five times is also less conspicuous, should you need to use it without anyone really noticing.

Once you finally do decide to unlock your iPhone or iPad, you are then taken to the Home Screen. Let us take a look at the Home Screen itself.

Home Screen

When you first look at the Home Screen on an iPhone or an iPod Touch on iOS 11, you may think that not much has been changed. On the surface, this is correct, but under the hood a whole lot has changed. There is always at least one single change for iOS. Each version of iOS has a new background, and the new one for iOS 11 is in the screenshot below, and through most of the screenshots within this book. The under the hood changes will be discussed in a little bit. Before we delve into that, let us look at an updated feature of iOS for the iPad, the Dock.

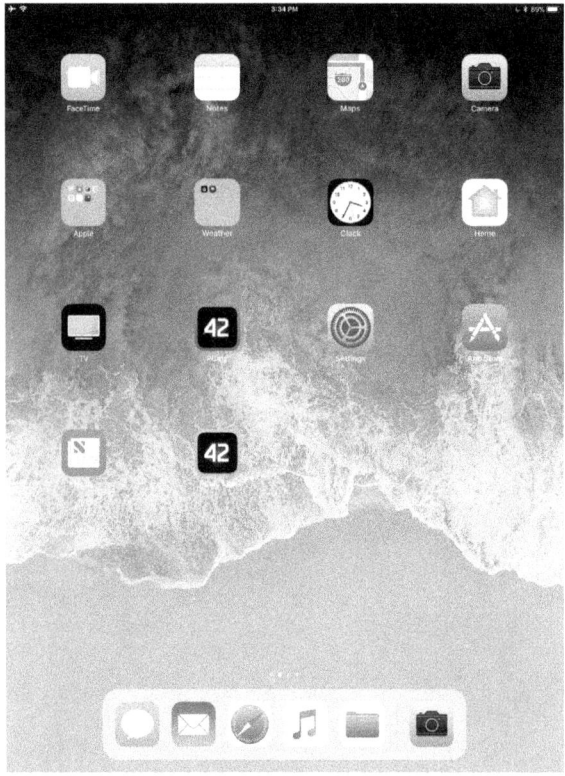

The Dock

Back in 2011, Apple said that it was going to begin bringing parity to applications on both iOS and, as it was called at the time, OS X, now macOS. This began with just name changes, but would eventually grow to include bringing groups of applications to each other platforms. Alongside this, if a concept from macOS would make sense on iOS, and Apple could bring the feature over, while maintaining the existing security and paradigms of the platform, they would do so. One of the concepts that was brought over to iOS, with the original iPhone, was the Dock.

The Dock under iOS 10 was effectively a larger iPhone Dock. It was capable having up to six total icons. You had the ability to add more applications to the Dock by using folders, but this is not always the best solution. With iOS 11, the entire Dock has changed.

The iPad Dock on iOS 11 is now capable of having more applications. The number varies on the size of the iPad. For the 12.9-inch iPad Pro you can have up to 15, yes 15, applications in the dock at once. For the 10.5-inch iPad Pro you can have 13 applications plus the three recent applications. The 9.7-inch iPads can also accommodate 13 apps and the three recent ones. and iPad Minis can have fewer icons.

The iOS 11 Dock mimics the behavior of the macOS Dock, in most ways. The primary way is that the Dock on iOS 11 will shrink the application icons as more applications are being added. You can have as many or as few applications in the dock as you would like. The dock is also somewhat more intelligent. Your most recent applications will be shown on the right side of the dock, which will allow you to quickly access your recent applications. If you have hand-off enabled, any applications that are offering an item to hand-off will be on the right most icon. This is where it differs from the macOS Dock. On macOS the handoff items are on the left side of the dock.

The second way the Dock on iOS 11 differs from its macOS brethren is in the fact that the icons within the Dock can be folders of applications, should you desire to place them there. On macOS, you can place folders, however these must be on the right-side of the divider on the Dock. On iOS 11, you can place them anywhere within the Dock, except for the right side, which is used for recents.

There is another slight change to the Dock in iOS 11. This change affects iPhones, iPod Touches, and iPads all the same. The name of the applications in the dock are now gone. Under iOS 10, the name of the application was prominently shown. This change makes sense given that if you have all 15 apps in the iPad Dock, you will not be able to read any of the names, even if they were shown.

The Dock is more than just a place for applications. If you long press, or force press, on an icon, it an provide some quick actions, just like any application. Developers have to provide these quick actions. Any application that already has quick actions should be able to perform these high from the Dock.

The final thing with the Dock is that is now accessible at any time. It will disappear when you are using an application, but you can easily access it by swiping up from the bottom of the screen. When you do this, the Dock will automatically appear, thus giving you access to your recent applications.

Earlier there were hints at some under the hood changes, now is the time to discuss those. We will start with Screenshots.

Screenshots

No matter how long you have been using iOS, there are likely time that you would taken a screenshot. The reason for taking a screenshot may be to post it to social media, inform a developer of a bug in their application, or just to document something in general.

When you do take a screenshot, you often want to be able to add information to the snapshot. In order to accomplish this, the workflow may look something akin to this:

1. Take the screenshot.
2. Locate an application to add some information.
3. Open the application.
4. Allow app access to your Photo Library.
5. Import the the screenshot into the app.
6. Add your information to the screenshot.
7. Save Photo back to Photo Library.
8. Open Photos.
9. Share the Screenshot.

This is not the simplest workflow just to be able to add information to a screenshot. iOS 11 takes this workflow and completely changes it. Here is the workflow under iOS 11:

1. Take a screenshot.
2. Tap on the screenshot preview in the lower left corner to enter Markup Mode.
3. Make changes to the screenshot.
4. Save or share the screenshot.

That is all it takes. There are only four simple steps to be able to modify a screenshot under iOS 11.

After you take a screenshot, there are two different functions you can perform. The first is to slide the picture off to the left. This gesture will dismiss the preview and it will be saved into your

Photo library. The second gesture is to tap on the preview. This gesture will open up the Instant Markup feature.

There are a couple of alternatives for taking screenshots via the hardware buttons on your iOS Device. If you are using your iOS device with a keyboard, you are able to hit the key combination, Command + shift+ 3. This will take a screen shot and show you the preview, as shown above. Alternatively, you can hit the key combination command + shift + 4 and this too will take a screenshot. The only difference is that it will immediately bring you into the screenshot editor; which is the next item to discuss.

Screenshot Editing

Being able to take a screenshot and instantly adjust it, without the need to locate an application will be a big boon to productivity under iOS 11. Once you do tap on a screenshot preview, you will be brought into the "Instant Markup" interface. Instant Markup is full of features to help you adjust and edit your screenshots. Let us look at different aspects of the interface.

Cropping

One of the basic tasks that any user will perform with a screenshot, or even a picture, is to crop the screenshot or photo. On iOS 11, the Markup interface has the ability to crop. This is delineated by the blue outline around your screenshot. You can

tap and drag any of the drag handles and move any of them. A dark overlay will be shown to indicate which areas will be removed. Once you lift your finger up, the screenshot will adjust and remove the darkened areas. If you have multiple screenshots, only the currently highlighted screenshot will have the crop handles. This means that only the current screenshot will be able to be cropped.

The Toolbar

The toolbar at the bottom is one of the most used areas. There are three different drawing implements. From left to right these are: a marker, a highlighter, and a pencil. Each of these has their own properties. The marker has a thick line, the highlighter has an even thicker line and functions just like a highlighter you are used to, and the pencil has a very thin line. Each fo these has its own uses. If you make a mistake and want to erase something you did, there is also the Eraser.

The item next to the erase is the lasso. The lasso will allow you take anything that has been added on top of the screenshot, group it together, and then move it about to another point on the screenshot. The underlying screenshot will not be removed or modified, it remains as it was originally.

There are six different colors that you can choose from: White, Black, Blue, Green, Yellow, and Red. You can use any of these six colors with the Pen, Highlighter, or Pencil.

There are three other buttons on the toolbar, two to the left and one to the right of the primary toolbar.

Undo and Redo

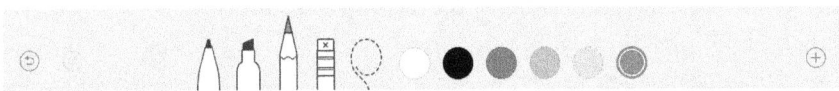

The two on the left are "Undo" and "Redo". If you make a mistake while editing your screenshot, you can undo your mistake by tapping on the "undo" button. If you initially thought that undoing was the way you wanted to go, but change you mind just tap on the redo button and the item that you thought was a mistake will be put back.

Additional Tools

The button on the right of the primary toolbar is a mini-toolbar of sorts. The "+" button contains three functions, and four different shapes. The three functions are:

- Text
- Signature
- Magnifier

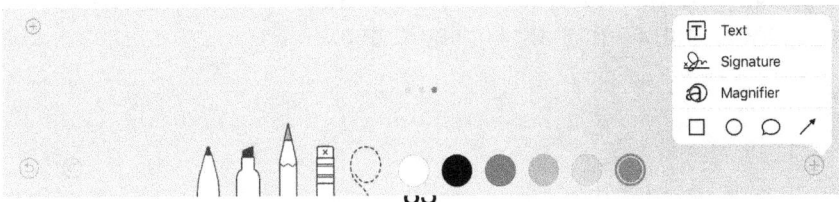

Text Function

The "Text" function will allow you to add text to your screenshot. Tapping on this button will add a box with the word "Text" in it. You can use any of the six colors to adjust the color of your text. To modify a text box, simply tap on the text box you want to modify and then tap the "Edit" button.

Once you are editing a text box, a new button will appear next to the "+" button, it is a "font" adjustment button. This button allows you to choose from three fonts, "Helvetica", "Georgia", and "Noteworthy". Helvetica is the default font. You can also use slider to adjust the size of your text. The last item to edit is the justification of the text. You can make it left, center, full, or right justified. Once you are done editing the text, simply tap anywhere on the screen and the editing dialog will disappear.

Signature

The signature button will allow you to add any already pre-saved signatures that you may have to the screenshot you are editing. If you tap on the "Signature" button, a popover with your existing signatures will be shown. From this dialog you can add or remove a signature.

If you tap on the "Add or Remove Signature" button you will be presented with something similar to this:

If you tap on the red "remove indicator" you will be prompted to verify that you want to remove the signature.

Tapping on the "+" button will allow you to add a signature. You simply sign your name, or initials, or whatever mark you want to use, and tap the "Done" button to save it. Even though it says "use your finger", if you have an iPad Pro and an Apple Pencil, you can use the Apple Pencil to sign your name.

Once you tap on "Done", your signature will be added to the screenshot. You can adjust the color by tapping on the Signature and then tapping on any of the six colors.

Magnifier

There are instances where you want to highlight something within a screenshot. This is where the magnifier tool can become your best friend. When you tap on the magnifier button, a round magnifier window is added to the screenshot. There are two adjustments that can be made to the magnifier.

The first adjustment is the zoom. This is done by dragging the green bubble from the top to the right. There is only 90 degrees of arc for adjusting the zooming. The closer to 90 degrees, or 3 O'clock if it is easier to think in terms of a clock, the more it will zoom.

The blue bubble is used to adjust the size of the magnifying glass. The range of sizes is quite large and should suffice for anything that you want to highlight. Just like the text boxes, you can adjust the colors of the bubble.

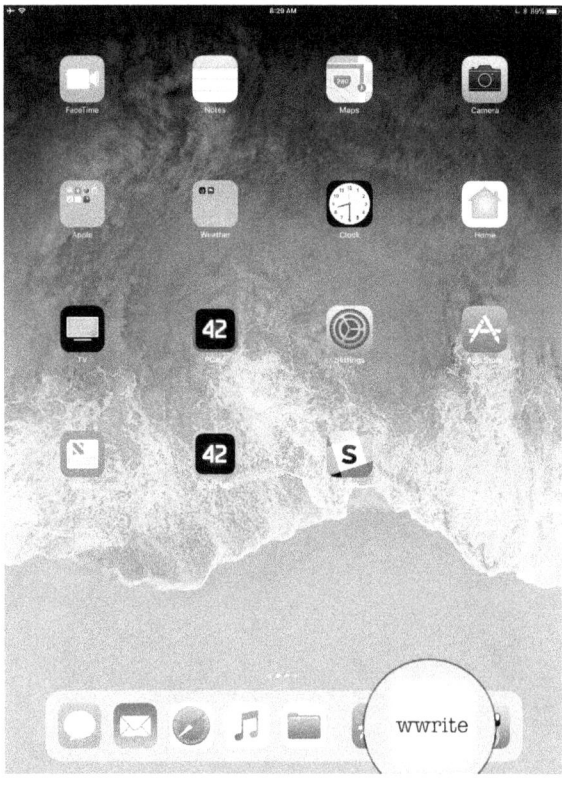

Sharing and Finishing

There are two last buttons to be aware of. The first is the share button. Once you have made the changes and additions to your screenshots, you will likely want to share them. This can be accomplished by tapping on the standard "share" icon in the corner. This is located in the upper right on the iPad and lower left on an iPhone or iPod Touch. This will show a standard share sheet. You can then send the image to any social media service, email, or even send it over messages.

The Done button provides two functions. You can either save the screenshots to Photos, or you can delete them. Alternatively, if you do make modifications and then hit the "home" button, your screenshots will be shown and after a few seconds they will disappear and will automatically be saved into Photos.

Screenshot Tips

There are a couple of tips that will help you with Screenshots under iOS11. The first is that you can take multiple screenshots and each one will be put onto a stack, similar to a stack of photos. If you tap on the entire stack all of the will open.

The second tip is that if you do have multiple screenshots in a stack, and you enter Instant Markup mode, each of these screenshots will have its own "undo" and "redo" queue. This means that any edits you make on a particular screenshot will be able to undone, or redone, only on that screenshot.

Final Thoughts on Instant Markup

The new Screenshots mechanism will make it much simpler to take a screenshot on iOS and then add some quick modifications and then either share that screenshot or save it to your Photos Library.

Even though it is a basic tool, there are still a ton of features included. The three different drawing implements will allow users to choose the best tool to express what they wish. The lasso tool will make it easy to grab a group of modifications and move them to another part of the screenshot.

The choice between six different colors will let people choose how best to express not only the drawings that they want to add, but also text as well as the magnification bubbles. The fact that there are different "undo" and "redo" queues for each image within a stack will help users keep everything organized.

Overall, the new Screenshots and Markup tools are a great addition to iOS and are likely to be used heavily by a variety of different types of users. Let us now turn to one of the biggest features of iOS 11, Drag and Drop.

Drag and Drop

When you use iOS 11, many aspects will look the same, with the exclusion of the Dock, which is mentioned above. But there have been a significant number of changes under the hood. The entire Home Screen mechanism, which is called Springboard, has been revamped and is now based entirely on Drag and Drop.

Drag and Drop on the iPad has been something that many users have wanted for quite some time. While it may seem like a professional-level feature, rewriting Springboard to use Drag and Drop has implications for all users. Let us look at when you want to rearrange your Home Screen applications. Under iOS 10, you would have to do the following:

1. Locate the application you want to move
2. Tap and hold on that application
3. Wait for the icons to start jiggling.
4. Tap and hold the application that you want to move
5. Drag the application to its new location, if this is on another screen drag the icon over to the side and wait for the home screen to move there.
6. Drag the icon to the new location
7. Lift up your finger to place the icon in its new location.

This procedure worked for a decade, since it was the original way to move applications. This was not too much of a burden if you were only moving one or two applications, but what if you wanted to move a half dozen at one time? It would get quite tedious. Imagine, if you will, if you could gather up all six of those applications and move them all at once. With iOS 11, this is exactly what you can do. In order to move more than one application at a time, perform the following:

1. Locate the applications that you want to move.
2. Place your finger on an application that you want to move until the delete icons appear.
3. Tap and drag the first application to the side.
4. Locate the next application that you wish to move. If it is in a folder, tap inside the folder (Yes, this is possible)
5. Tap the icon of the second app you wish to move. It should appear on top of the first app, much like a stack of cards. Repeat this for all applications that you want to move.
6. Move the entire stack to their new location.
7. Lift up your finger to place the items in their new location.

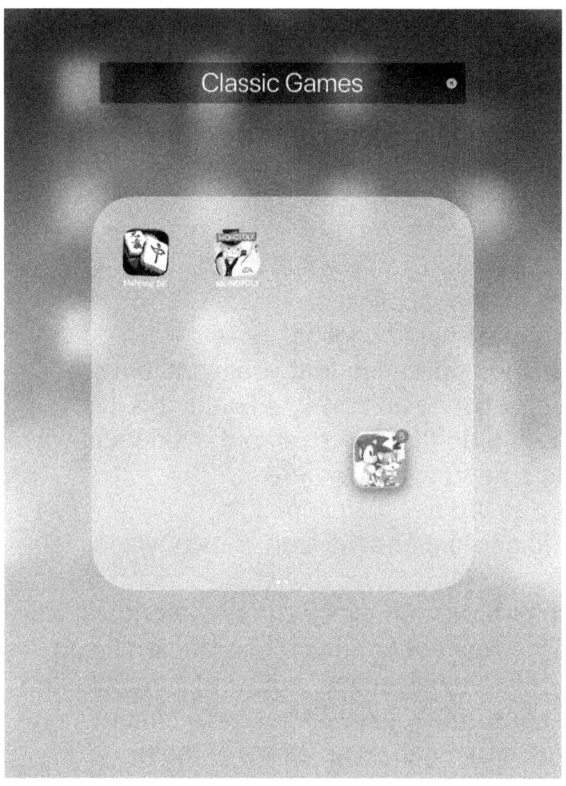

The ability to move multiple applications will make it much easier to manage your applications. Moving applications is just one possible use of Drag and Drop. There is more to Drag and Drop, but before we delve more into Drag and Drop, let us look at some multitasking changes for the iPad.

Multitasking on the iPad

One of the biggest features of iOS 9, released in 2015, was the ability to run multiple applications, side-by-side. Initially this was only possible on the iPad Air 2 since it was the only iPad capable of handling multitasking due to it having 2GB of RAM. In October of 2015, Apple released the 12.9-inch iPad Pro, which was the device that was really designed to take full advantage of multitasking. The downside to this is that multitasking did not change much under iOS 10. Under iOS 11 though, multitasking has received a number of new features that will help productivity.

The first of these features is how you are able to use Slide Over and Multitasking. Under iOS 10, when you initiated Multitasking, you had to choose which application was to be considered the "primary" application. Once you had selected the primary application, you could then choose which application would accompany the primary application. This would be done by sliding over from the right of the screen, towards the left side of the screen. When this gesture was performed, a menu of applications that would support multitasking would appear. You could select any of these applications and it would run.

If you wanted to have both of these applications on the screen at the same time, you could tap the divider to have the application always be present. This was provided that the application actually was able to work in Split View mode, some applications cannot. The manner in which you begin multitasking has completely changed, for the better.

Now with iOS 11, this is a much simpler procedure; it is as follows:

If you have an application open, swipe up to bring up the Dock.

If the application is in your Recent apps on the Dock, tap and drag the application on top of the currently open app. That's it, you are done.

1. If the application is not in your recent applications, locate the app
2. Open the application
3. Swipe up to bring up the Dock
4. Tap on the first application you opened
5. Swipe up to bring up the Dock
6. Tap and drag the app you wish to use in multitasking on top of the currently open application.

It may seem like it is more complicated, however in practice it is not more difficult, it is more intuitive. There are a couple of benefits to Multitasking on iOS 11. The first is that by default, when you start an application in multitasking, it sits on top of the currently open application. If you want to have the apps be side by side this is easy to accomplish. Presuming that you have two applications open, you can perform the following:

1. On the app that is floating on top of the "primary" application, tap and hold on the bar that is at the top of the floating app.
2. Drag your finger down, the screen, the "primary" application will slide out of the way so the secondary app can sit side-by-side to the primary application.

At this point you can adjust the size of each app to your own liking. The second benefit to the redesigned multitasking is that applications can now be on either the left or right side of an application and can be more easily swapped between the two positions.

To move an app from one side to the other, perform the following:

1. Tap and hold the bar at the top of the application.
2. Drag the bar down until the secondary application appears on top of the primary application.
3. Lift up your finger so the secondary application can float.

4. Tap and hold the top bar on the floating app.
5. Drag the app to the other side of the screen.
6. Lift up your finger so the secondary application can float.
7. Tap and hold the bar at the top of the application.
8. Drag the bar down until the secondary application appears to the side of the primary application.

There is something to keep in mind with this new arrangement. The application on the left is still considered the "primary" application, provided that the application is not taking up half of the screen. To know whether or not an application is considered the "primary" application, just look for the bar at the top of the screen. If there is one present, it is not the primary application and can be adjusted to float or to be moved to the other side.

There are times that you wish to be able to have the same applications open simultaneously. This could be something like a Twitter Client and Slack, or Safari and Notes, or any other combination of applications that support Multitasking. Under iOS 10, many users became frustrated that they could not group applications together. If a user removed an application from Multitasking, an re-opened the application it was not with the other application that they would like. This has changed in iOS 11.

Grouping Applications

If you have ever used the Spaces feature of macOS, you know that it can be frustrating to group applications together. There are a few options for Spaces on macOS. You can assign an application to "All Desktops", "This Desktop", or "None". Each of these has their own use. If Apple were to bring this mindset over the iOS, it would be cumbersome. Besides, iOS does not have the concept of "Spaces", there is only one "Desktop" on iOS, Springboard. So how does one go about grouping applications together on iOS 11. This is probably the simplest thing to do in iOS 11. Just perform the following:

1. Use the two applications together in Multitasking.

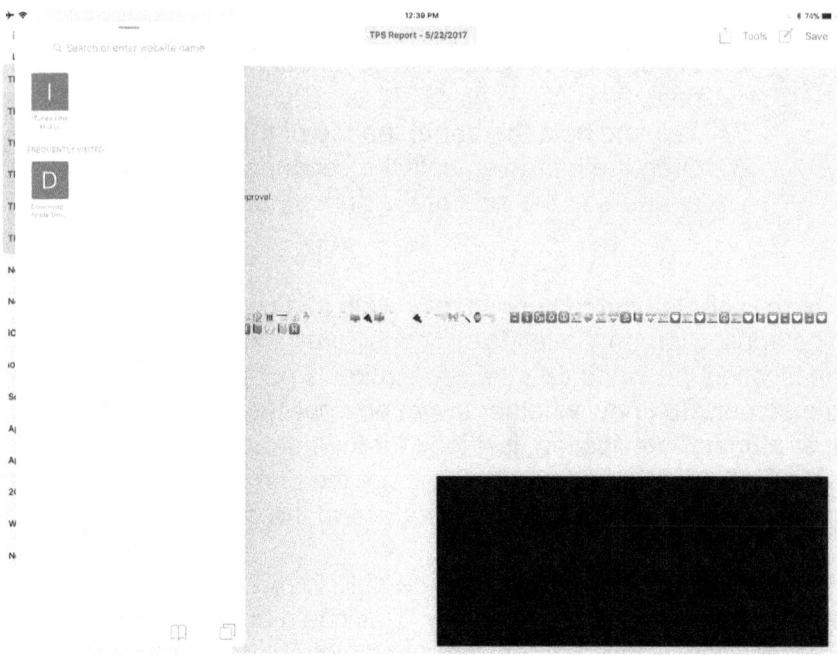

Yes, that is all that you have to do. Once you use applications together in Multitasking, they will be grouped. For instance, let us say you have a note taking application and Safari as one group. If you open either of the applications, the other will open. If you remove an application from the group and open that application, only that application will open.

To see which applications go together, you can simply open up Control Center on the iPad. This will show all of your applications that are grouped, provided that they are open. When applications are grouped together, when you quit one application, the other grouped application will quit as well. When this is done, it will also break the grouping.

Now, imagine if you were able to drag and drop items between applications, it would provide some great productivity gains, would it not? Guess what iOS 11 provides this capability, that is right, you can Drag and Drop between applications.

Multitasking Plus Drag and Drop

Even if Drag and Drop stopped with the ability to easily move applications, it would be a great improvement. Given that iOS 11 is built entirely on Drag and Drop, the ability to implement Drag and Drop items between applications becomes much easier.

In order for an application to fully take advantage of Drag and Drop, developers will have to do to do some updates to their applications. However, there are a number of built-in controls that support Drag and Drop. Why this is important to you is because having support for these built right into the operating system means that as soon as you upgrade to iOS 11, many of your existing applications will already have Drag and Drop support, without the developer needing to do anything. This is the exact behavior I noticed with my application when I first upgraded to iOS 11, I was able to drag and drop text without needing to do any updates to my own application. This alone will be huge for both users and developers.

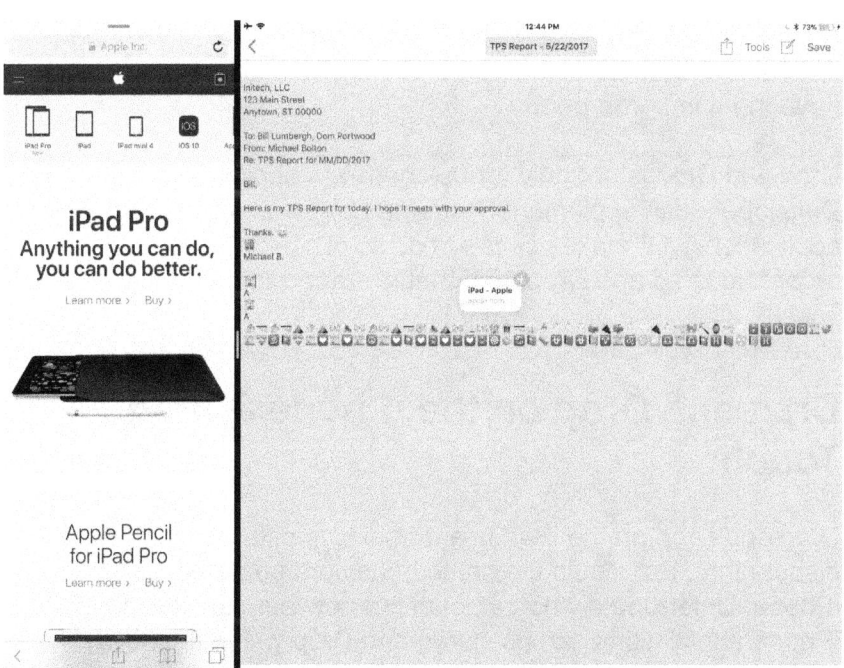

Some of the items that automatically support Drag and Drop include, textfields, text views (scrolling text fields), table views and even collection views. What this means in practice is that you can drag and drop a URL from Safari into another application. You can also take an entire block of text and drop it into a document.

Text is not the only type of object that you can drag and drop. You can also drag and drop images. The only caveat for images, as is the case with anything you wish to drag and drop, is that the application must support the importing of those types of documents.

If an application does support a particular file type, when you drag the files over the application, there will be a green + button in the upper corner of the stack of images, along with a count of the images. If an application explicitly forbids a file type, it will have a red circle with a line through it. If you attempt to drag and drop a set of files, and it fails, it is likely because that particular application does not support that type of file.

As mentioned before, applications do have to explicitly support drag and drop to be able to drop entire files into an application and have them import properly.

Drag and Drop is not only for use between applications. Developers can implement Drag and Drop within their own applications, if it makes sense to do so. There is one last caveat regarding Drag and Drop, and that is around the iPhone and iPod Touch.

Drag and Drop on the iPhone & iPod Touch

Drag and Drop on the iPad is a fantastic addition, no one would dispute that. But, could the same behaviors be brought over to the iPhone. Unfortunately not, at least not between applications. iPhone applications can use Drag and Drop within their own application without any restrictions. The data just cannot leave the application. This is due to the limited screen space available on an iPhone or iPod Touch. Being able to drag items out of the way and then using another finger to manipulate the interface would provide a bad user experience. It is not that Apple could not bring this functionality to the iPhone and iPod Touch in the future, it certainly could. However, for now, it is not possible.

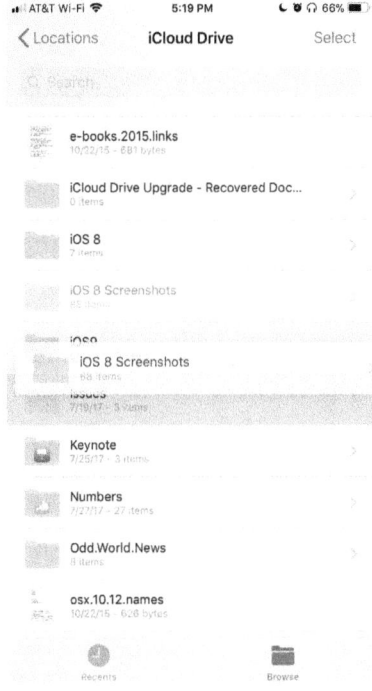

Final Thoughts on Drag and Drop

Drag and Drop on iOS 11 brings a slew of new features and productivity gains. The ability to move data between applications while using Split View will really assist some users. Having built-in support for some of the standard operating system components will provide an even better experience for users since developers do not necessarily need to implement Drag and Drop in order for their applications to work.

Springboard, as mentioned above, is entirely based on Drag and Drop, which allows for easy manipulation of applications, which will make customization of iOS an even easier proposition.

As good as Drag and Drop is between applications, Would it not be great if you use Drag and Drop within iCloud Drive to manage all of your files stored in iCloud?

iCloud Drive App

Prior to iOS 9, applications could store their own files in iCloud. This came with some benefits as well as some downsides. The benefits are that your files were not stored on your devices, so if some tragic happened to your device, your files would be safe. A second benefit is that your files were also available across devices, so if you updated a file on one device, and subsequently opened it on another, it would be the most up to date version. One of the downsides of this, is that you could not open files created in one application with another application. At least not very easily.

In iOS 9, Apple unveiled a new application, iCloud Drive. The iCloud Drive app was designed to allow you an easy view into the files that were saved in iCloud. From the iCloud Drive app you could open up any stored file. it has remained largely unchanged since it's introduction. However, that has now changed with iOS 11. The iCloud Drive app has been renamed to Files. Along with it, comes some new functionality.

Files App

As the internet has become more ubiquitous and reliable, users have begun to store more and more items "in the cloud". When people say things are stored in the cloud, what they really mean is that it is stored outside of their own devices and is available at all times. There are millions of files stored outside of our devices. When we do store these files, they can become strewn across a variety of providers. Some of these may include, iCloud, One Drive, DropBox, Box, and countless other providers. One of the downsides of having files in various locations is that it becomes difficult to locate the item that you need.

This can be very similar to a physical filing system, where one set of files is in one cabinet, while another similar set is in another filing cabinet. The best way to remedy this is to consolidate all of the files into one file cabinet. While this would be ideal, it is not always possible. One of the biggest culprits of this inability to consolidate is that there is no physical room to do so. The Files app provides a solution, but only for your digital files. Unfortunately, you are left to figure out your own physical filing system.

The Files app takes what iCloud Drive had done, and expands upon it. Files can now include more than just iCloud Drive, in fact it can include any storage provider, like One Drive, Dropbox, Box, or even an enterprise storage solution. This depends upon the developer adding the functionality. The Files app replaces the iCloud Drive app, but adds some nice functionality in the process.

Some of this includes the ability to move files, delete files, or even view information, along with a variety of other tasks. The first thing you will notice with the Files app is that there is an all new structure to the application. In particular, there are now two buttons on the tab bar at the bottom of the screen, "Recents" and "Browse". Let us look at the Recents tab first.

Recents

The Recents tab is quite simple, it provides a look at all of the recent files that you have been using, or that have been added to your storage. By default on the iPhone there only six of your recents are shown. While on the iPad in portrait orientation there will be ten displayed and in landscape there are fourteen. There is a "Show All" button in the upper right corner. This button will, as one might suspect, shows all of your recent items. When you first view your recent items, a preview of each of the files will be shown. For text files, you will get a small preview. For images, a thumbnail will show and for any other file that Quick Look knows about, you will also get a preview.

If you do not want to view your recents as tiles, you can tap on the list icon in the upper right and the display will change to a more detailed view. The detailed view shows the file's name, when it was last updated, an option to download, and the file's size. You can download any file that you wish, or you can simply tap on a file and it will open in the appropriate app.

Besides just your recent files, it will also show the tags that have been recently used. When a recent tag is used, a preview of the files will also be displayed. This will provide a fast way to be able to see the files with that tag.

Let us say that you are previewing a text file. Once you tap on this, the preview should open right within the Files app. There are a couple of actions you can perform. The first is to tap the "list" button in the upper left, this will display all of your other recent items. The second action is to tap on the "Share" icon in the upper right. This will bring up the standard share sheet, where you can email a file, or open it in another application. There is another

option within the share sheet, but that will be discussed in a little bit. For now, let us move over to the Browse tab.

Browse

If you use other storage providers besides iCloud Drive, this will be one pane that you will use quite a bit. That is because the Browse tab is the basis for all of your storage. Under "Locations" should be listed all of the places where you have storage, again, provided the developer has updated their application to allow access to the storage. With the Browse tab you can locate the file you wish to open and then simply tap on the icon and it should open.

Let us say that you do not remember which storage apps you saved the file in, there is a solution for this: Search.

There are two different contexts for searching. The first is under the "Browse" screen. If you perform a search while on the Browse screen it will search all of your storage for whatever string you enter. If you want to limit searching to a single storage location, you can do so simply. Tap on whichever storage location you wish to search, and there should be a search bar at the top of the screen.

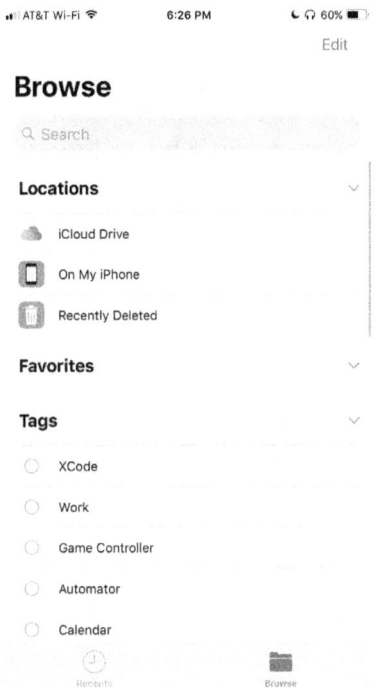

Recently Deleted

Under "Locations", besides your storage locations, there are two other locations; "On my iPhone", or "On My iPad", and "Recently Deleted". The "On My iPhone" location is a list of everything that is downloaded to your device. The Recently Deleted folder will show everything that has been recently deleted. The recently deleted items are to be considered unavailable. This is because depending on the retention policy of the storage provider, the files can be deleted at any point. The Files app will stop you from opening the items. You do have a coupe of options. You can perform the following:

- Recover
- Delete
- Get Info

Tapping on "Recover" will put the file back from where it was deleted. Clicking on "Delete" will bring up an alert to verify that you want to delete the item. The "Info" option will allow you to see some information about the item. You can see the date it was created and deleted, as well as whether or not it is currently downloaded to your iOS device. You can also add a tag to the item.

Favorites

The next section is "Favorites". Favorites is designed for folders that you want to have quick access to without the need to perform a search. A good example may be a project that you are currently working on, or even just a folder that you reference quite a bit. To add a favorite you can do the following:

Locate the folder you want to make a favorite.
Tap and hold on the folder. A popup toolbar should appear
Tap on Favorite. It should now be a favorite and appear in the Favorites drop down.

Favorites are a great way to always have access to the your most frequently used files, without the need to search or browse to their location. There is another way to quickly access and organize files. This is done by using the Tags function.

Tags

The last section is Tags. Tags were introduced to macOS back in OS X 10.9 Mavericks. Tags are a mechanism for allowing a user to organize their documents and files in an easier manner. Tags have not been present on iOS before. If you had tags already set up with macOS, all of these tags will be synchronized over to iOS. This will allow you to easily find all of the files that you have already tagged, provided they are stored on iCloud Drive. You can tag any individual file that you wish to by performing the following:

1. Locate the file, this can be done with browsing or by search
2. Tap and hold on the file. A popup toolbar should appear.
3. Tap on "Tags". A tagging sheet should appear.
4. Select the appropriate tags.
5. Tap done. The file should now be tagged.

When you are tagging a file, or folder, you may not always have an appropriate tag defined, this is where setting a new tag can be helpful.

Creating a new tag.

Creating a tag in iOS is pretty simple action. It can be done by performing the following:

1. Locate any file
2. Tap and hold on the file. A pop up toolbar should appear.
3. Tap on "tags". A popover window with all of your tags should appear.
4. Tap on the "Add new tag" text box
5. Enter in the name of your tag
6. As an optional step, select a color for the tag. The tag should now be available for use.

Tagging an item is a quick method of being able to organize a file. There are those times, however, when you want to reorganize your files.

Rearranging Items

There are instances when the list of tags that you are using are not arranged in the most efficient order. You can adjust the order of of any of the sections of the files app. This includes the tags. To adjust the order of any of the objects, tap on the "edit" button of

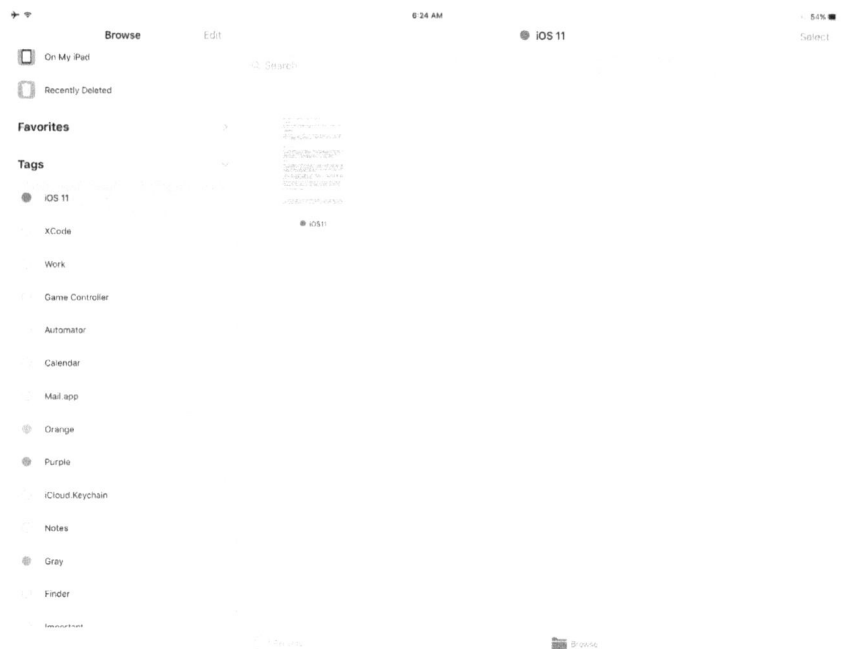

the "Browse" window. Depending on the section, some new icons will appear.

In the Locations section, toggle switches will appear next to each storage provider. This will allow you to hide any provider. The only item that you cannot hide is the Recently Deleted location. This location must remain and will always be at the bottom.

Under "Favorites" and "Tags", you are able to delete any of your favorites or tags. When you delete a favorite, or a tag, the items associated with that favorite or tag will remain, but the folder will no longer be a favorite. Alternatively, you can also locate the actual folder, tap and hold on the folder and select "Unfavorite" to remove the folder as a favorite.

The second icon that will appear is the rearrangement icon. You can simply tap and hold on any tag that you wish to rearrange and then you can drag your finger yo the desired location for the tag. Lifting up your finger will save the item in that spot. These changes should sync to all of your devices.

Moving Files

There are different scenarios when you may want to move files from one location to another. This may be from one folder to another within the same storage location, or even from one storage provider to another. With the Files app, this is entirely possible to do. There are a couple of different ways of moving files, depending on your preferred method. You can follow either of these procedures.

Process 1: Traditional Method

7. Locate the file, or files, that you wish to move
8. Tap on the Select Button, to begin the file selection
9. Select the items you wish to move.
10. Tap on the "Move" button at the bottom.
11. Select which storage provider that you wish to move the files to.
12. Navigate to the destination folder
13. Tap on the "Move" button in the upper right. The files should move to that location.

Process 2: Drag and Drop

1. Locate the file, or files, that you wish to move.
2. Place your finger on the first item you wish to move, it should change the border
3. Drag your finger away from its original position.
4. Locate any other files you wish to move
5. Tap on the file to add it to the group to be moved.
6. Navigate to the destination location
7. Place the items over the location.
8. Lift up your finger, the files should move to the location.

There is one thing to note. If you are transferring files between storage locations, they will be removed from the original storage location and moved to the destination storage provider. If the destination storage provider has an error, your files could be lost. If the application follows all of Apple's guidelines, it should not be an issue. However, there is always the possibility of an issue. The second thing to note is that *Procedure 1* can also be used for duplicating or deleting files, just without moving them.

Files app and the Keyboard

One area where Apple has been putting forth more effort is in the realm of the professional iPad user. One of the ways that Apple has accommodated this contingent of users is by providing keyboard options within iOS. While it is not present within every Apple application, there are those where keyboard shortcuts have been created. One of those applications is the Files app. The list of keyboard shortcuts within the File app are:

Command	Keyboard Combination
Create Folder	command + shift + N
Copy	command + c
Duplicate	command + d
Paste	command + v
Move Here	command + shift + v
Delete	command + delete
Select All	command + a
Search	command + f
Show Recents	command + shift + R
Show Browse	command + shift + B
View as icons	command + 1
View as List	command + 2
Go to Enclosing Folder.	command + up arrow

You can invoke any of these by performing the key combination listed. While the inclusion of a set of keyboard shortcuts may seem trivial, they can go a long way for those users who do not want to remove their hands from the keyboard just to perform an action which can be more easily completed by using the keyboard.

Closing Thoughts on Files.app

Files.app provides users with a richer experience for interacting with all of their files. The addition of Copy, Move, Rename, and tagging will allow power users to be able to better manage their files across all of their storage locations. One of the benefits of the Files.app is that everything should be synchronized across your devices, meaning that if you perform an action on one device, it should be reflected on your others, even cross-platform from iOS to macOS and vice versa.

The ability to have all of your storage centrally manageable, as well as searchable, will make the task of accessing all of your data that much easier. The ability to tag individual items will provides and easy mechanism for users to be able to strategically organize their files and also provides quick access similar items. The integration of Drag and Drop into files will make it much simpler for those who are very accustom to using touch interactively on their iOS device. One of the most common interactions is using Control Center and closing applications. Let us look at Control Center first.

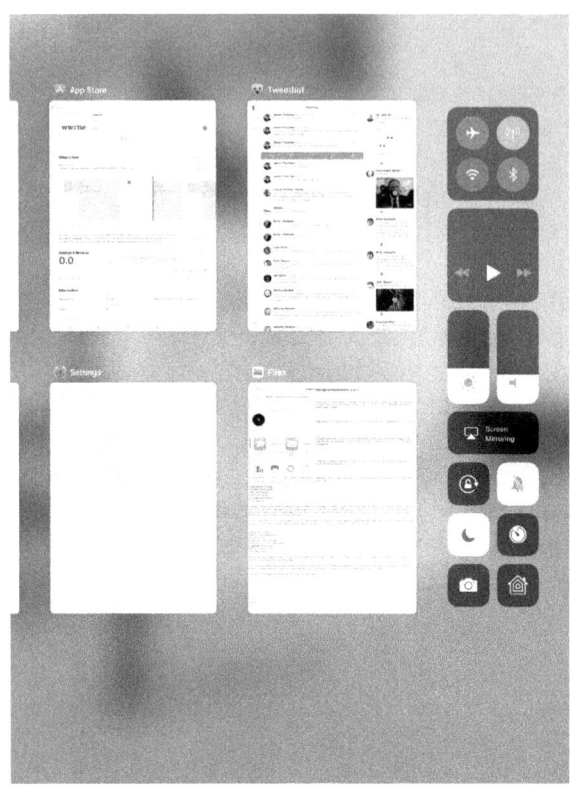

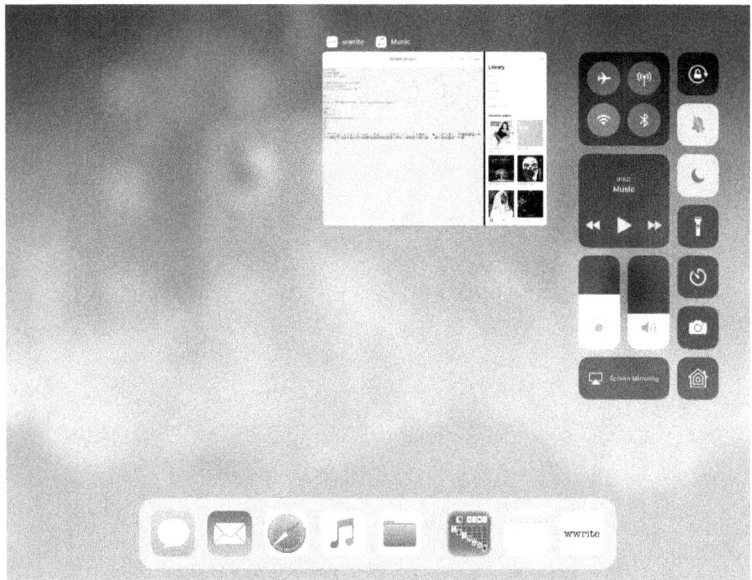

Control Center

Control Center was introduced with iOS 7 in 2013. When it was first released, it brought quick access to certain functions of the operating system. The items that were accessible via settings were: Airplane Mode, Wi-Fi, Bluetooth, Rotation Lock, and display brightness. There were also some quick access to applications, like Calculator, Timers, the Camera, and a new function, at the time, flash light. Also present were AirDrop and AirPlay, as was quick access to the now playing controls.

In iOS 8, it was only slightly redesigned. In iOS 9, it remained unchanged from iOS 8. However, with iOS 10, Control Center got an update. Instead of everything being on a single pane, it expanded to three panes. One for the system controls, one for the now playing screen, and one for "Home", if you had HomeKit enabled devices configured. This would have certainly continued to work in iOS 11. However, Apple chose to make some improvements.

While three panes is certainly not too much to handle, how would Apple handle adding more functions? Would it expand to four panels, or even five? Instead of that, Apple has chosen to completely redesign the Control Center. Under iOS 11.

The New Look

If you used Control Center on a regular basis you will immediately notice the difference in Control Center. In iOS 11, the idea of the three panels is gone. Now, there are a bunch of icons that correspond to different functions. One of the biggest requests for Control Center is the ability to customize the functions. This is now possible under iOS 11.

Customizing Control Center

By default Control Center has, the System Controls, Now Playing, Rotation Lock, Do Not Disturb, AirPlay, Brightness, Volume, Flashlight, Timers, Calculator, and the Camera icons. If you have HomeKit enabled devices, the Home app should be shown as

well. These are the same that are available under iOS 10. However, there are even more options. You can add the following:

- Wallet (iPhone Only)
- Apple TV Remote
- Notes
- Low Power Mode
- Alarms
- Text Size
- Accessibility Shortcuts
- Guided Access
- Magnifier
- Stopwatch
- Voice Memos.

There are two other additional options, but we will cover those in a bit later. In order to customize the actual Control Center, do the following:

1. Open Settings

2. Tap on Control Center
3. Tap on Customize Controls. A list of options should be displayed.

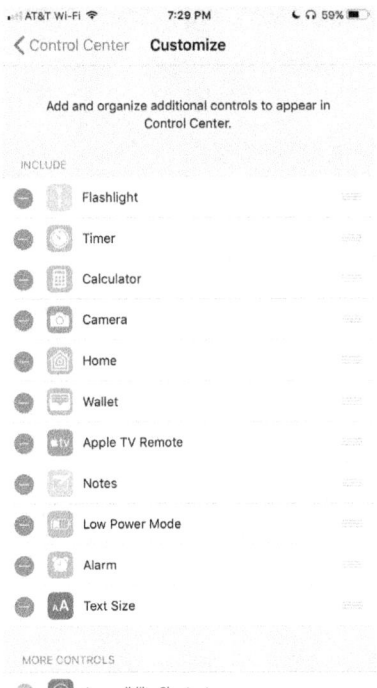

Once on this screen you can now customize not only what is shown, but the order of the items. To add an item, simply tap on the "+" button under "More Controls". To remove an existing control tap on the "-" button next to an item. If you want to rearrange the icons, you can click on the drag indicator to the right of any of the enabled items, and move it up or down, depending on where you want to position the item.

The items under "More Controls" should be listed alphabetically, whereas the items in the "Include" section should be based on your own ordering. Once you have added your items, you can return to Control Center.

System Functions

Let us look at each of the individual functions available in Control Center starting with the System functions.

There are some settings that either toggle the item when you tap on it, or are simply a shortcut to some settings. These toggles and shortcuts are:

- Accessibility Shortcut
- Alarms
- Calculator
- Guided Access
- Low Power Mode
- Magnifier
- Night Shift
- Screen Rotation Lock
- Timer
- Voice Memos

Having the ability to add any of these toggles or shortcuts will provide quick access, which can therefore increase productivity. The Calculator does provide a quick action. That action is to copy the last result, which is convenient if you did a calculation and need to paste it elsewhere in the system, or to another application.

Control Center System Functions

The system functions in Control Center provides quick access to six different functions. These are:

- Airplane Mode
- Cellular
- Wi-Fi
- Bluetooth
- AirDrop
- Personal Hotspot

By default, AirDrop and Personal Hotspot are hidden. These can easily be viewed by tapping and holding on any of the icons in the System Functions box. If you tap on any of the icons, it will toggle that function. Next let us take a look at Music on Control Center.

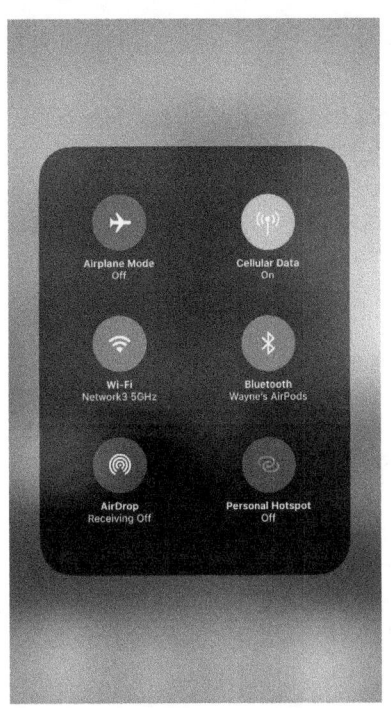

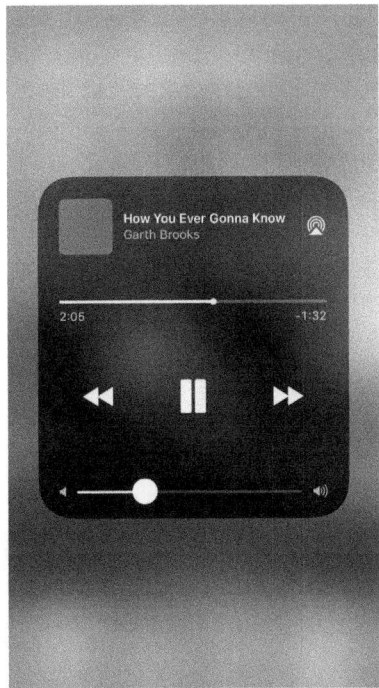

Music in Control Center

There have been Now Playing controls in Control Center since its inception. The ability to pause and start audio from the Lock Screen has been around even longer. As time has progressed, iOS has also added the ability to choose the output destination for the media that is currently playing. This is done through Apple's AirPlay protocol.

The proliferation of wireless headphones, wireless speaker systems, and the ability to wirelessly send media via AirPlay has necessitated a way to quickly switch between output devices. This is easily accomplished via the Now Playing section is in the upper right corner of Control Center.

There are three Now Playing functions that are immediately available in Control Center. These are reverse, pause and forward. Tapping on any of these will perform that action. This is very convenient.

Similar to the System Functions, you can tap and hold on Now Playing icon and it will expand. Here you will have only a few options. You can see the currently playing media. You can also scrub through the item, reverse, go forward, and even adjust the volume. The last icon is the AirPlay icon in the upper right. Tapping on the AirPlay icon will reveal all of the possible audio destinations for the media. You can then tap on any of the destinations and the media will begin streaming to the selected device. If you playing audio, using AirPlay is a great way to play that audio on another device. Ye, there are times when you want to be able to show exactly what is on your screen. This is where Screen Mirroring can come in handy.

Screen Mirroring

Whether you are playing a game, demoing an application, or just want to have a shared experience with others, mirroring your iOS device's screen can be an effective way of doing just that. Control Center in iOS 11 provides a simple shortcut to be able to choose

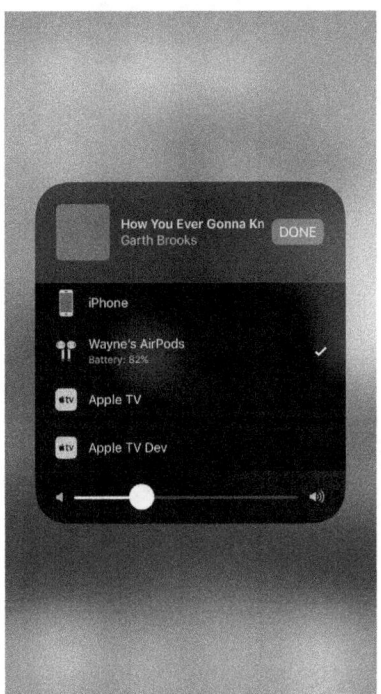

the destination. To share your screen via Control Center simply tap and hold on the Screen Mirroring button. A popup will appear providing you the destinations for mirroring your screen. These differ slightly from the Now Playing, since the devices listed in this section must be able to do video. A common destination is the Apple TV. Tapping on any of these destinations will begin displaying your screen on that device.

Once you are finished mirroring your screen, you can go back to Control Center, tap and hold on the Screen Mirroring button and tap on "Stop Mirroring". Even though you may be done screen sharing, you may still want to be able to use your Apple TV to do something else.

Apple TV Remote

One of the trends of technology is to make things smaller. In most cases, this is a great benefit. Who wants to lug around a 15 pound laptop? No one does. However, there are times when this can

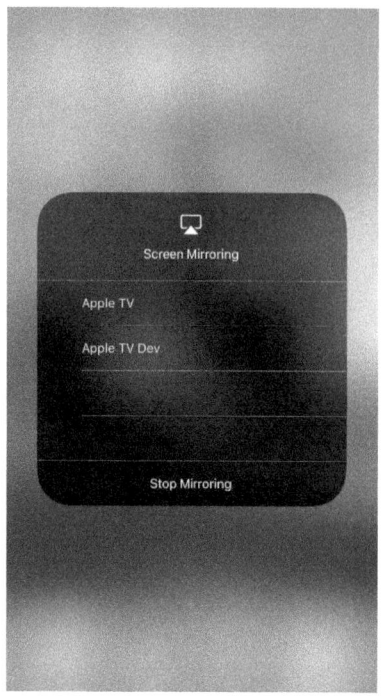

become a bit problematic. For instance when it comes to remotes for devices. Remotes often get lost. When they do it can be quite inconvenient to have to find the remote in order to use a device.

Apple is fully aware of this issue, and for that they have the Apple Remote app. Even with this, iOS users tend to have many applications installed on their devices and it can be difficult to locate the Apple TV Remote application. To make things a bit easier on everyone, Apple now has the Apple TV Remote built directly into Control Center.

The functionality of the Apple TV Remote in Control Center is the same as the actual application. You get the same functions, Play/Pause, Home Button, Siri, and the large Touch Pad on the top. Just like in the full application, if you need to enter text, a keyboard will appear. Below are a couple of screenshots comparing the full Apple TV application and the Control Center Apple TV Remote.

Now the question becomes, how do you adjust the volume of the Apple TV while you are mirroring your screen. That can be done via Control Center as well.

Volume Adjustment and Brightness

As mentioned above, you can adjust the volume of the audio via Control Center. This is done via a slider on the far right. You can adjust the volume by simply moving your finger up and down. You can also press and hold to get a larger version of the same control.

Similar to Volume adjustment, you can adjust brightness of your device using the same type of slider. This is located directly to the left of volume. It works in the same exact manner and also has a larger slider that can be accessed by tapping and holding on the Brightness slider. There are times however, that you need quick access to the Camera.

Camera in Control Center

At times life can be fleeting and at these times you want to quickly be able to capture a moment. If your iPhone or iPad is locked, you can simply swipe to the right and gain access to the Camera. Although, if you device is not locked then you have to try and find the Camera application and most of the time when you do find it, it is too late. Yes, you could quickly lock your device and then swipe to the right, but this is not ideal. Instead, Apple has provided the ability to put a Camera shortcut into Control Center.

There are a couple of different options with the Camera. Simply tapping on the Camera button will bring up the camera. You also have the option of tapping and holding, or force pressing. When you do this you get a few options. The quick actions you can complete are:

- Take a Selfie
- Record Video
- Record Slo-mo
- Take a Portrait

Tapping on any of these will bring the camera up directly into that mode. If you tap on the Camera button at the top of this popup, you will be brought into the standard Photo mode of the Camera. When you are done taking your picture and want to get back to watching what were on the Apple TV, you may need to adjust some of your Smart Home Devices.

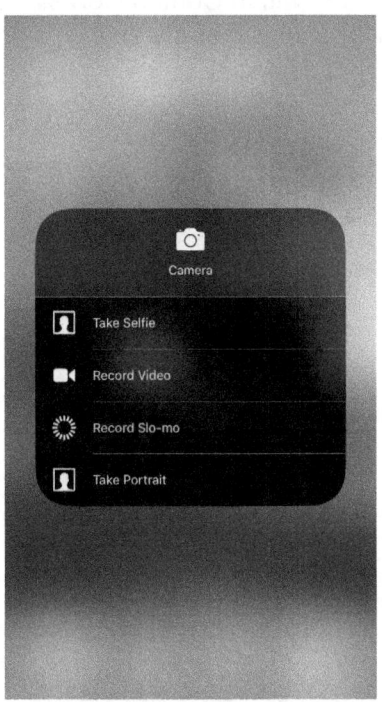

Home in Control Center

In iOS 10, Apple expanded Control Center to the three panels. One of these panels, the one on the far right, was for quick access to your Smart Home devices that are configured within the Home app. iOS 11 continues to have this feature. Under iOS 11, you can simply tap on the Home icon and the Home app will open. Alternatively, you can tap and hold on the Home icon and a popup will appear.

In this popup, you will have quick access to your Favorite Accessories as well as any scenes that you have configured. Tapping on any of the accessories or scenes will toggle that device. If your device has any options, say like a light, you can tap and hold, or force press on that individual item and its options will appear. In the case of a light, a slider for its intensity appears.

The inclusion of HomeKit enabled devices within Control Center is a continuation of the functions in iOS 10 just with some nice enhancements.

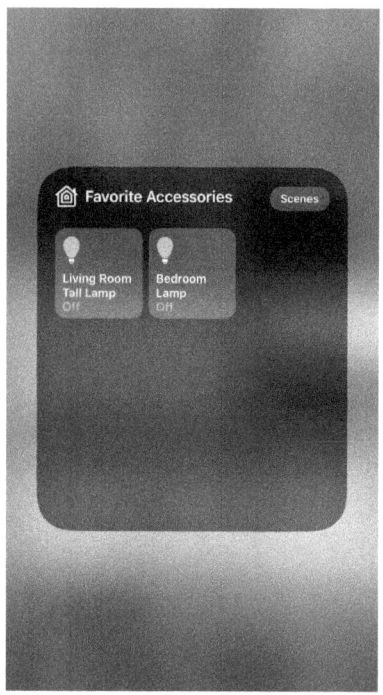 

Timers

Sometimes you want to be able to set a timer. You can open the Clock app and tap on Timers, and then set your timer. Alternatively, you could set a timer in Control Center. To do this, simply Tap and Hold, or Force Press, on the Timer icon. Similar to other functions, a popup will appear. Here you can select the length of your Timer. The options are:

- 1 Minute
- 2 Minutes
- 3 Minutes
- 4 Minutes
- 5 Minutes
- 10 Minutes

- 20 Minutes
- 30 Minuts
- 1 Hour
- 2 Hours.

You can either tap on one of the options, or you can slide your finger up and down to get the right time. Once you are ready to start the timer, simply tap not the "Start" button at the bottom.

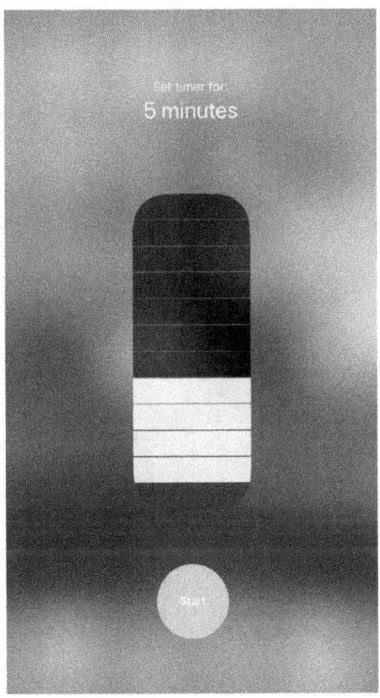

Accessibility in Control Center

Everyone's needs for an iOS device are all different. Some users can get by on a smaller font size, whereas others cannot. In order to make thing easier for those users who need to adjust the text size, there is not an option within Control Center on iOS 11 to quickly adjust the size.

Just like many other controls, tapping and holding or force pressing on the Text Adjustment icon will show a popup. Also similar to the Timer popup, you can drag your finger along the slider to find the proper size, or simply tap on one of the options.

There is one thing that is a bit different to this popup, as compared to others. The Text Adjustment takes into account whether a user has set the "Larger Fonts" accessibility option. If they have, they will receive more options to choose from. This is nice feature to have.

The ability to quickly adjust the text size may come in quite useful when using a shared iPad. Instead of needing to find the option within Settings, you can quickly adjust it right from within Control Center.

Notes

There are absolutely times when having quick access to make a

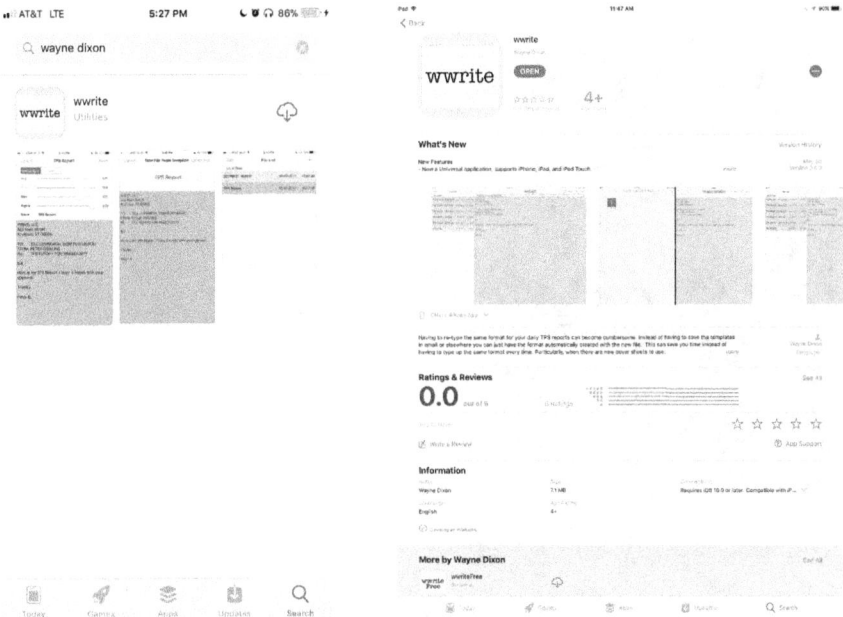

note would come in very handy. Similar to the Camera mentioned above, you could go and find the Notes app, but it would be cumbersome to do so. Instead, you can now have quick access to Notes right from within Control Center.

If you tap on the Notes icon, you will be brought directly into Notes, where you last left off. If you tap and hold, or force press, the Notes icon, you will receive a popup with some options. Here you can create a:

- New Note
- New Checklist
- New Photo
- New Sketch

Tapping on any of these will bring you directly to that function within Notes. If you tap on "New Photo" it will bring up the Camera

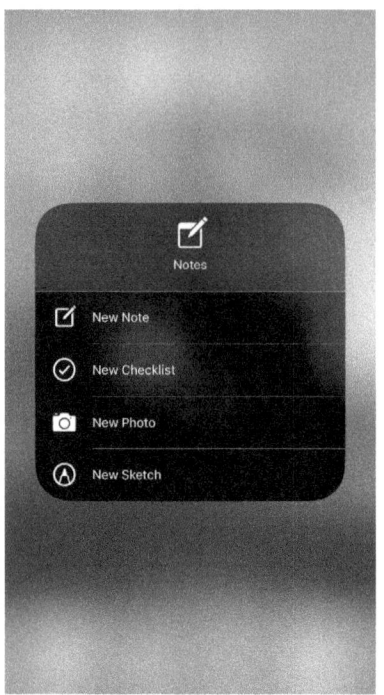

and any photo you take will be automatically imported into a new note within notes.

You can also tap on the Notes icon at the top of the popup and you will be brought directly into Notes. If you are one who uses notes on a regular basis, having quick access to your Notes from anywhere will be a productivity improvement.

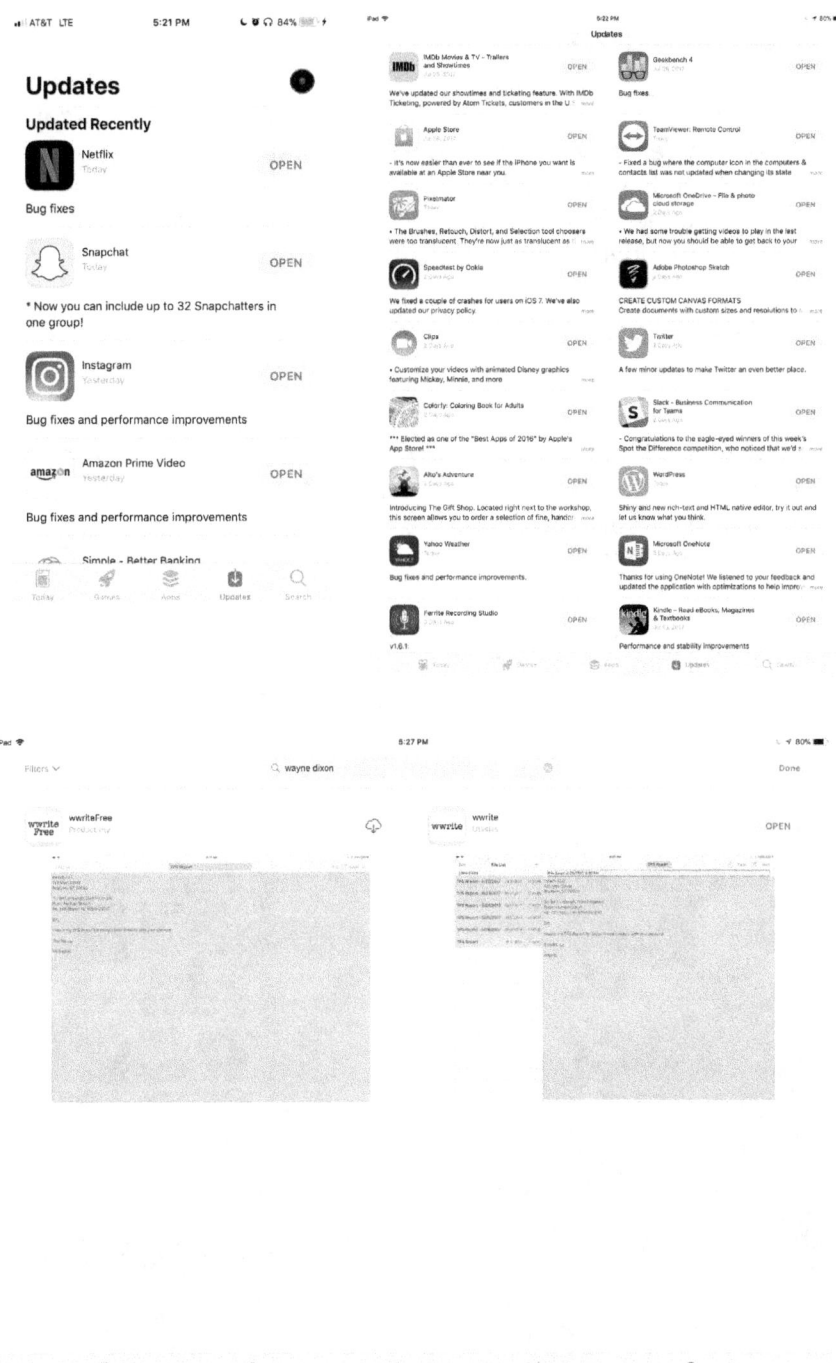

New Features

There are two items that were specifically omitted earlier, because they are entirely new items. The first is Screen Recording and the second is Do Not Disturb while Driving. Screen Recording is available on the iPhone as well as the iPad whereas Do Not Disturb while Driving is only available on the iPhone.

Screen Recording

Have you ever been trying to help someone with an issue on their iPhone or iPad and no matter how hard you try, they do not seem to understand the steps to accomplish the task that you need them to? In these cases it may be easier to just record a video and then send it to them.

If you have a Mac, you can setup QuickTime Player to record your screen. But that can be a pain. Plus, what if you are not near your Mac, or do not even have a Mac. There are tools for Microsoft Windows, but this is not a solution because many individuals do not own a computer. This is where Screen Recording can help.

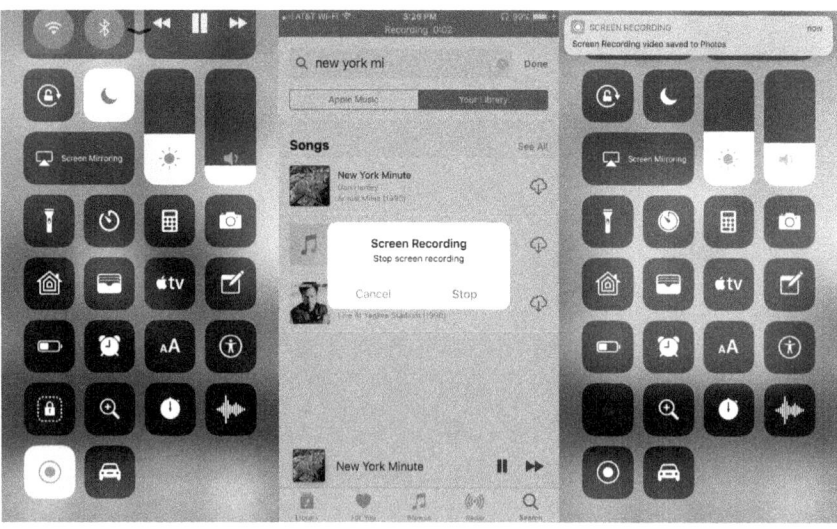

With iOS 11, it is now possible to record your entire screen at any point. Screen Recording is available for iPhone, iPod Touches, and iPads. After adding Screen Recording to Control Center, within Settings, you can simply tap on the Screen Recording button and a recording session will begin. Alternatively, you can also tap and hold on the Screen Recording icon. You will see another option at the bottom of the screen, "Microphone Audio". By default, anything this toggle should be off. Tapping on the microphone button will enable it and it will become a bright red color. Also on this screen is the option to start recording.

When you tap on the Screen Recording button without having the popup arise, or whether you do enable the popup, the Screen will immediately begin recording.

The first thing you will notice once recording begins is that the Control Center icon changes from white to red. This is done to indicate that it is recording. If you manage to not notice the icon change it is not likely that you will also miss the bright blue banner at the top of the screen. This will absolutely let you know that the screen is recording. Anytime that the screen is being record, this bar will be shown and it will be shown during the entire session. There is no way to turn this feature off. The reason that this is required is so that applications cannot surreptitiously begin recording a screen without a user's consent.

While the screen recording is occurring, all output from your iOS device will be included in the recording. If you enable the microphone, any audio that is playing on your device will stop. However, if the microphone is off, all system audio will continue to play.

You can stop the recording via three different methods. The first is by tapping on the blue "Screen Recording" bar at the top of the screen. When you do this, an alert will popup verifying that you want to stop recording. The second method is by going into Control Center and tapping on the Screen Recording button again. The final method is to Tap and Hold, or Force Press, the Screen Recording button and tapping the text that states "Stop Recording".

The video file will then be created in the background. Once it has finished being created you will receive a notification indicating that the video has been saved to your Photo Library. If you tap on the notification, you will be taken directly to the newly created video in your Photo Library.

As the adage goes, a picture is worth a thousand word, which means a video must be worth the removal of a headache and long time on the phone attempting to walk someone through a task. Particularly since now you record a video and send it to someone directly on your iOS device. On the subject of headaches, driving can be a headache for some people. To help with driving, there is a new feature specifically for the iPhone, Do Not Disturb While Driving.

Do Not Disturb While Driving

When cars were originally introduced to the world, safety was not the highest priority. At that time, there were not many cars, so there was less potential to crash. Given the newness of driving as well as the minimal interiors made it easier to focus solely on driving. Fast forward a hundred years and today's modern cars are chock-full of screens and technology. All of these can become distractions while driving. The biggest distraction is typically the one that we carry with us, our iPhones.

The iPhone has become the center piece of the modern world. It holds all the access to our memories and our access to interactions with others. We are constantly bombarded with an unlimited number of distractions. The ability to have instant access to anybody in the world has trained many to want instant

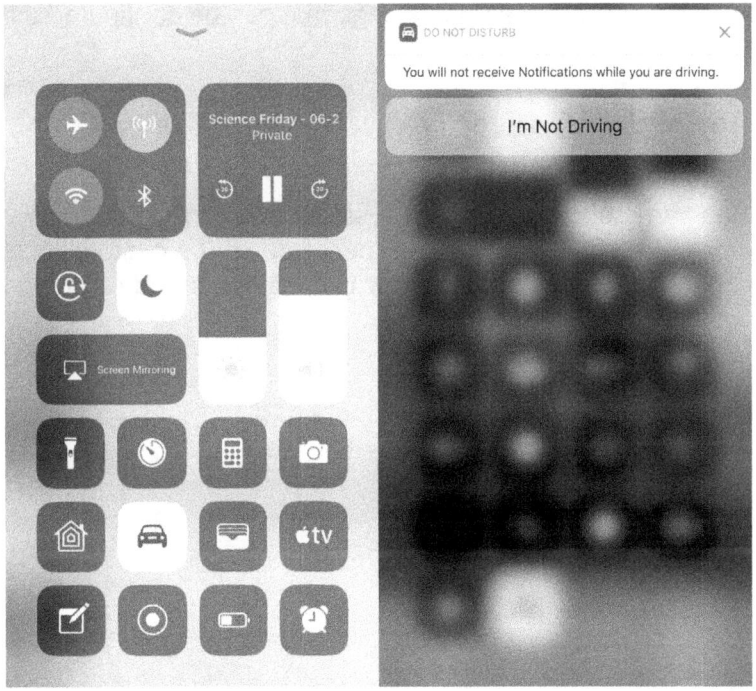

gratification as well as instant access to knowledge.

When we are at a stop light, we have all looked around and observed drivers not paying attention to their surroundings. If this is the behavior that is exhibited when these drivers are at a stop light, what is their behavior when they are actually driving?

There is a rise in the number of accidents that occur every year. In some instances this is directly attributable to distracted driving. To help attenuate this trend Apple has introduced Do Not Disturb While Driving.

Do Not Disturb While Driving is a new feature for iOS 11 which will enable drivers to set the parameters of when this feature is enabled. You can add Do Not Disturb While Driving to Control Center through the customize Control Center tab within Settings. When Do Not Disturb While Driving is enabled, you will still receive notifications, but they will not be displayed on your device, nor will there be any haptic or Taptic feedback when a notification is received. There are some settings that can be configured as well.

Customizing Do Not Disturb While Driving

As many are able to attest, a one-size fits all configuration does not work, in most cases. Instead there need to be customizations available. Do Not Disturb While Driving can be found by doing the following:

1. Open Settings
2. Tap on Do Not Disturb

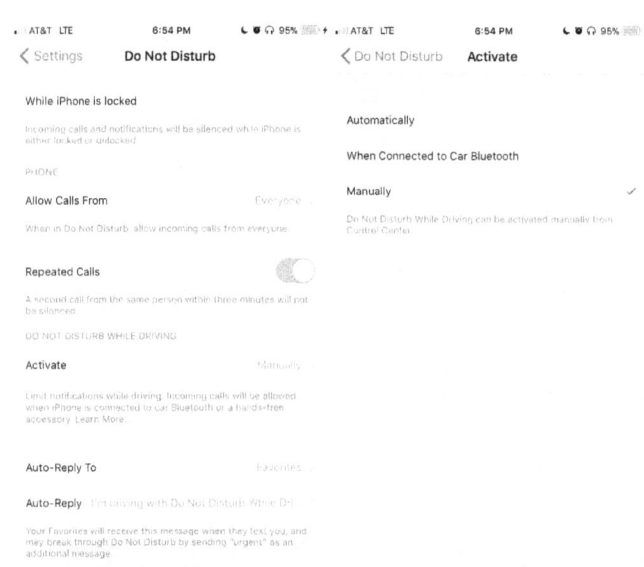

At the bottom of the screen, there should be a section titled "Do Not Disturb While Driving". There are three options within this section. "Activate", "Auto-Reply To", and "Auto-Reply".

If you tap on "Activate" you will see three different options. "Automatically", "When Connected to Car Bluetooth", and "Manually". The default option is "Manually". If you select "Automatically", Do Not Disturb While Driving will be enabled based on motion. If you are going ten miles, or sixteen kilometers, per hour, it is likely that Do Not Disturb While Driving will be enabled.

Selecting "When Connected to Car Bluetooth" will do as it states, automatically enable when an iPhone is connected to Bluetooth stereo within a car.

The "Auto-Reply To" section provides four different options, "No One", "Recents", "Favorites", and "All Contacts". You can select whichever group best fits your situation. By default "Favorites" is selected. It seems a bit strange that the default would be Favorites when it would make more sense that "All Contacts" would provide a wider range of individuals, hence would limit distracted driving even more.

"Auto-Reply" is the message that you would like to send when someone messages you while Do Not Disturb while Driving is enabled. The default message is:

"I'm driving with Do Not Disturb While Driving turned on. I'll see your message when I get where I'm going."

What remains unclear though is if Do Not Disturb While Driving while someone is on a bicycle. Although, if it did automatically enable at five miles per hour while someone was on a bicycle, it would not be a negative thing. This is because the cyclist should be paying attention to their surroundings, much like drivers.

Final Thoughts on Control Center

Control Center in iOS 11 has received a significant re-design. Many of the functions now have quick access to be adjusted.

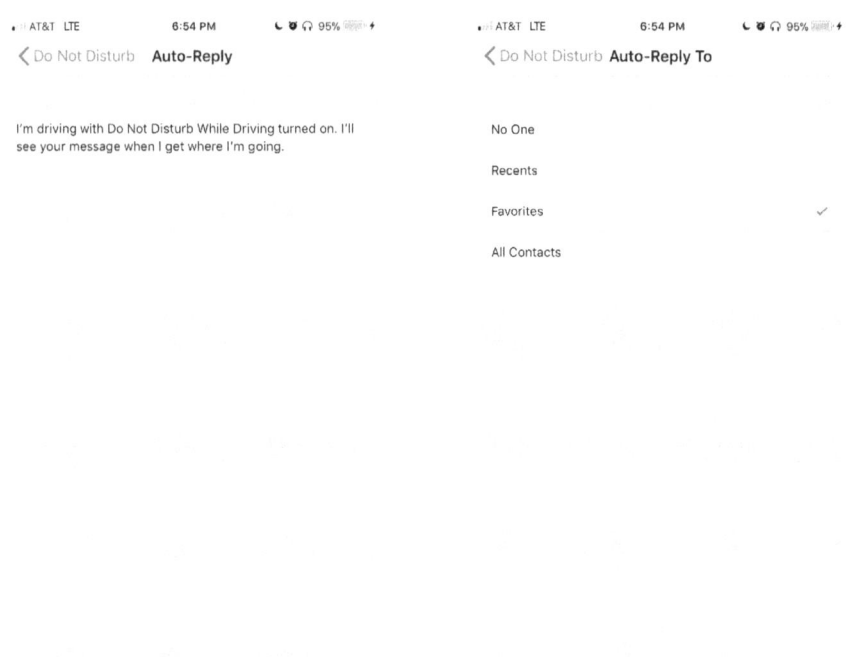

Combine this with the ability to toggle some functions on and off quickly and you have a real productivity boost. The biggest gains, however, may be in the ability for users to customize their Control Center. The customization will allow users to create a more personalized experience. An experience that can be tailored to what will work best for that user.

The inclusion of quick access to Screen Recording and Do Not Disturb While Driving will make great additions to an already feature-rich Control Center, but now that Control Center is customizable users will be able to add and remove features as they see fit.

The fact that the Text Size Adjustment takes into account a user's preference is a nice touch and something that one has come to expect from Apple, when it concerns accessibility options. Control Center is now capable of expanding should Apple add other features, or allow 3rd-parties to add Control Center icons, at some point in the future.

App Groups on iPad

Despite already covering app groups earlier, it is probably a good time to revisit them again. But this time in the context of switching applications. The app switching view has changed dramatically under iOS 11, but only for the iPad. On an iPhone or iPod Touch, the app switcher remains as it was it was under iOS 10, where each application appears as a tile in a horizontal scrolling view.

Under iOS 10, the iPad's application switcher was effectively, a larger version of the iPhone's application switcher. With iOS 11, this has changed. The primary reason for the change is that now when you swipe up from the bottom and look at Control Center, immediately to the left are all of your open applications.

The open applications are organized with the most recently used on the right and going from top to bottom. If you have two applications grouped together, you will see both of these together. What you see is a snapshot of the screen when it was last open, as is the case on previous versions of iOS. The difference with this is that each application, or application group, in its entirety. Meaning, that there is no more overlapping on application on the application switcher on the iPad.

Closing applications under iOS 11 remains the same as it was for iOS 10. You slide the application up to close it. This is the same behavior that is used to close an application group. It would be beneficial to have the option of closing just one of the applications within an application group, but it is not possible. Instead you have to close the entire group.

The redesign of the application switcher for the iPad is not revolutionary, instead it is evolutionary with the full viewable tiles and snapshot of each application as well as Control Center being on the right side. This is not the only redesign that has occurred, there have been some overall design changes that users may notice while using iOS, starting with Apple's assistant, Siri.

Siri

One of the features that many users have come to rely on is Apple's personal assistant, Siri. Siri began its life as a standalone application and was purchased by Apple in April of 2010 and integrated into iOS and released in October of 2011.

Siri Data

Over the intervening years, Siri has seen some significant improvements. From being able to play songs, to providing sports scores, helping with the definitions of words, and even finding the files on your Mac. One of the downsides to Siri has been that it has not been your personal assistant. What is meant by this is that each of your macOS and iOS devices has its own instance of Siri. While some of your data is shared, your actions and things that are learned about you on one device are not transferred over to other devices. With macOS High Sierra, this is no longer the case.

Under macOS High Sierra and iOS 11, Siri will now be able to synchronize the data it has learned about you to each of your devices. What this means for you is that you will now have one Siri assistant with all of your data. This is done by encrypting all of your Siri data and sending it between devices. This means that Apple will not be able to see your Siri data. That is not the only thing that has changed with Siri under macOS High Sierra.

Siri's Voice

One of the aspects to Siri that has changed over the last six years is the voice. It first changed in iOS 7.1. It still had the same general sound but was improved. Siri still had the hint of being a bit robotic. The Siri voice is changing again with iOS 11 and macOS High Sierra. The voice now has more fidelity, more natural pausing, and even better inflections. Ultimately, it sounds even more natural than before.

The new Siri voice is even more natural than before. When Siri reads out sentences, and responds it sounds a lot more natural and what people are accustom to hearing from fellow humans. It is perfect, no, but the Siri Voice is a lot better.

Translations

The world is becoming smaller and smaller, not in terms of physical size, although that may be happening as well, just on an imperceptible scale. People are able to get from one end fo the planet to the other faster than ever. This results in more interactions amongst people of different cultures and ethnicities. Alongside this comes different languages. If you are able to travel with a translator, your work becomes much easier. However, this is not always possible. To assist in this, Apple has added some translation capabilities to Siri.

The languages that are you able to translate from and to are:

- English
- French
- German
- Italian
- Mandarin
- Spanish

You are able to translate to and from any of these languages. In order to have Siri translate a word, just perform the following:

1. Activate Siri. This can be done by using the trigger phrase "Hey Siri", or holding down the Home button.
2. Siri will activate and then you can proceed to ask Siri to "Translate a word". Siri should respond asking which language to translate to.
3. Select the language that you want to translate to by either speaking the language or tapping on the language.
4. Siri should then translate the word. A card should appear within the Siri transcript. On this card should be the native phrase you stated, the translated phrase, and an audio version of the translated phrase.

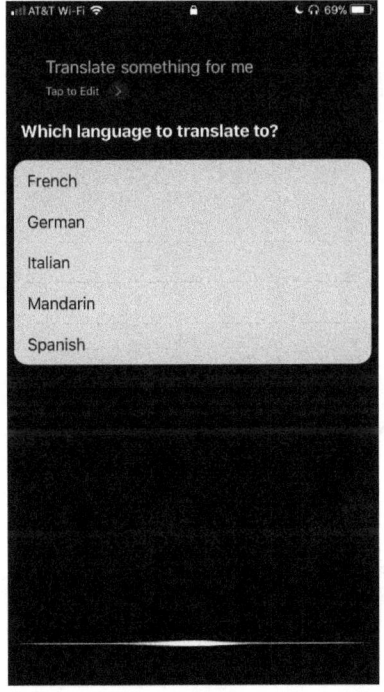

Siri translation is as beta feature. Not only because of the actual translations, but also because interacting it can be somewhat interesting at times. Regardless of its beta status, it will be helpful feature for anyone who has as need to translate between the languages that Siri can translate. There will be more languages coming in the future, but that will take some time to be able to fully finish. Translation is not the only new feature with Siri on iOS 11.

Additional Siri Capabilities

Each release of iOS, or macOS, provides an opportunity for new capabilities with Siri. With macOS High Sierra, and iOS 11, Siri gains a couple of new functions. Most notably, the ability to be your personal DJ. You can ask Siri to play any music that you might be in the mood for.

Besides this, Siri can also read out thing about album notes, and provide additional information about songs, albums or artists. All you have to do is ask.

Siri keeps getting better and better with each new release. The added functionality will allow you to do even more than you could before. The ability to have a single assistant across all of your devices will make Siri feel even more like your own personal assistant. Let us look at some other elements that you might notice when using iOS 11.

New Design Elements

One of the big feature of iOS 9 was the redesigned Music app. Besides Apple Music, the redesigned Music app brought a new look and feel to iOS applications. When you first use iOS 11, you may notice that many applications now look quite similar to the Music app, this is not a coincidence. One of the focus points regarding iOS 11 was to update the design. The biggest thing one might notice is that some applications now have a larger title and font at the top of the screen. An example can be seen below. The one of the left is the Music app, whereas the one on the right is the opening page for Settings app. As you can see, they both show the same general type of design aesthetic.

Besides the larger titles, there have been some other enhancements with tab bars. Tab bars are at the bottom of the screen that provide a number of selections, as in the Music app or the App Store. Tab bars can now display custom icons that will scale. For instance, if you have larger font accessibilities enabled, you are able to press and hold on icons in tab bars. When you do this, a popup should appear that will show a larger version of the icon and display some text below it.

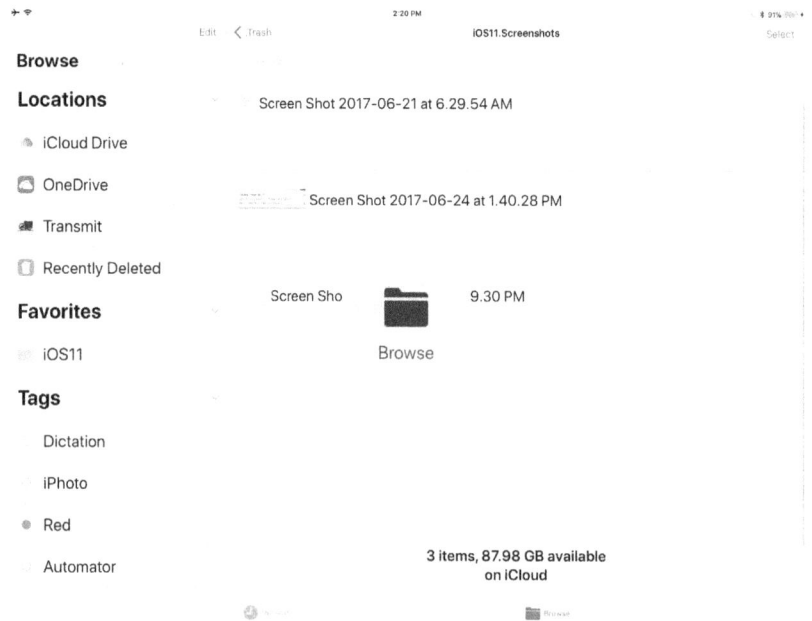

On the topic of the App Store, it has also received a major redesign.

App Store Under iOS 10

General applications are not the only thing to see a redesign. The iOS App Store app has received updates throughout the years, however, it has just received its first major since it was introduced. When you opened up the App Store app under iOS 10, and previous versions, you were presented with five buttons at the bottom. The four buttons that were consistent between versions included "Featured", "Top Charts", "Search", and "Updates".

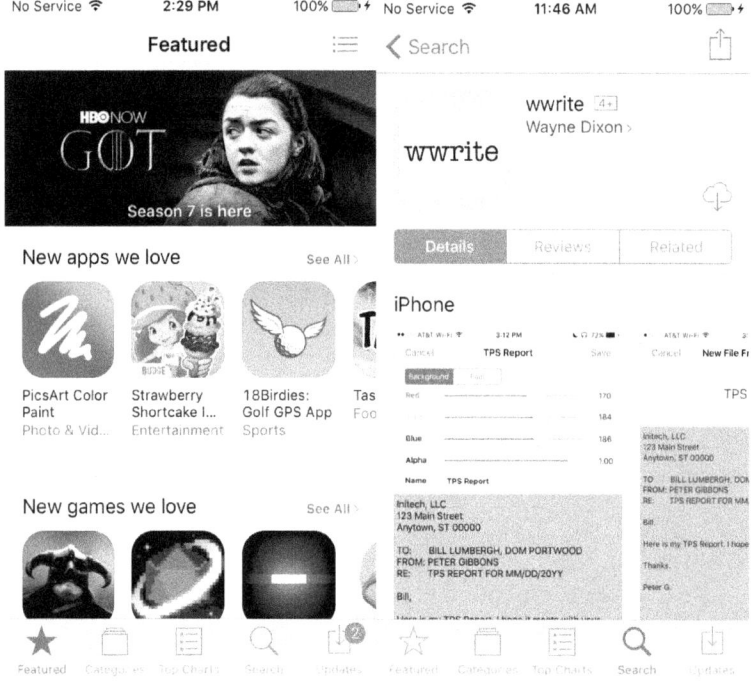

Featured highlighted a variety of different types of applications, including items that the App Store editors love, new games, and many more.

The Top Charts were, as one might expect, the best selling applications. There were three sections, "Paid", "Free", and "Top Grossing". The Paid applications were those that were available for purchase, where as Free were ones that could be downloaded for free. The Top Grossing section could be either paid or free applications that have made the most money.

Search would allow you to search for any type of application you would like. The search could be for a specific application name, a genre, or even a keyword.

Updates is where you would go to update the applications on your iOS device, if you did not have auto-updates enabled or if you wanted to manually update your applications. Under iOS 11, this is all changes.

App Store On iOS 11

When you first open the App Store, you will notice that the button options at the bottom have changed. There are still five, but they are not all the same. The options are, "Today", "Games", "Apps", "Updates", and "Search". Let us look at these in turn.

Today

The Today tab is designed to provide users with a collection of apps that are highlighted. This was done previously under "Featured", but there is more than meets the eye. What will show up is under the charge of the App Store's editorial team. They will be choosing what to highlight and what gets featured.

The possible items that will be highlighted include apps and games. The App Store will not just list apps and games, but instead will provide longer pieces about the apps. With longer editorials about the applications, are you going to have to scroll

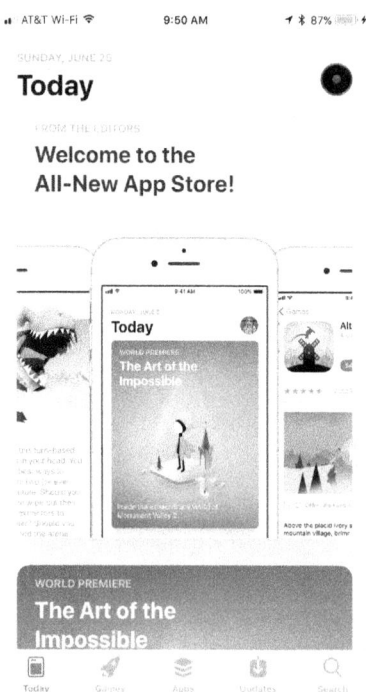

forever just to get to the next item. No, you will not. Instead, everything is displayed using a large tile. If you tap on any tile, you will then be shown the information about the app. At the bottom of every tile is a link to either get, or purchase the app.

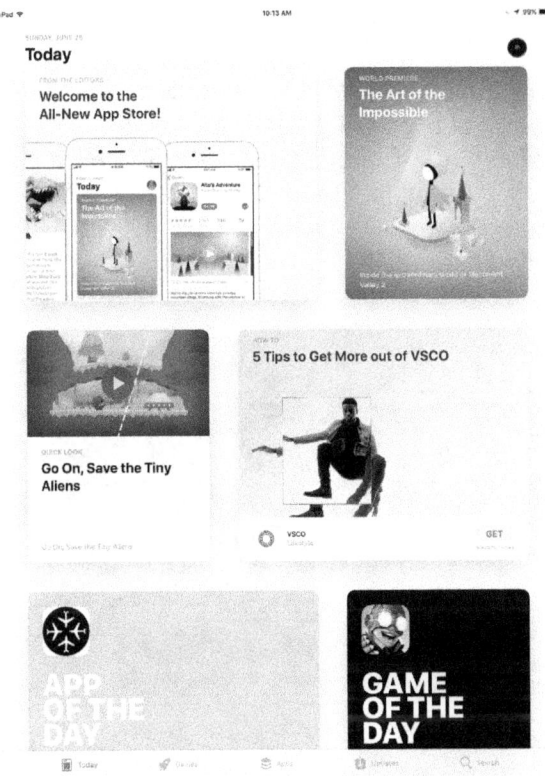

The information will be updated every day. Each day there will be an App of the Day as well as a Game of the Day, A Collection, a Daily List. Other topics may include "How To," "Quick Looks", or even "Favorites" of the App Store editors.

You will be able to scroll back through the days to see anything that you may have missed. What is highlighted may be timely, given events that are occurring around that time. For instance, June is the time for things that remind you of Summer. As an example, on June 24th, one of the highlighted items was the NBA Finals, as well as a topic called "Rule at Road Trips".

Games

According to Apple, Games is the biggest category within the App Store. In order to acknowledge that fact there is now a dedicated section in the App Store just for games.

When you open up the Games tab, you will be presented with an arrangement of different games. Some of these may include "Games We Love", " New Games", "Editor's Choices", "Top Paid", "Top Free", "Top Categories", "Beautiful Games", "Games You May Like", and even specific categories.

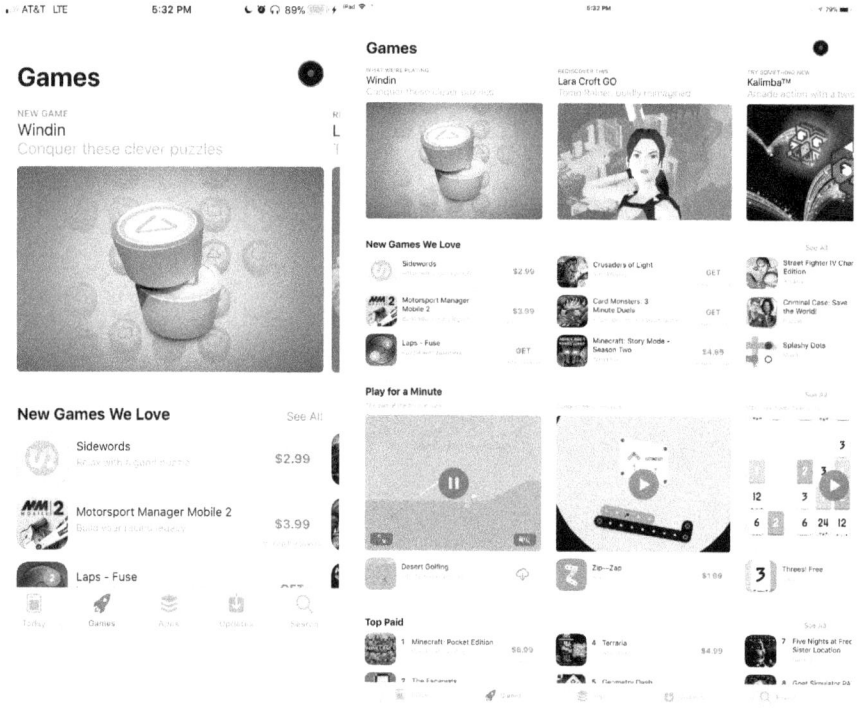

The separation of Games will allow popular applications, that are not games, to be seen in the "Top Charts" area, of the next item, Apps.

Apps

With Games being the biggest section of the App Store, that means that all other non-games go under the "Apps" tab. The Apps tab is configured similarly to the way the Games tab is set up. You have the Highlighted apps at the top, will "Apps We Love", "Top Paid", "Top Free", "Top Categories", and other special categories.

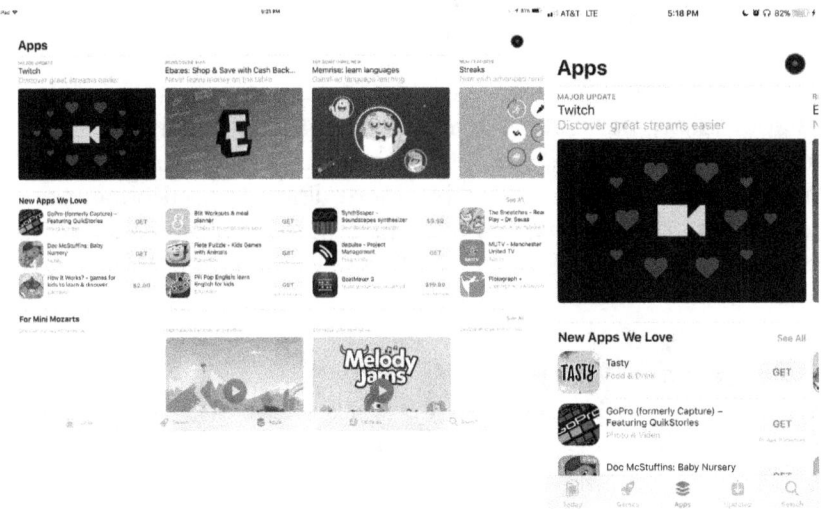

Updates

Updates provides the same functionality as one might expect, it is where you go to update your apps. Even with this though, the Updates tab has received some improvements as well.

Under iOS 10, you are presented with a list of apps that needed to be updated as well as a list of recently updated applications. At the top of this list is a link for your purchased applications. If you wanted to know what was new with the update, you could do so by tapping on the "What's New" link at the bottom of the bottom of each updated application. With iOS 11, you will now be able to see the first two lines of the update notes.

This added benefit will allow you to decide if you want to update the application, particularly if you know of a bug and it is mentioned within the notes. If there are more than two lines in the update notes, you can tap on the "More" link. On an iPhone, or iPod Touch, the notes will be expanded, just as in previous versions. The behavior is slightly different on an iPad. When the

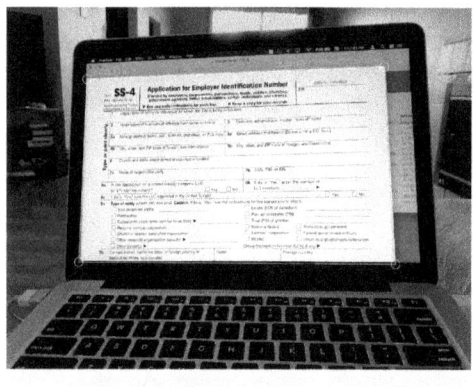

"More" link is tapped on an iPad, a popup with the release notes will be shown. You can dismiss the notes by tapping anywhere outside of the popup.

The location of your Purchased application has changed. Now, instead of tapping on a link to see your purchased applications, you now have to tap on the icon for your account in the upper right corner of the screen. When you do this, you will have a few options. These include "Purchased", "Redeem", "Send Gift", and "Sign Out".

The last little change is the the button to either update or open an app. Instead of being a white button with a blue border, the button is now rounded with a gray background.

The changes to the "Updates" tab may be small, but they are nice improvements that add to the experience of updating applications. The movement of Redeem and Send Gift to under the Account button makes complete sense since those items affect your account. The last tab in the App Store is Search.

Search

When you hear of a new application, whether it be from a website, podcast, or someone you know. You often want to look at what the application has to offer. The primary method of finding apps is by searching for them. This is where the Search tab in the App Store comes in handy.

The initial search page has not changed much, it still shows the searches that are trending. The only change to this page is that there are now a search icon next to the search term, as well as line under each of the different search terms.

When you do search for an application, you are presented with a list of possible applications that match the search term. The app information is still the same, you see the name of the app, it's category, it's current Star Rating and one or two screenshot previews, depending on if you are using an iPad or an iPhone or iPod Touch. Once you tap on an app, you will see that the App's page has changed quite a bit. Let us look at this in detail.

App Pages

Each App on the iOS App Store has its own page. These individual pages have changed significantly under iOS 11. All of the changes are for the better.

If you viewed an app's page on iOS 10, you would see the name of the App, its icon, the developer at the top, and the app's rating. Following this were three tabs, "Details", "Reviews" and "Related". The Details tab included Screenshots, the description, version notes, general information, and links for the version history, developer website, and other apps by that developer.

The Reviews tab included ratings and reviews for the application. You could toggle between the reviews for the current release and all versions of the application.

The Related tab is for similar applications to the one you are looking at. This is useful in case you do not think the current application that you viewing will meet your needs.

The biggest change with the App Store pages in iOS 11 is that there is now only a single page that will display all of the same information. The iOS 11 App Store pages start off this same with the App's icon, the app name, and the developer at the top. You will also notice that at the top that the current ratings are shown. Right next to this, age rating for the application. These are followed by the latest release notes, and then screenshots for the app. Following the release notes are the description, the developer information, and detailed Ratings and Reviews. The last section is the app information, additional apps by the author and other applications you might be interested in.

The biggest changes that one notices immediately is that the most important information is the largest. This includes What's age rating and the app's current ratings. These being the largest indicate that these are what users are most looking for when it comes to evaluating applications. This make sense given that an application needs to be appropriate for the audience whereas ratings help users decide if the app is worth downloading.

There is a factoid to keep in mind when it comes to ratings. Prior to iOS 10.3, developers could not opt-out of resetting their ratings for their applications. Every time that they did an update, their application's rating would reset.

Now, they have the opportunity to keep their existing ratings when an application is updated. This change will allow developers to determine when it is best to reset ratings. The likely reason that a developer would reset their ratings is due to a bad update being released, but there could be other reasons. For instance, when a new major version comes out, it may be time to reset ratings to see how users react.

Purchasing Content

The iOS App Store is great for being able to generate revenue. According to Apple, they have paid out more than $70 Billion to developers since the App Store's inception in 2008. To many this is an unfathomable number. Conceptually, it is not difficult to understand, but imagining that much money in one spot is not really something one can truly imagine.

When a user purchases an application, or an in-app purchase, they must confirm that they want to purchase an item. On iOS 10, this was merely a confirmation to put in their password. While this did indeed stop any errant purchases, it was not the most ideal when it comes to user experience and user confidence in what they were doing. To remedy this, Apple have completely revamped what you will see when you buy, or download an app from the iOS app store.

This is what the buying experience looked like in iOS 10.

It is not super inviting nor does it really indicate what is being purchased. Contrast that to what it looks like in iOS 11.

There is definitely a big difference. Under IOS 11, you get a pay sheet that is similar to one that is seen when using Apple Pay. The information that is provided on this pay sheet is::

- The name of the app
- The developer of the app
- The app's icon
- Whether it is an app purchase, or a free app.
- The app's rating
- The account that will be purchasing the app
- A "Cancel" button
- And either an "Enter Password" link or "Touch ID" button.

This last item depends on whether or not your device is capable of Touch ID and whether you have logged into the App Store since you last restarted your iOS device.

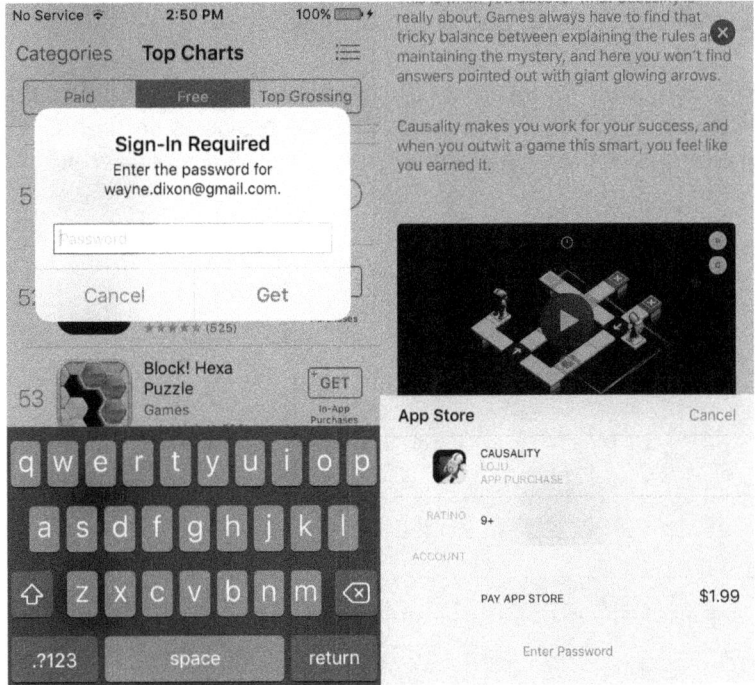

The new iOS App Store purchasing workflow is a significant improvement over the iOS 10 workflow. There is no more information when you go to purchase, or download, an app from the iOS 11 app store. This should vastly improve not only the user experience but also the confidence that a user understands what it is they are getting.

Final Thoughts on the App Store Redesign

The redesign of the iOS App Store is a much needed improvement over the previous iterations. The redesign brings all of an App's information into a single screen, which allows for information to be at a user's fingertips.

The addition of daily updates to the "Today" screen will give users a chance to check out new applications that they may not know about, but also provides the possibility of rediscovering an app that might have been forgotten. The App Store redesign is a thoughtful one, where much care and consideration was put into changing the way that the pages are displayed.

The new "pay sheet" for when a user purchases or downloads an application is a significant improvement over previous versions. The App Store is not the only application to receive a refreshed look.

Messages

Messages is one of the most used applications on iOS. Messages is full of a variety of features, including combining all of your conversations in one place, allowing attachments, sending audio messages, and even iMessage apps.

Introduced in iOS 10, iMessage apps can be just about anything that a developer can imagine. This could be a game, a productivity application, or even just a sticker pack that can be used to adorn your conversations. One of the issues that occurred with iOS 10 is that when you had a variety of iMessage apps installed, finding the application that you wanted was not an easy task. Besides this, managing your iMessage apps could be a bit cumbersome. The display and management of iMessage apps has changed under iOS 11.

Display of iMessage Apps

As mentioned above, the display of iMessage apps under iOS 10 was not ideal. With iOS 10, it was not easy to locate your iMessage apps. When you in a conversation and want to use an iMessage app, you would have to try and figure out which button to hit in order to show all of your iMessage apps. It was, and still is, the App Store icon. When you did hit the App Store button, a sheet would be shown with all of your installed applications. If you had a bunch of applications, more than could fit on one panel, it would expand to additional panels. While this worked to keep it organized, it was not easy to find the apps.

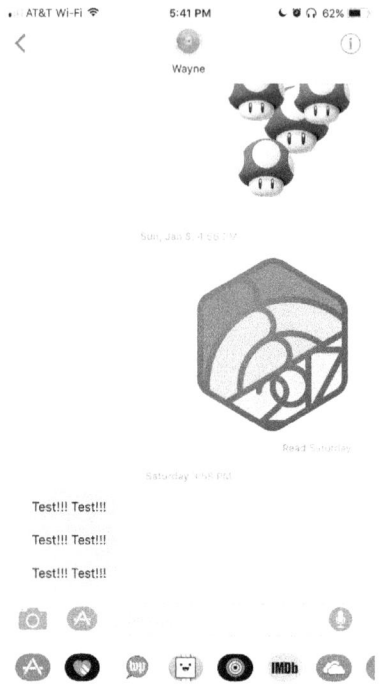

With iOS 11, accessing your iMessage applications is a lot easier. Here are the steps:

There are no steps. This is because all of your iMessage applications are now available at the bottom of the screen. The iMessage app tray consists of two sections, on the left are your favorites. You can tap and hold on any iMessage application and drag it to your favorites. The right hand side is all of your iMessage applications in order from most recently used to least recently used.

So now you can easily locate the applications that you want to use. When you use the horizontal scrollbar, the icons for the iMessage apps will get larger and include names. As was the case under iOS 10, you can simply tap on an iMessage app and it will appear. The display of iMessage apps has improved, how about management of the apps?

Management of iMessage Apps

Management of iMessage apps under iOS 10 heavily mimicked the way that you managed apps on the iOS Home Screen. You could tap and hold on any icon and it would begin to jiggle and a small x would appear. While this did work, it was not ideal. Managing iMessage apps with iOS 11 is much simpler.

The steps to enable or disable an iMessage app are as follows:

1. Scroll over the far right of your activated iMessage apps.
2. Tap on the "..." button.

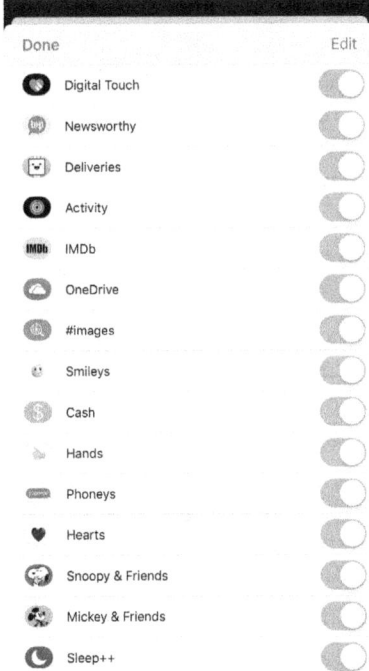

Here you will see all of your enabled applications. If you tap on the "Edit" button toggle switches will appear for each installed application, including the ones that are not enabled. Simply tap on any of the toggle switches and it will be enabled, if it was disabled, and disabled, if it was enabled. Once you are finished, tap on the "Done" button.

That is all there is to management of iMessage apps in iOS 11, but not all there is to Messages in iOS 11. There have been some interaction enhancements that developers must adopt.

Enhanced Interactions

iMessage apps were somewhat limited in what they could do. For instance, iMessage app developers were limited in terms the type of content that they could display to users. Developers were required to include most of the assets that they wanted to use within the iMessage application. Under iOS 11 this is no longer the case. Developers can automatically adjust the content within an app, if it makes sense.

One of the tasks that could be accomplished with iMessage applications was the ability to pay individuals right from within a conversation. This is being enhanced with iOS 11, with the introduction of Person to Person Apple Pay.

Person to Person Apple Pay

Have you ever been out to dinner with a group of friends and everybody is going to chip in? Even with this situation, it is typically that one person will end up paying and everyone else will either have to give money, or send money via an app. If there are a bunch of people people who all have iOS devices running iOS 11, you are now able to use Apple Pay for direct person-to-person payments. This begs the question, what happens when the money is sent, where does it go? With Person to Person Apple Pay, you have an Apple Pay Card. Let us look at the Apple Pay Cash Card now.

Apple Pay Cash

The Apple Pay Card is where any payments sent to you will be stored. With the Apple Pay card you are able to do the following:

- Send the money to your bank
- Send the money to others
- Use the card to pay for items in the App Store or iTunes Store
- Use the card in apps and websites that support Apple Pay.

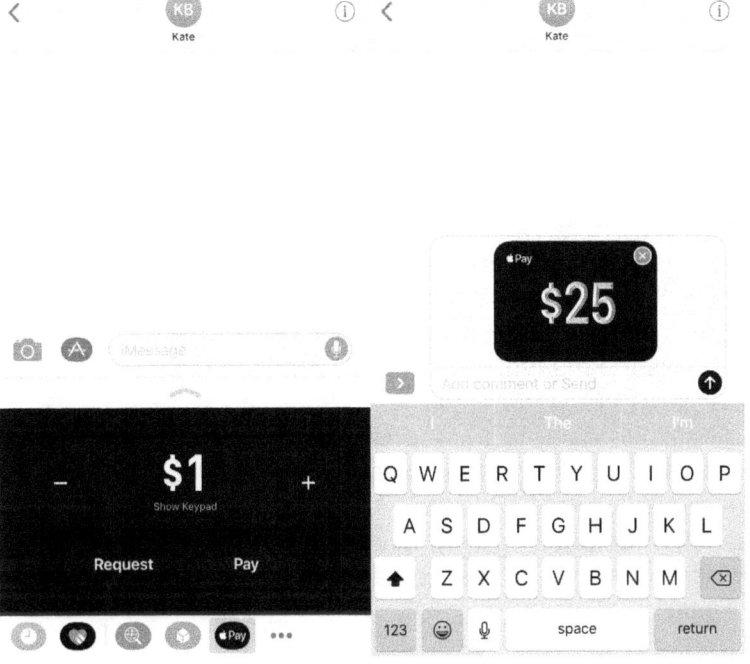

The Apple Pay card will be very versatile in what it will allow. There are many scenarios, beyond the one outlined above. Some of these may include, Parents providing their children will money for apps and in-app purchases, paying a baby sitter, or even as a way to buy stuff at a local farmer's market. The possibilities are endless.

There is one last interaction that would be a lot easier if it could be done in iMessage and not necessarily requiring you to use the web. That would chatting with businesses. This is where a new service, Business Chat will be useful.

Business Chat

Business Chat is a new services that Apple will offer to businesses that will allow them to interact with customers directly within iMessage. Business Chat could be used for customer support, after sales support, or any other interaction that you as a user could do with a business. There are a couple of key things to know about Business Chat.

The first thing to know is that you, the customer, will have to initiate the conversation. The service is specially designed in this manner to allow you to control when and how often a business will be able to contact you.

The second thing to know is that it be a standard iMessage, with a caveat. That caveat is that the color of the bar a the top is different. It will be a gray color. This is done to let you instantly know that this is not a conversation with an individual over iMessage. This means that you can use iMessage apps with these Businesses.

The third item is that since it is a standard iMessage, you have full control over notifications. This means that you can mute the conversation or delete it entirely. Once the conversation is deleted, the business will not be able to contact you unless you initiate contact again.

Conversations with Business Chat can be "long-lived", meaning that you could start a conversation before purchasing a product and then follow up with an order status a week or so later and then even with post-sales support questions afterwards. There is one last new feature of Messages.

Additional Screen Effects

With iOS 10, Apple added a new capability to Messages. That ability was to send a message with a whole screen effect. These effects allow you to add a bit of splash to messages that you send. Under iOS 10, there are a total of seven full screen effects. These are:

- Balloons
- Confetti
- Love
- Lasers
- Fireworks
- Shooting Star
- Celebration

These are some great effects. With iOS 11, there are two more full screen effects to add to your repertoire. These effects are:

- Echo
- Spotlight.

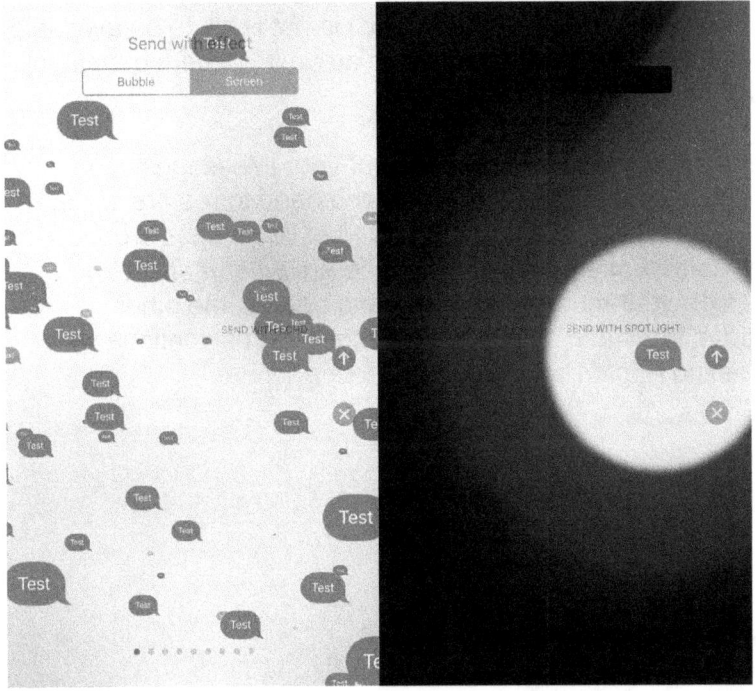

The "Echo" effect will duplicate your text multiple times on the screen and it will then make them all disappear. The "Spotlight" effect will shine a spotlight on your text for a few seconds and then expand the spotlight across the entire screen.

The two new effects will be great for adding some additional emphasis to some of your communications.

Final Thoughts on Messages

The improvements to Messages provide significant user enhancements. The ability to more easily manage iMessage apps, as well as indicate favorites will allow users to customize iMessage to their liking.

The expanded capabilities within iMessage applications, as well as the addition of Business Chat, will provide more interactions between different entities. The fact that initiation of the Business Chat is initiated by the customer means that they will be in full control of when the conversation ends. Business Chat will not be available to businesses until 2018, so it is not likely to be available for users until mid-2018. Once it does arrive it will be a benefit for both businesses and customers.

The fact that you can now backup all of your iMessages into iCloud will be a huge boon for users who need to restore or get a new device but want to keep all of their old iMessages around. The new screen effects will allow a different type of effect and emphasis on your messagesThere have been some other applications that have seen some changes, let us continue with the remaining Apple Pay changes.

Apple Pay Changes

One of Apple's core concerns is privacy and the securing of its user's data. One of the downsides to modern society is that there are many people who are out to get the information of others. In a similar manner to the securities that are in place in Safari under iOS 11, is the feature Apple Pay.

Apple Pay was introduced in October of 2014, with the introduction of iOS 8.1. Apple Pay brings the ability for users to add their credit and debit cards to their iPhone, Apple Watch, iPad, and even their Macs. You can use Apple Pay on any website that offers it, as well as within applications. There have been a couple of changes to Apple Pay, besides the ones mentioned previously in the section about changes to Messages.

The only other change is a minor one. That change is that the screen is now has a bright white background instead of a dark background..This change was done for a couple of reasons. The first is to make it easier to see the cards that have been added. The second is to provide an alternative to changing the screen to full brightness, which was the behavior under iOS 10. This is a minor change but take into consideration the other changes, the inclusion of the Apple Pay Cash card and the person-to-person Apple Pay, and all of these changes make for an even better Apple Pay experience. Let us now take a look at some changes to a highly used app, the Camera.

Camera

The camera is one of the most used hardware features on any iOS device. The camera allows us to capture what we are seeing for posterity. It provides a mechanism to be able to look back and recall those important moments. Even though the Camera is primary used to take photos it does provide a myriad of additional options, like magnification and color adjustments. The hardware of the camera within an iPhone is quite capable, but it cannot do its function without the software within iOS.

The camera has gained quite a bit of functionality over the years and iOS 11 brings even more features to the Camera. The first new feature is the filters.

Filters

iOS has had filters for many years now. The filter set has remained unchanged. The filters that were available under iOS 10 were:

- Mono
- Tonal
- Noir
- Fade
- Chrome
- Process
- Transfer
- Instant

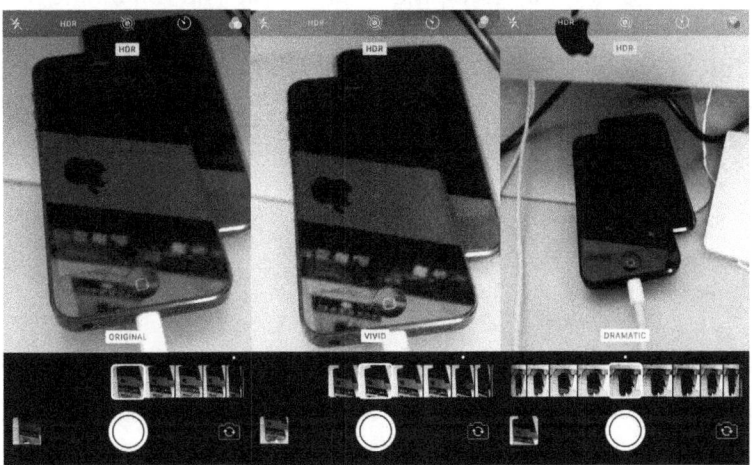

Each of these added its own feel to a photo. iOS 11 brings an new set of filters for users. The filters available under iOS 11 are:

- Vivid
- Vivid Warm
- Vivid Cool
- Dramatic
- Dramatic Warm
- Dramatic Cool
- Mono
- Silvertone
- Noir

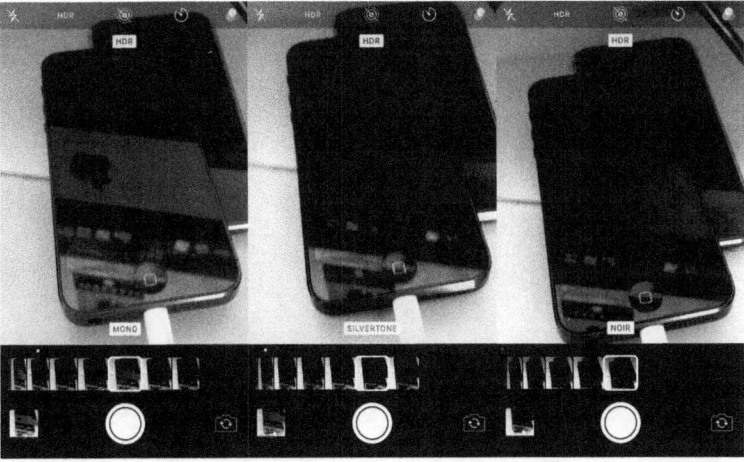

Only two of these are the same, Mono and Noir. The remaining ones are all brand new. These new filters will allow you to evoke just the right mood to your photos. The new filters are not the only new feature of iOS 11's camera. There is another around barcode scanning.

QR Codes

Everyone encounters barcodes, of one sort or another, every day. If you go to the grocery store every product you put into your cart has a Universal Product Code, or UPC, on it. Barcodes have made it easy to scan items for identification. Despite all of their uses, barcodes are limited in what they can represent. They can only represent letters and numbers. There is another representation that works a bit better Quick Response, or QR, codes.

QR codes are represented two dimensionally. Their benefit is that they are able to contain a wider variety of different types of information. The idea for QR Codes started twenty years ago in 1997 by the Association for Automatic Identification and Mobility. Over the last twenty years it has slowly gained traction within the market. You can now read QR Codes with iOS 11. Let us look at some potential uses.

As mentioned above, QR Codes can contain a myriad of different types of information. These include:

- URLs
- Email Address
- Telephone Numbers
- Contact Information
- SMS Links
- Geographic Information

And anything else that someone can define. The camera app within iOS 11 will be able to decipher any of these, plus wireless network information. You can use this example below to test out iOS 11.

Let us say that you do scan the QR Code above, the Camera app should provide an notification asking if you want to continue to proceed to waynedixon.com. The URL will actually bring you to my e-books page.

If you tap on the notification, you should be able to open Safari and bring you to the webpage specified in the QR Code. Having the camera be able to read QR Codes will help everyone, but particularly those in Asia where QR Codes are used heavily, particularly with the WeChat app.

Even though the new features of Camera are not revolutionary, they will be significant benefits for all types of users. Now that the Camera has been covered, let us turn our attention to Notes.

Notes

One of the applications that can be quite useful, particularly if you also use its macOS counterpart is Notes. Notes is a general purpose place that can be used for jotting down text, images, urls, and even sketches. There are a couple of new features available in Notes for iOS 11, starting with the inclusion of tables.

Tables

The first new feature is that you can can now add tables to your notes. In order to add a table to your note, simply do the following:

1. Locate the note that you want to add a table
2. Open the Note
3. Tap into the text area of the note to bring up the keyboard. Once this has been done, the toolbar will appear above the keyboard. On an iPad, the toolbar will be next to the predictive text area.
4. On the toolbar, tap on the icon that looks like a spreadsheet table. Once you tap on the table icon, a new table with two columns and two rows should be added.

You can add more columns if you need them. To add a new column simply tap on the three dots above any column. A popup menu should appear asking if you want to add or delete a column. Similarly, you can add a row by tapping on the three dots to the left of any row.

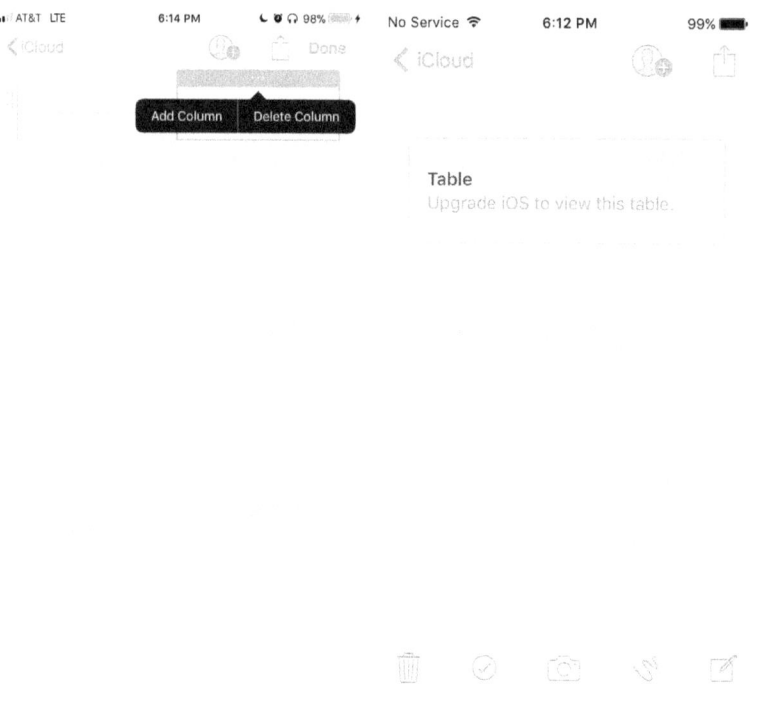

You can then enter in any information that you would like into the new table. When you are entering text into a table, you do not need to tap to go to the next cell, you can simply tap on the "Next" button in the lower right of the keyboard to advance to the next table cell. If you need to add more rows, you can simply enter text and keep hitting next. If you hit "Next" on an empty table cell, it will be interpreted as though you want to begin typing text outside of the table. **Tip:** If you need an empty row at the end of your table, just put a space in either of the table cells in the last row, and the row will effectively be empty.

If you need to move an entire column or row, you can do this by tapping on the three dots above a column, or to the left of a row, and then dragging it to the location that you want. This will move the entire column or row.

There is one thing to be cognizant about regarding notes about older iOS devices and notes that contain tables. If you have an iOS Device that is running an older version of iOS and a note that contains a table is synchronized to that device, the older device will not be able to view the table. It will, instead have a message similar to "Table: Upgrade iOS to view this table". An example is above.

Text Choices

The second new feature is some enhancements to the font selection. You can now select to have a monospaced font, within your note. This is extremely helpful if you need to line up some text, or if you want to add a bit of emphasis but do not want to use **bold** or *italics*, or underline.

iOS 10 had a couple of options for formatting. These included Title, Heading, and Body. Under iOS 10, these were presets. These options are still available in iOS 11, however you can now optionally select a couple of different options for text. You can now select the components individually. You can choose between bold, italics, underline, or ~~strikethrough~~, which is a new option. Whatever options you select will remain, until you decide to change them. There is one last option in this panel. You can now select to indent from the panel too. This is particularly helpful on an iPhone where you may not have a keyboard attached. These new font options are great for Notes users. There is still one new feature, which may be extremely useful for some users.

Pinned Notes

The third feature that has come to Notes in iOS 11 is the ability to make sure your most important notes are at the top, with the new feature called Pinning. To pin a note in iOS 11 perform the following steps:

1. Locate the note you want to "pin".
2. Slide from the left to the right on the title of the note. A "pin" icon will appear
3. Click on the pin button and the note will be pinned.

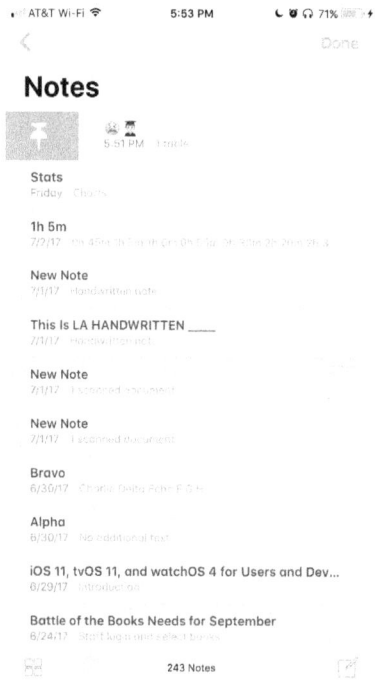

All of your Pinned notes will synchronize on all of your devices that are running iOS 11 or macOS High Sierra. The contents of the notes will sync to devices running other versions of iOS or macOS, but they will not be pinned.

Scanning Documents

As modern technology users, we all like to capture fleeting moments with our Cameras so that we can look back on those times with fond memories. This could be a monumental moment, a picturesque nature shot, or even just your friend making an idiot of themselves after they have had too much to drink Yet, there are those times when we need to save more mundane pieces of information. When these incidents occur there are ways of saving that information. The easiest is to take a picture with the camera on your iPhone. While this works, there are some issue with this. The most common one is that it is difficult to get a clear picture of what you are trying to save. If you do get a clear picture, it may not contain everything that you need or the entire picture may be skewed.

There are some third-party solutions to this issue. Even with these solutions, for some users they can be a lot more than fits their use case. For this, Apple has introduced a new feature of Notes in iOS 11, the ability to Scan Documents. If someone were to say "You can scan documents with notes", a response may be, "I can just add a picture to a Note". Which is true, but as mentioned above, there are some issue with that approach. Notes takes into account all of these issues and provides a quite robust document scanning interface.

To Scan a document in Notes, do the following:

1. Open Notes
2. Create a new note, or find a note where you want to add.
3. Tap the "+" button to bring up the action popup menu.
4. Tap on "Scan Documents". This should bring up the Camera.

Once the camera appears, you can then align the document you are trying to scan. The camera will create a yellow box around what it detects as a form. Once the yellow box appears you can take a picture. Once you take a picture, the picture will appear, with the form area highlighted.

This is where you can fine tune what it found. You can do this by moving the corners to the corners of the form. Once you are satisfied with the selection, tap on the "Keep Scan" button in the lower right corner to save that document. If you are not satisfied with it, simply tap on the "Retake" button in the lower left. At this time, you can either scan the next document, or tap the "Save" button to save the scanned document.

After you tap on the "Save" button, the scanned document will then appear in the note. Opening up the scanned document will allow you to do some minor adjustments. The adjustments you can make include:

- Rotating the scan
- Doing some fine tuning on the cropping
- Adjusting the color.

All of these are simple to perform. On an iPhone, or iPod Touch, you will find the toolbar at the bottom of the screen, whereas on an iPad, the toolbar will be in the upper right. Rotating the scan is simply done by tapping on the document with an arrow icon. Cropping can be done by tapping on the "crop" icon. Adjusting the color is accomplished by tapping on the three circles icon. There are four color choices. These choices are:

- Color
- Grayscale
- Black and White
- Photo.

Tapping on any of these color choices will adjust the scanned document to match the selected color. These color adjustments can be done on a document by document basis. This is particularly useful in case there is variations between the scanned documents. The ability to Scan Documents will be very helpful for those who need to be able to scan documents for later use.

There is one thing to be aware of with notes that contain Scanned Documents. If you have an iOS Device that is running an older version of iOS and a note that contains a table is synchronized to that device, the older device will not be able to view the table. It will, instead have a message similar to the one below. If you are running macOS High Sierra on a Mac that is logged into the same iCloud account, your documents will synchronize over and you will be able to view your scanned documents.

This is not the end of new features in iOS 11. There is one last feature.

Quick Handwriting

The last new feature of Notes in iOS 11 is one that is for the iPads. You can now easily start a handwritten note by simply beginning to write with your Apple Pencil. There is no longer a need to start a sketch or anything like that. As soon as you begin writing with the Apple Pencil. This is a nice touch particularly if you need to start writing quickly. There is an additional feature that comes with this quick handwriting.

Unlike tables and Scanned Documents within notes, handwritten notes will be able to be seen on older iOS devices. This is because the handwritten portion is converted to an image, and Notes on older iOS versions can recognize images.

Optical Character Recognition

One of the benefits of using an iPad Pro with the Apple Pencil is that you are able to take handwritten notes using the Notes app. This is great for those who cannot type as fast as they can write. The ability to do handwritten notes was present with iOS 9, when the first generation iPad Pro was released. There was one feature that was missing, the ability to search handwritten text. This is now available in iOS 11.

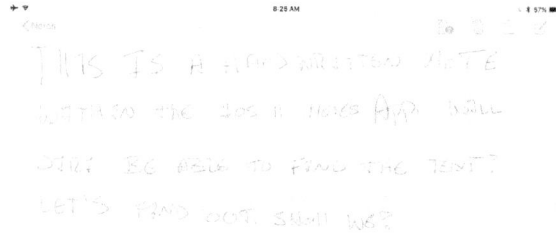

There are some caveats for handwritten messages. The first is that you can only search for the text via Siri. This can be via typing in the text in the Siri search. The second, and probably bigger caveat, is that is it is not perfect. For example, I wrote out the following:

"This is a handwritten note within the iOS 11 Notes App. Will Siri Be able to Find the Text? Let's Find Out. Shall We?"

Once the handwriting has been detected, it can take a minute, the note note will be updated to include the first part of the handwritten note. This means that it can be opened from a Siri Search. The search preview was missing some letters, and some of the words were wrong, but it did correctly locate the note. It is not a perfect feature by any stretch of the imagination, however it can be a useful feature.

Final Thoughts on Notes

Notes in iOS 11 adds to an already extensive feature set. The ability to adjust fonts more easily, without the use of a keyboard will help those who want to better organize their notes. The new Scan Documents feature will help people be able to scan documents, without the need of a third party application. Plus, the fact that it will allow fine tuning of the form area and that any skewing is accounted for makes it a very necessary feature for some users. The new capability of quickly starting a handwritten note that will have some optical character recognition applied to it will enhance the experience for those users who use handwritten notes on their iPads.

Music

The Music app on iOS 11 has not changed much, at least not in terms of direct user facing features. However, you may be seeing more applications that begin integrating music. This is through a new developer framework called MusicKit. There is more on that developer aspect to that framework in the developer section of the book. For now, let us look at how you, as a user, might be impacted.

In order to property talk about music, let us travel back to the early 1990's, If you were alive during this time you probably remember all of the hits, like "Baby Got Back" by Sir Mix-a-lot, "Nothing Compares 2 U" by Sinead O'Connor and who can forget "Ice Ice Baby" by Vanilla Ice. These were all hits in the year 1990. There were a few different methods of listening to the song. You could listen to the radio, where the song would probably be played at least once an hour. Alternatively, if you had the means, you could go out to the record store and buy either the album, or the single. You could buy albums or singles in two different formats, cassettes or CDs. For those who were not around in the 1990s, this was the norm for the time.

If you were going to go out and buy a cassette of an album, you were looking at paying between $11 and $12 for each cassette. If you wanted the CD, you were going to pay a premium and pay closer to $15. The thing with the cassettes and CDs is that it was an all or nothing deal. There was no cherry picking songs that you wanted. If you bought it, you had all of the songs.

One of the trendier things to do during that time was to create a mix-tape. This is how many individuals were able to listen to popular songs at the time. Friends would either have a tape or CD with the song and then would go ahead and record tracks off the CD or cassette, or even the radio, in order to create a mix tape. The thing with Mix tapes is that there were times when your friend would just go ahead and put a bunch of songs that they thought you might like. While the "mix tape" itself may have gone the way of the dodo, there is still a new way of getting music recommendation from your friends.

Sharing Music

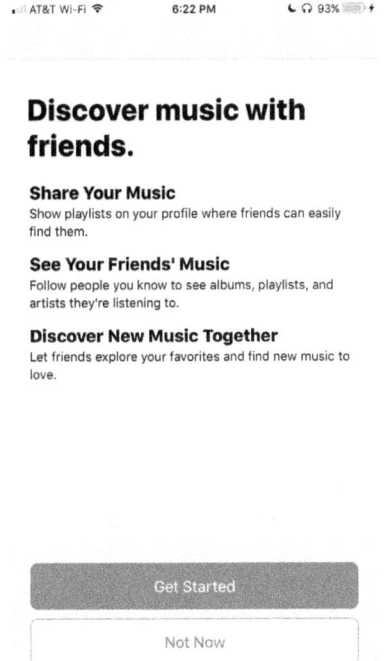

Apple's first attempt at a music-based social network did not go well at all. The service, which was called "Ping" was social network for users to follow artists and get song recommendations, akin to a service like Twitter. The "Ping" social network did not last very long, two years to be exact. The ability to connect to artists and get music recommendations is still around, provided you are a subscriber to Apple Music.

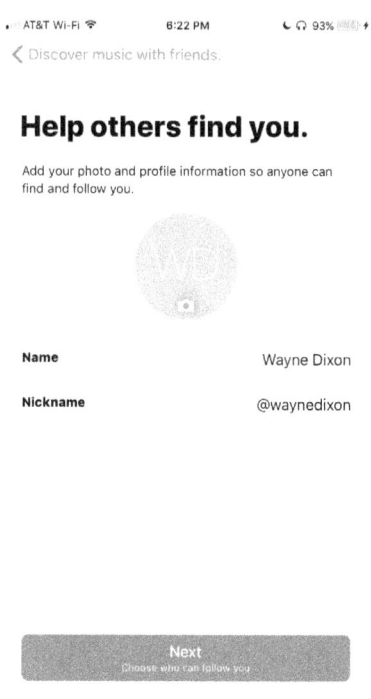

As mentioned above, there are still those times that you want to be able to get recommendations from your friends and see what they are listening to. This is possible with some additional social features within iOS 11, and iTunes on the Mac. You are now able to create an account that will allow others to find you and be able to see what you are listening to.

Setting Up Your Profile

As with any other sharing service, you need a profile. This profile will be how others can find you. The first step is to enter in your name, select a profile photo and choose a nickname. The nickname is how people will end up finding you.

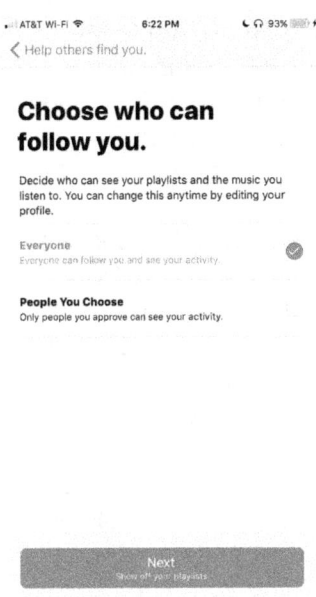

The second step is determining who can follow you. You have two options, "Everyone", or "People You Choose". If you select "Everyone", then anyone will be able to follow your music habits. If you opt for "People You Choose", anyone will be able to request to follow, but you will be able to approve, or reject, individuals.

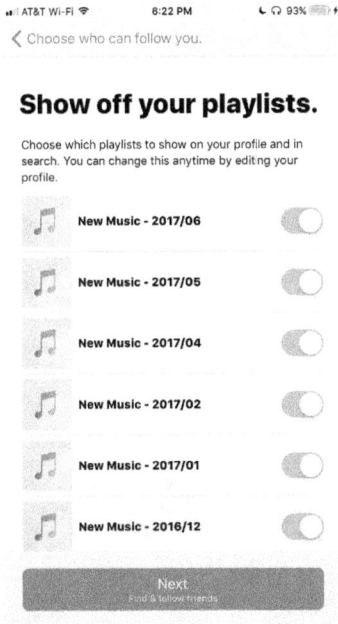

The third step is to choose which playlists to share. Apple Music will suggest some of the playlists within your Music Library to share. By default, it will enable a selection of your playlists. You can simply tap on the slider to not share a particular playlist. Do not fret, you can add and remove playlists at any time.

Step four is to follow your friends. Apple Music uses Facebook to find your friends. With Facebook having more than two billion users, it would make sense to use the largest social network in the world. However, this is very limiting for some because they do not want to have a Facebook account. If you do not want to use Facebook to find friends, you do have an option of sharing out your profile link to others as well.

The last step is to choose what notifications to receive. You can choose either of the following options. "Friends", and "Artists and Shows". The "Friends" option will send you notifications when your friends either join Apple Music or start following you. The "Artists and Shows" notification will let you know when your favorite shows, music, and radio shows have new episodes. Both of these are enabled by default, but can be disabled by tapping on the switch. After you have finished setting up your profile you will be brought to your newly created profile page.

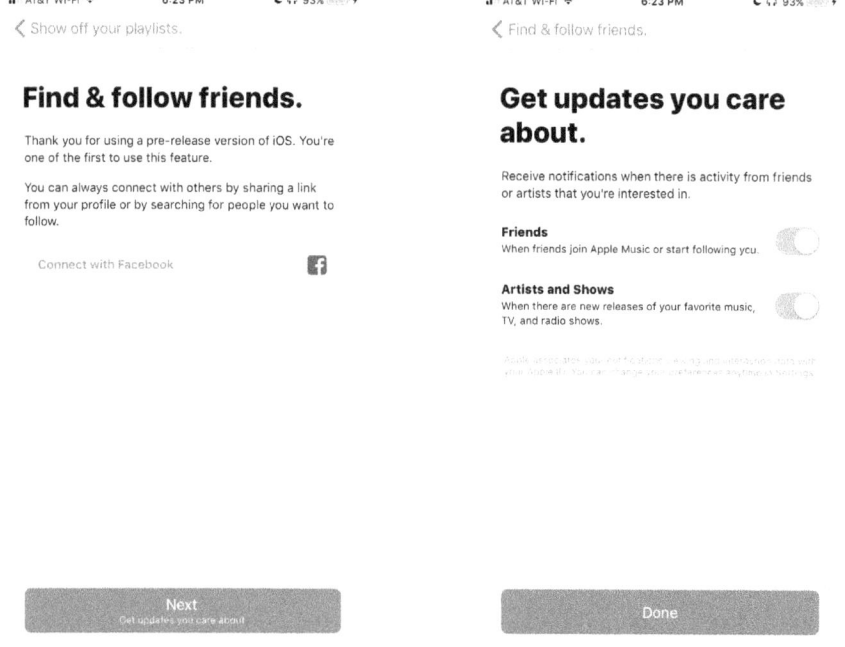

Your Profile Page

There are a couple of different aspects to your profile page. As you might expect, it shows the music that you have been listening to. There are two distinct sections. The first is playlist sharing. You control what playlists are shared out to others. By default there are eight playlists shown, but you can always tap on the "See All" link to see You can add new playlists, as well as remove a playlist at any time.

The second area is "Listening To". The "Listening To" section is comprised of items that you have listened to recently. These could be songs, playlists, or albums. Again there are eight items shown by default. And also as with the playlists, there is a "See All" button that will then show all of your recently listened to items. Unlike the playlists, you cannot remove any of these items. They are displayed most recently to least recently.

The information on your profile should update automatically.

Adding or Removing Playlists

As mentioned above, you can add or remove playlists at any time. There are two different methods of accomplishing this. The first is by editing your profile. On iOS 11 perform the following steps:

Method 1:

1. Open Music.
2. Tap on the "For You" tab bar item.
3. Tap on your picture in the upper right corner. This will bring you to your Apple Music profile.
4. Tap on the "Edit" button below your name.
5. Scroll down and a list of playlists will be shown.
6. If the playlist you want to share is in the list, simply tap on the circle on the left. A checkbox will appear.
7. Once you have finished adding playlists, click the "Done" button in the upper right corner.

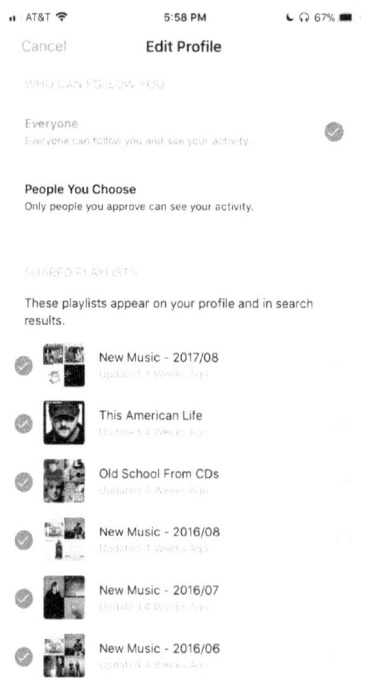

This first method will be useful if you want to add a playlist suggested by Apple. However, the more likely thing that you will want to do is add a specific playlist. There is a way to accomplish this as well.

Method 2:

1. Open Music.
2. Tap on the "Library" bar button item.
3. Tap on "Playlists".
4. Scroll down to the playlist you want to share.
5. Tap on the Playlist you want to share.
6. Tap on the "Edit" button in the upper right corner.
7. Tap the slider next to "Show on My Profile and in Search".
8. Tap the "Done" button in the upper right corner. The playlist will then be shown on your profile.

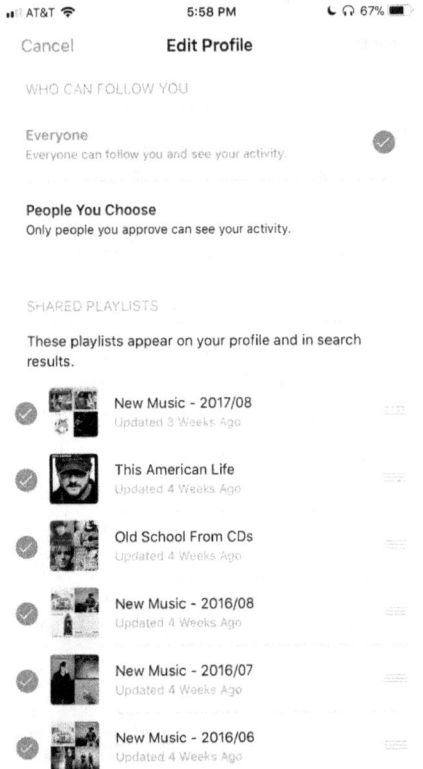

Items to Note

There are a couple of things to know about with adding and removing playlists. The first is that you cannot share Apple curated playlists. This means that the "My Favorites Mix", "My New Music Mix", and "My Chill Mix" will not be shareable. They will appear in the "Listening To" section, but cannot be shared. Similarly, if you have any automatically updating playlists, that are in your library, these too cannot be shared.

The reason that these playlists cannot be shared is because they are constantly updating. Instead, the sharing features of Apple Music are designed to allow you to share your own curated playlists. Let us now turn to how you can find friends.

Finding Friends

As mentioned above, during the Apple Music profile setup, you can use Facebook to connect to friends on Apple Music. To find friends, perform the following:

1. Open Music
2. Tap on the "For You" tab bar item at the bottom.
3. Tap on the "profile" icon in the upper right corner.
4. Scroll down to the bottom of the screen.
5. Tap on the "Find More Friends" button. A popup will appear.
6. Tap on the "Find More Friends" link with the Facebook icon. Another popup will be shown, asking you to "Connect with other apps you already use to find friends on Apple Music." The only option is Facebook.
7. Tap on the "Facebook" button. A different popup will appear prompting you to log in to facebook. Doing so will allow Apple Music access to your friends list to connect you.
8. Once you log in, you will be shown a confirmation indicating that you want to allow Facebook access to your public profile and friend's list.

This will show you a list of individuals, whom you are connected to on Facebook, and who are sharing music with Apple Music.

When you go to Follow individuals, some people may already be shown. If there are individuals shown, it is because they are already in your contacts list. You can invite those individuals to use Apple Music.

If you do not want to use Facebook there is another method of sharing your profile.

Sharing Your Profile

When you set up your Apple Music account, a profile was created for you. This profile is also available on the web. It follows the pattern of "https://itunes.apple.com/profile/username" where "username" is the name that you used to set up your profile. You can get this link by performing the following:

1. Open Music
2. Tap on the "For You" bar button item
3. Tap on the "Profile" icon in the upper right corner.
4. Tap on the three dots, "…" in the upper right corner.
5. Tap on "Share Profile". A standard iOS share sheet will be shown.

Here you have two options. The first is to share via Messages, or via Mail. You can tap on the "More" button to give you additional options for sharing.

Once you have this link you are able to share on whatever social platform you prefer. This could be Twitter, Facebook, Instagram, Snapchat, or any other platform of your choosing. You can also put it as a link in your social media platform of choice.

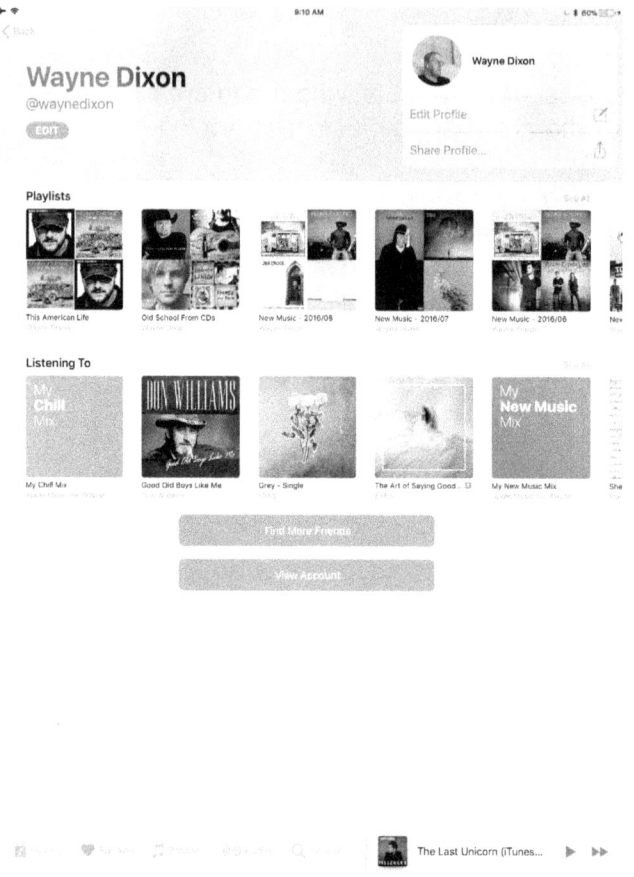

Final Thoughts on Sharing

The ability to find your friends to share music will let you keep in touch with your friends in a musical sense. The ability to share playlists will help you surface new music to your friends. If they follow you, they will be able to see what you are listening to, start playing one of your playlists, and then add any songs that they like to their own Music Library.

Curated Playlists

If you are a subscriber to Apple Music, you get an option of having Curated playlists. Under iOS 10, there were two introduced, "My Favorites Mix", and "My New Music Mix". The Favorites mix is a list of twenty five songs that are ones that you play a lot. This list is updated every Wednesday. The "New Music" mix is a collection of twenty five songs that Apple Music thinks you will like, based on your listening tastes. This list if updated every Friday. There is a new curated playlist, this one is titled "My Chill Mix".

My Chill Mix

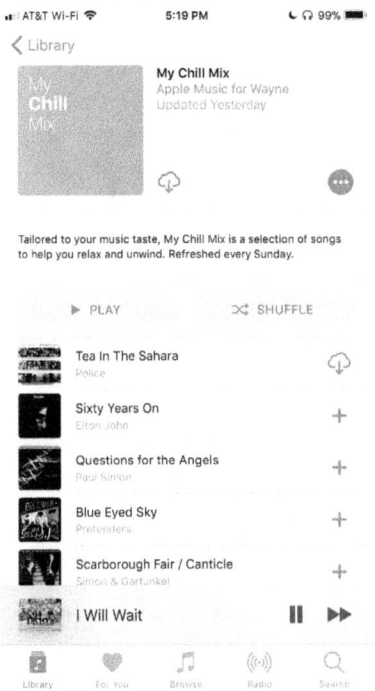

There are those times when you want to be able to sit and relax. During these times it is important to have music that will reflect your mood. This what the "My Chill Mix" playlist is intended to do. Just like the other personal playlists, this one is designed to allow you have a list of twenty five songs that will help you relax. These songs are typically slower than other songs. This playlist is available for Apple Music subscribers and is updated every Sunday.

MusicKit

Imagine if it were possible to have service create a mix tape for you. Apple has done some of this with the "For You" section within Apple Music, but they can only do so much. There are many other companies that would be capable of providing suggestions. The thing that these companies would need is access to your Music collection. This is what the MusicKit framework provides to developers.

If you provide access, applications will be able to have access to your music collection. They will be able to suggest tracks, albums, or even artists. They will also be able to provide a music player right from within their application. This means that you will not need to leave the app just to be able to change the song.

The key thing to know is that they will not be able to access your music library if you do not give permission. This is like any other permission within iOS. It must be explicitly given for them to be able to access your music library.

The ability to integrate music right into your app is something that may ultimately benefit users, as long as developers implement it. There is one additional feature of Music under iOS 11.

Music is important to many individuals and is deeply personal for everyone. There is another area that is also very personal, that is a user's passwords. Let us look at some of the changes around accounts and passwords next.

Accounts and Passwords

There are often times that you need to see if you have an account saved locally and there are also times that you need to authenticate with a service. Under iOS 10 and prior versions, when you needed to login you would have to copy and paste the information from the Settings, by going to Settings -> Safari -> Passwords. This may no longer needed, for some cases, in iOS 11. There is a new feature, Autofill for Username and Password within applications.

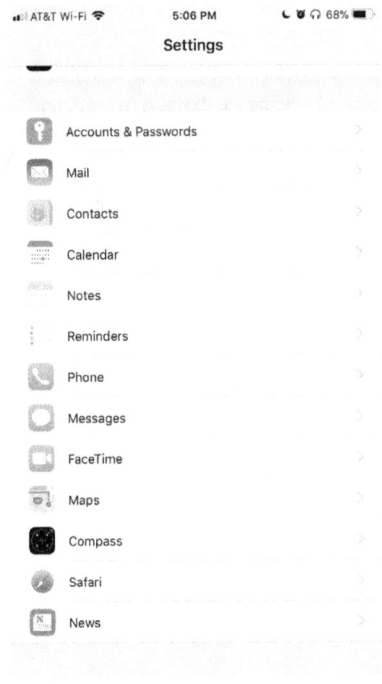

Autofill for Username and Passwords

One of the most frustrating things to occur is that you have to enter in your username and password into an application. Many people use the same user name and password for all of their logins. This is not good practice.

In reality, you should be using a different password for every website. This can easily be done by allowing Safari to suggest a password when you are signing up for an account. Now, if you do this, it will become difficult to remember all of your usernames and passwords. This can be remedied by enabling iCloud Keychain. iCloud Keychain is a service provided by Apple that will automatically synchronize all of your logins and passwords. iCloud Keychain is not a requirement for Autofill, but it is recommended if you want to be able to have all of your information across all of your devices. With all of that information, let us look at autofill.

Autofill for Usernames and Passwords is a new feature of iOS 11 that will automatically attempt to match the application that you are using with its web-based counterpart. If a website owner and developer have done some work on the back end, this matching will be automatic and work 100% of the time. However, if the developer has not done all of the work to setup this feature, you will still be presented with a lock on the quick type keyboard. Tapping on this key will allow you to select a username and password to fill into the proper fields.

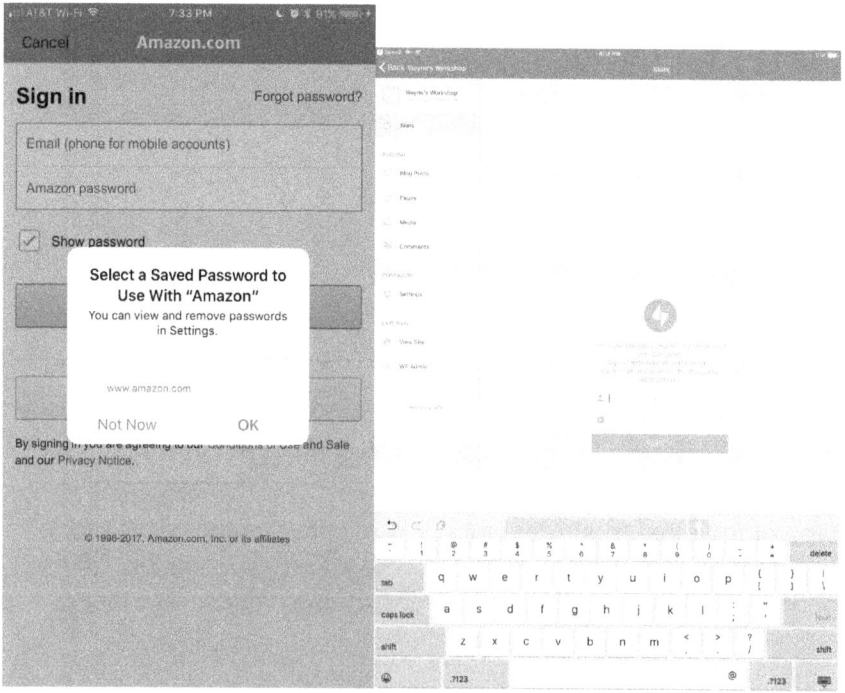

This will be a very convenient feature for users provided that developers implement the necessary items on their websites as well as within the applications. You may even see some applications that automatically work with the feature, without needing to update the application. When you do enter in usernames and passwords, you have to use the keyboard. There have been some keyboard improvements within iOS 11.

Keyboard Improvements

The keyboard is one of the primary input mechanisms for iOS 11. There are many times that you cannot hold a phone with two hands and are forced to use it one handed. When this occurs it can be problematic to try and type, particularly on the larger iPhone screens. Reaching over to the far side of the screen can cause you to drop your phone. When you drop your device it could easily result in a damaged device. None of us want that to occur.

To help accommodate this issue of typing with one hand, there is a new option for typing. This is only for the iPhone and iPod Touch. You now have the option of enabling a one-handed typing mode. To enable one handed typing perform the following:

- Tap into a textfield or text view to bring up the keyboard.
- Tap and hold on the Emoji icon in the lower left corner to bring up the keyboard selector.

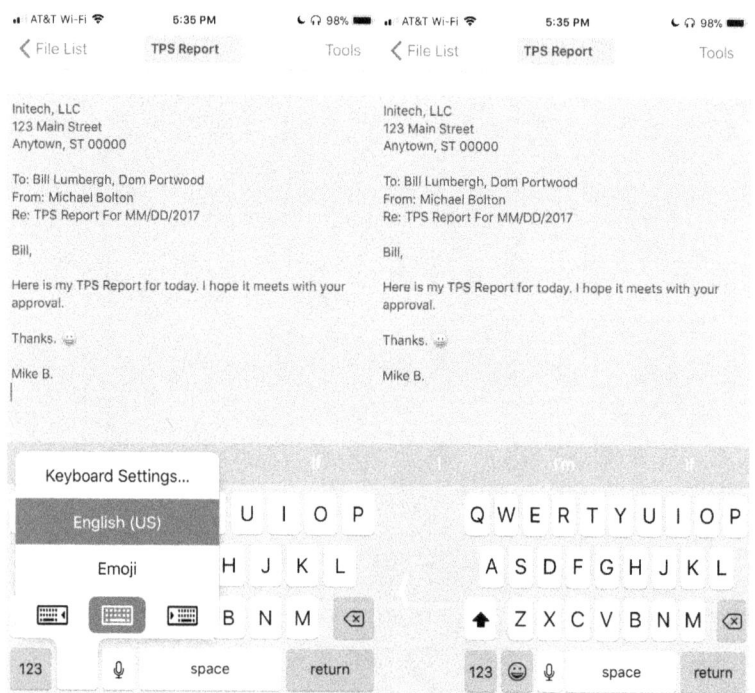

- Tap on either the "Left Handed" keyboard, or "Right Handed" keyboard to enable the one-handed keyboard.

To disable the one-handed mode, simply tap on the left or right arrow on the keyboard and it should return to the full-sized keyboard. There are a few things to keep in mind regarding the one-handed keyboard.

The first thing to keep in mind is that this only works when the iPhone or iPod Touch is in portrait mode. If you switch the phone to be horizontal, the full keyboard will appear. However, if you switch back the one-handed keyboard that you chose will return.

The second item to keep in mind is that this is a system-wide change. This means that if you select a one-handed keyboard in a social media application, it will remain that way in Safari and even in other third-party apps.

The new one-handed keyboard option will help those who want to be able to quickly type with one hand on their iPhone or iPod Touch. The fact that it is system wide means that users do not have to keep changing keyboard modes when switching between applications.

Photos

One of the most used applications on iOS is the Camera. When you use the camera to take photos, or video it gets stored in the Photos. Photos contains a slew of features introduced in previous iOS versions. Some of these features include, Memories, editing, and even facial recognition. There have been a couple of improvements to Photos in iOS 11. The first new change revolves around facial recognition.

Facial Recognition

One of the most useful features of Photos on iOS is the capability of Photos to do facial recognition. One of the downsides to this is that the facial recognition engine must attempt to find and analyze faces on each of your devices independently. This not necessarily the case with iOS 11.

Now with iOS 11, if you explicitly add a name to a person in Photos, that information will now be synchronized across all of your devices. The information that is synchronized will then use machine learning to analyze the photo library on that device. This means that if you tag a person in Photos on your iPhone running iOS 11 it will be transferred to your Macs, and vice versa. This is not the only enhancement that has occurred. There have been some changes to Live Photos as well.

Live Photos

One of the most notable features on iOS is the ability to create a Live Photo. A Live Photo is a combination of still images and video to create a miniature video. With iOS 11, Live Photos are gaining a couple of new features.

You can now select which still image is the preview image. This is called the "Key Photo". Previously, the Key Photo was the picture taken right before the video start. This change will help for those times when your live photo starts off a bit blurry.

To select a key frame, perform the following:

1. Open Photos
2. Locate the photo that you want to edit
3. Tap on the "Edit" button. A new screen will appear.
4. At the bottom of the screen a timeline will be shown. Drag your finger across the timeline to find your preferred key image.
5. Tap on the "Make Key Photo". The select image is now the Key Photo for the Live Photo.

The second new feature with Live Photos is some new effects that can be added to a Live Photo. These new effects are:

- Loop
- Bounce
- Long Exposure

Loop will allow you to have the live video loop. This effect is great for a shot that lends itself to be able to repeat. Bounce will take a Live Photo and after playing, reverse it, so it looks like the subject is bouncing off and reversing. Long Exposure is an effect which is similar to the capabilities of a Digital Single Lens Reflex Camera. When you use the Long Exposure effect it will add some nice shadow effects to your Live Photo.

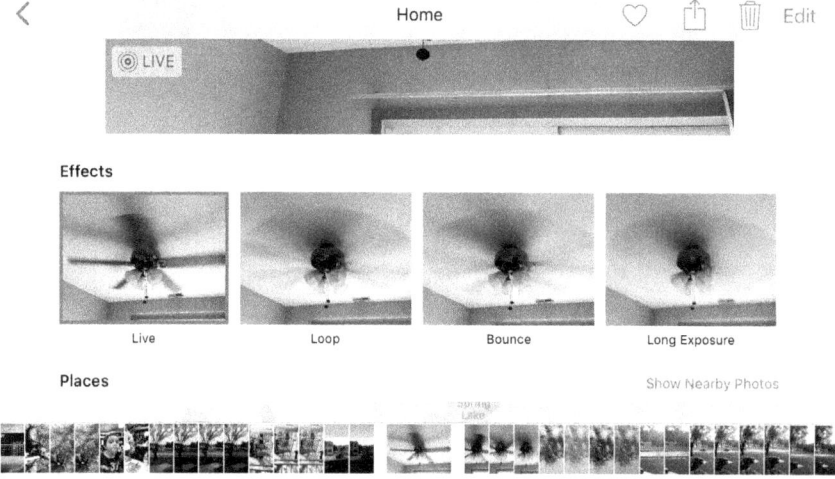

To add any of of the effects to your Live Photo, simply swipe up from the Photo and a preview of each of the different effects. You can tap on one of the effects and it will apply to your Live Photo. With all of these new effects, how is everything going to be stored?

Media File Formats

One of the topics that may not seem to be super important, and can be somewhat uninteresting to some, is the topic of file formats. What makes file formats uninteresting is that unless they offer some sort of new feature, they are a bit too technical for the average user.

The main interaction that users have with file formats comes into play when they cannot open a file because they do not have an application that can open the file, or when the files are taking up too much space on their iOS device.

One of the primary causes of excessive space on iOS devices is also one of the biggest uses, taking photos. There are a few common standard image formats that are in use today. These are primarily, Joint Photographic Experts Group (JPEG or JPG) and Portable Network Graphics (PNG). These were released in September of 1992, and October 1st, 1996 respectively. They have been around over twenty years and have become the standard for sharing images on the internet. When these formats were conceived and introduced, these image formats provided a means of being able to take a larger picture and reduce the size to allow for sending over the internet in a more efficient manner.

Since these formats have been around for so long, they have become the de-facto standards for images, even though better formats have been introduced. Given that almost any device that can display an image can read JPG and PNG files, there has been some significant inertia to changing this. One group that could effect this type of change is the largest phone maker, Apple.

If you use your iPhone or iPad regularly to take photos and you look at what is taking up the most storage on your device, it is likely to be Photos, particularly if you keep all of the full quality photos on your device.

One of the changes in technology in general over the past decade has been the transition from traditional spinning hard drives to solid state media for storage. The size of solid state storage has been smaller than traditional spinning hard drives, at the same price points. This means that many Macs have a lot less storage on them now than they did in the past.

Apple has implemented a few features over the past few versions of iOS to assist with the storage space on iOS devices becoming full. Some of these features include Photos in the Cloud, as well as a few new options under iOS11, which will be discussed later. But for now, let us discuss a couple new file formats, starting with the High Efficiency Image Format.

High Efficiency Image Format

High Efficiency Image Format, or HEIF, is a new International Standards Organization (ISO) standard. HEIF is designed to provide the same, or better, image quality as JPG has for the last twenty-four years.

Apple had a few requirements for any potential replacement file format. These requirements are:

- Alpha channel and depth channel as primary asset types. This is for transparency in images and depth for Portrait Mode on the iPhone 7 and iPhone 7 Plus.
- Support for GIF, Live Photo. This is because Live Photos are a big feature of iOS.
- Image sequence compression, photo bursts. This is needed because there are some users who intentionally

- take a large number of photo bursts, not just those of us who accidentally end up taking them.
- Partitioning of image into rectangular tiles. This is necessary to be able to pan and zoom images quickly.
-
- HEIF met all of these requirements. Under iOS 11, and macOS High Sierra, the new default file format for still images is HEIF. Still images were not the only new format for iOS 11. There is also a new file format for video.

High Efficiency Video Codec

The High Efficiency Video Codec, or HEVC, will do the same for video, as HEIF will do for still images. This means that besides images being significantly smaller, video will also be smaller. Up to 40% smaller to be exact.

HEVC had similar requirements as HEIF, with some additional video-specific ones. The video-specific requirements included:

- Still compatible with H.264
- Delivers significant compression improvement over H.264
- Adopted in the industry

HEVC met these requirements. Overall it can deliver up to 40% better compression over H.264. The next question becomes "What do these new file formats mean for users?"

Impact on Users

The last requirement is that any new file format must not take up more space than the existing JPG file format. HEIF also met this last requirement. The fact that HEIF and HEVC met all of the above requirement, for each of their respective groups, as well as not taking up more space, meant that HEIF and HEVC could be a possible candidate for replacements. During Apple's testing, they saw significant reductions in file sizes.

There will be a rather large impact on users regarding the amount of storage space available on iOS devices. The amount of available storage should actually go up, not just on your iOS device, but also within iCloud.

One of the challenges that one faces with a new image format is that it is not supported by a large number of applications. In order to help work around this possible limitation is that anything exported out of Photos under iOS 11 will be in standard JPEG format. Similarly, when you export an HEVC file, it will be transcoded to a standard H.264 file. As the adoption of HEIF and HEVC progresses, there will come a tipping point when the two formats are just as common as JPEG and H.264 are today. Once this occurs, the need to transcode these formats will be obviated.

There is one thing to keep in mind. These formats will only be used for photos that are taken after installing iOS 11. You cannot retroactively go back and apply the new format to old files, at least not natively on iOS 11. You may be able to do so with aa third-party application, but doing so may destroy the original photo; so it is best to proceed with caution.

Final Thoughts on Photos

Photos in iOS 11 brings a few new features. Most notably the synchronization of People data across devices. The new Live Photo effects will allow for an added pizzazz to existing Live Photos and the ability to always be able to have the sidebar available will be a nice benefit for those who need it.

The new file formats will end up saving users space not only locally on their iOS devices, but also within iCloud, and it should also reduce the space used for backups and on all of your Macs as well. Even though the changes made to Photos may be minor, they will be something that a variety of users can enjoy.

Weather

There has been a slight change in the way that weather information is shown within the Weather application. The Weather app consists of five sections. These sections are:

- Current Weather and Temperature
- 24 Hour Forecast, by Hour
- Nine Day Forecast
- Today's Forecast in longer form.
- Weather Details.

The first four sections have remained the same, but the Weather Details section has received a new look. The same information is present, but it is displayed in a bit more pleasing manner.

Under iOS 10, the items were in two columns, with the Description and data meeting in the middle. Under iOS 11, the information is still in two columns, but now the information is larger. The labels for the items that were on the left column, are now above the data.

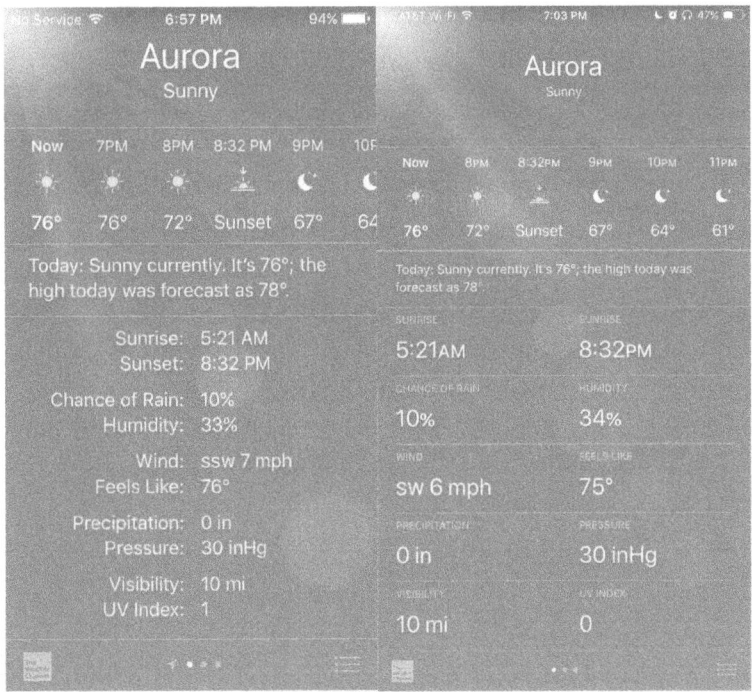

In the left column you will find Sunrise, Chance of Rain, Wind, Precipitation, and Visibility. In the right column you will find Sunset, Humidity, Feels Like, Pressure, and UV Index. The corresponding values for each of these is beneath the label. While this is a minor change, the larger font will make it easier for those users who have difficulty with their eyesight to be able to be able to more easily read the current weather information.

Home

One of the features released in iOS 8 was HomeKit. HomeKit is a set of APIs that would allow smart devices to be controllable via Siri. Any smart device that was configured would be stored in a centralized database and would be available over all of your devices. This setup worked, although it was a bit cumbersome. Last year, with iOS 10, Apple introduced the new Home App.

The Home App took all of the capabilities of HomeKit and instead of relying on third party applications to control features, bundled them into one application. With the Home app you are able to control all of your "smart devices". The Home app could be used to trigger events while you are away; provided that you had a 4th Generation Apple TV or an iPad that stayed at home.

Home is able to control a myriad of devices. The entire list includes:

- Lights
- Locks
- Temperature Controls
- Plugs and Switches
- Sensors
- Shades
- Air Treatment
- Camera Accessories
- Doorbells

There are two new categories that can be added to the already existing list. The new types are:

- Sprinklers
- Faucets

The ability to add sprinklers and faucets will mean that you do not need to worry about accidentally leaving these on, since you can turn the off with your iOS device. The addition of these also lends towards preserving the environment by conserving water. Preserving the environment is one of Apple's core tenets.

There was one feature that developers and users requested, the ability to trigger events when someone arrives home and when everyone leaves. Under iOS 10 it was possible to have just an automation occur when one person entered or left, but many homes have more than one person in them. The ability to trigger an event when everyone has left, or when someone is the first person to arrive, has been added to HomeKit with iOS 11.

Entering or Leaving

There are situations where it would be quite convenient to be able to have a HomeKit automation event trigger when a user leaves or enters a home. An example might be that when the last person leaves, you will want to be sure that the front door is locked, the garage door is closed, all of the faucets are turned off, and the lights are all off. This is now possible with iOS 11.

To add an automation that uses these new options, simply do the following:

1. Open the Home app
2. Tap on Automation
3. Tap the "+" button to add a new automation
4. Tap on either "People Arrive Home" or "People Leave Home"
5. Tap on the individuals to include
6. If you have more than one Home configured, select the specific Home.

7. If you need to set a specific time, tap on Time and select the time.
8. Tap Next to move to select the scenes or configured devices
9. Select a scene or individual devices
10. Tap Next to bring up the "When" tab.
11. If you want to add a delay tap on the "Timer" toggle and select the delay.
12. Tap the "Done" button to save the automation.

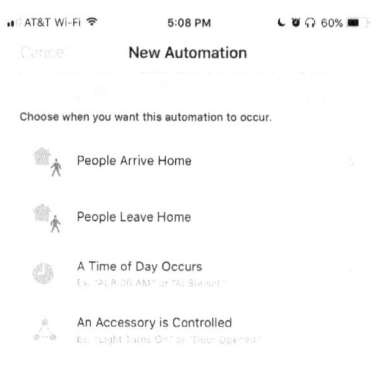

The new automation should be listed and should trigger when the selected individuals enter or leave the selected home.

Other Home app Changes

There have been a few other changes to the Home app, one that you may not initially notice. The first of these is that the icons are now the same consistent icons. They no longer change when you tap on an icon. The second small change is one that was mentioned above. The "New automation" button is now in the upper right corner of the screen, instead of being a large button at the bottom of your list.

The last little feature is that you can use offsets from Sunrise or Sunset. What this means is that you can schedule an automation event to occur up to one hour before or one our after either Sunrise or Sunset. This is handy in case you want to start your sprinklers for a half hour before Sunset, but then turn them off a half hour after Sunset.

Even though the user-facing features of the Home app are subtle changes, they can be important, particularly if you have a need to trigger events to occur sometime near either Sunrise or Sunset.

Safari

Safari is likely one of the most used applications on iOS. You may be using Safari and not even really notice. If you are within an app and tap on a link to a website, it may be using Safari to display that site. There have been some slight improvements to Safari, that users will notice.

The first improvement is that developers can now make the colors for some elements of Safari, while used within their apps, the same color as their apps. This means that you will be able to more easily tell which app you are in, should you switch back to an app that has Safari open.

The second change is a security-related one. When you use Safari within an app, any cookies or browsing data will be restricted to that app. What this means is that your data cannot be easily seen by other websites. One thing to keep in mind with this is that sites that you are logged into using the primary Safari browser will still be logged in when you use Safari within an app. The ability to limit cookies and browsing data is being by a feature called "Intelligent Tracking Prevention".

Intelligent Tracking Prevention

Have you ever been shopping on Amazon, but then logged into Facebook and see an ad for the exact items you were searching for appear? How is this done? Simple, it is via tracking cookies.

One of the most pervasive practices in use on the internet today is to track users. There are entire companies whose sole purpose is to be able to aggregate and sell your information to third-parties. Apple, through its web-browser Safari, is going to attempt to stop this practice.

Safari has been blocking third-party cookies, by default, since its inception. Safari was the first to block them by default. With Safari 11 on iOS, Apple is going beyond simply blocking tracking cookies and doing some intelligent tracking prevention. According to the Webkit Team (WebKit is the engine that powers Safari):

"In our testing we found popular websites with over 70 such trackers, all silently collecting data on users."

Imagine seventy trackers on one website. How is Safari attempting to stop this behavior. It is quite ingenious. When you visit a site, we will call it example-cool-gadgets.com, Safari will track what resources load on that domain, look at your taps, clicks, and even text entries and throw all of this information into a bucket, specifically for that example-cool-gadgets.com. Safari will then use some machine learning, which happens entirely on your iOS device, and it will start to look at different factors. If the Intelligent Tracking Prevention engine determines that example-cool-gadgets.com has the ability to track users across different sites, that is when it will act.

Action Taken

If the Intelligent Tracking Prevention engine determines that example-cool-gadgets.com does have the ability to track users across different websites it will then begin to take action to limit the tracking.

If you have not visited example-cool-gadgets.com in the last 30 days, all of its data is immediately purged. If new data comes in for that domain, it is also immediately purge.

If a user has interacted directly example-cool-gadgets.com in the last 24 hours, the stored cookies will behave in the following manner:

If less than 24 hours, the information can be used for third-party access. If it has been more than 24 hours, but less than 30 days, the data cannot be used for third-party tracking, but can still be used on example-cool-gadgets.com. If the data is more than 30 days old, it is removed.

What all of this means is that if you only use example-cool-gadgets.com once a week, you will stay logged in, depending on if the site allows you to stay constantly logged in. All of this happens without any interaction from you.

Autoplay

One of the more maddening things that can happen when you are browsing the web is that a video begins to play automatically as soon as it can. Not only does this possibly disrupt you, it is even more annoying when you are reading something and an autoplay ad appears and begins playing. Safari in iOS 11, will begin to learn about the sites that autoplay videos and it will no longer allow them to do so. This should make for a better user experience. There have been some other changes to video, but these are around the full screen video playing experience.

Video Player Changes

On the topic of video, there has been some changes to the way that the video playback under Safari is displayed. Under iOS 10. The playback was divided between the top and the bottom of the screen, with translucent bars. The top section contained the "Done" button, the time scrubber and the zoom button. Whereas the bottom divider contained the volume, playback controls, and the full screen button.

While the two sections are still divided, the translucent bar at the top is now gone. Additionally, the layout has changed a bit. The "Done" button has been replaced with a large X. Right next to the close button lies the full screen toggle. On the far right is the volume control, which is reduced down to a small button, yet will still expand to allow fine tuning of the volume. At the bottom of the screen is the playback controls, which are now 15 second backward and forward buttons. The biggest change is that the time scrubber is now on the bottom. If you are accustom to the scrubber being on the top, this can be an issue. Also at the bottom is the AirPlay button. The color of the bars is more of a brown instead of the light gray they were under iOS 10. These are some minor tweaks, but all of the video playing experience is consistent across all sizes of iOS devices.

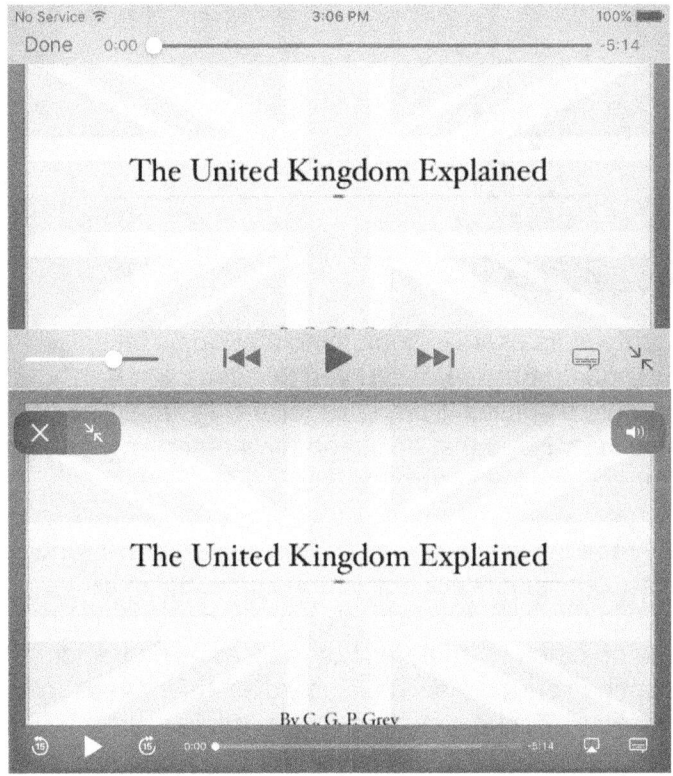

Insecure Connections

There has been one last subtle change to Safari. This one is regarding information about non-secure websites. As mentioned

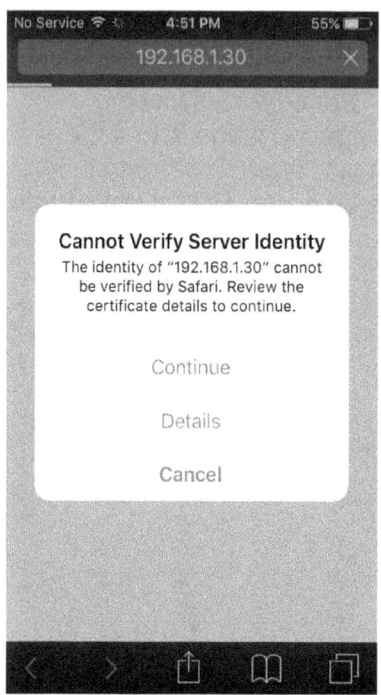

before, the security of its users is something that Apple takes seriously. Many modern browsers alert you to issues when connecting to secure websites. Safari has for a long time. The most common security issue that arises on the web is likely to be an insecure connection. to a secure website.

There are many reasons why this may be the case. It may be due to only using a security certificate that is not signed by a valid Certificate authority or it could be due to an expired certificate. There could also be other, more nefarious reasons. A bad actor could be intercepting your connection. Regardless of the reason why, when an insecure connection, to a supposedly secure website occurs, Safari will tell you about it. Under macOS Sierra this dialog was not very informative and not easy to understand. The manner in which you are notified about a connection that is not private has changed.

Under Safari on iOS 11, you will be presented with a slightly more informative and attention grabbing warning. The information has remained the same. You can still view the certificate to verify that you want to connect, you can continue on as before, or even go back. It may be a small feature, but showing the user that there is an insecure connection in an more attention grabbing feature may help some users stave off releasing some of their personal information.

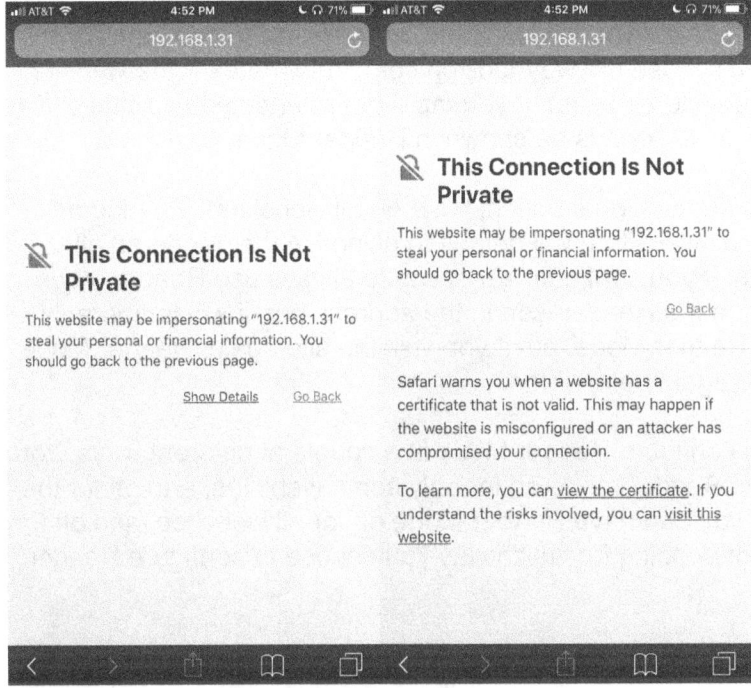

Reader Mode Enhancements

The internet has significantly changed since its initial introduction. In order to sustain many websites, there has been an increase in the amount of advertising on websites. One of the consequences of this has been the increasing difficulty in reading websites. A possible solution to this is to block the advertising. This solution may just remove the ads, but keeps the location for the ads. Apple has an alternative. One that was introduced with Safari 5 in June of 2010. It was brought over to iOS with iOS 5 in 2011.

Reader Mode is an option within Safari that will reformat a webpage to remove the ads, sidebars, and most of the formatting.

The only remaining images and the actual text of the page. While Reader mode has been really helpful for many users. There is an option that has not been available is the ability to have an "always on" mode for reader. This is now available with Safari 11 on iOS 11. Enabling Reader Mode is the same as under iOS 10, tap on the "Reader" icon in the address bar.

However, now if you tap and hold on the Reader Icon, you have a new option, "Use on 'waynedixon.com'", or whatever the website you happen to be using. If you tap on this, when you visit the website, it will always be shown in Reader Mode.

There is an additional option, "Use on all websites". Tapping on "Use on all websites" will default to using Reader Mode on all websites. If you configure a website to always use Reader Mode and tap on the Reader icon in the address bar, it will temporarily disable Reader Mode, but if you visit the site again, Reader Mode will once again be enabled.

You can configure Reader Mode in a couple of different ways. You can have Reader mode on for only some websites, and off for the rest, or, you can have Reader Mode on for all websites, and off for others; depending on which way you choose to configure Reader Mode.

The ability to have an "Always On" Reader in Safari will make browsing and reading the web that much easier, particularly on those sites that have chosen to put a large number of ads on their sites.

Final Thoughts on Safari

Safari in iOS 11 will see a minimal number of new features that directly affect users. Users will see apps being able to change colors when they are using Safari within apps, as well as the adjustments to the video player, but the remaining changes are all under the hood. These changes will allow better protection of a user's privacy by limiting what types of third-party tracking can occur. It may sound like no big deal, but if you do not know you are being tracked, how can you stop it? Luckily, with Safari on iOS 11, you do not have to know about how everything is being done because it is all handled automatically. The autoplay blocker will be a nice touch and the revamped controls for video playback may confuse users at first, but ultimately does make for a better user experience.

Calculator

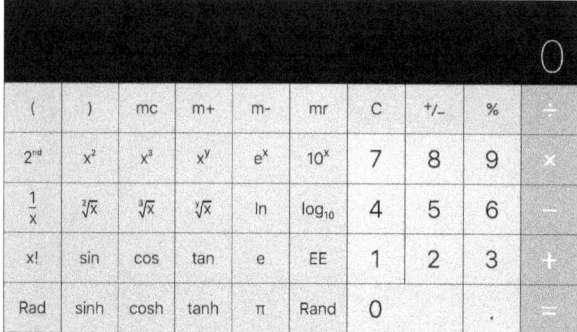

One of the applications that has been on been on the iPhone since it was originally released in 2007 is the Calculator. The look and feel of the calculator has remained unchanged for many versions of iOS. The Calculator on iOS 8 is the exact same as the one on iOS 10. iOS 11 changes this.

The calculator's functionality has not changed at all, but the entire look and feel of the calculator has been updated. The buttons are now rounded instead of being squares with borders around them. This is purely a cosmetic change, but a refreshed Calculator is a nice touch for iOS 11. There have been some other refinements within the operating system. Let us look at some of those, starting with Messages.

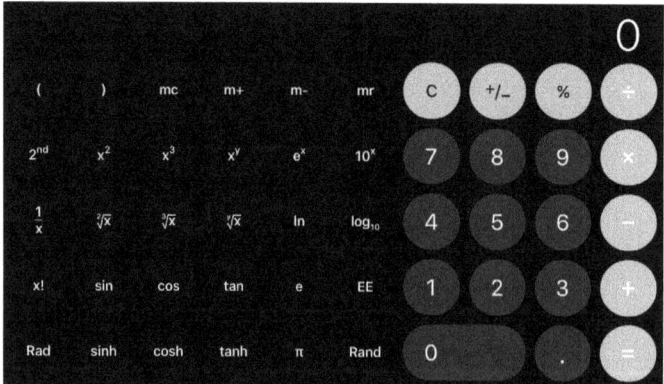

Other System Refinements

Each new version of iOS brings with it, a few slight enhancements. These may be subtle changes that you might not even realize have been changed. These are outlined in this section. We still start with the Settings app and its changes, which are actually quite extensive.

Settings

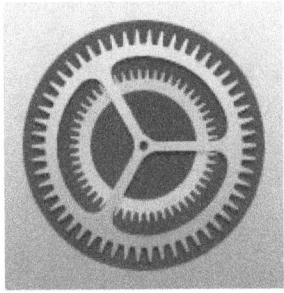

Settings is the general all-purpose location for adjusting many of the different options in iOS. Over the last ten years, what is contained within has expanded greatly. In iOS 10.3, the location of iCloud settings changed and a giant banner with your name was added to the top of Settings. This was done to provide quicker access to your iCloud settings. There have been some subtle changes to these settings.

iCloud Settings

iCloud is Apple's cloud-based storage location for users to be able to store files outside of their devices. Apple provides 5GB of storage for free and offers various tiers for storage. These tiers are: 5GB, 50GB for $0.99 per month, 200GB for $2.99 per month, and 2TB for $9.99 per month. You can easily manage your storage, however under iOS 10, this may have been difficult to find. Under iOS 10 you had to perform the following:

1. Open Settings
2. Tap on Your Name
3. Tap iCloud
4. Tap on "Storage" under iCloud.

This was a bit confusing for some, so now there is a separate button titled "Manage Storage". Tapping on the "Managed Storage" button will perform the same actions as under iOS 10, but it is just more obvious how to adjust your storage.

You may notice a slight change to the display of your storage. The colors have now been changed. Under iOS 10, Photos was blue, Backup was yellow, Docs were green, and email was orange. These colors were very pastel in nature. On some screens, and for some users, they were likely difficult to discern. iOS 11 has changed the colors for these items.

Photos is now yellow, Backup is now purple, and Documents is now orange. All of these colors on iOS 11 are a deep shade of each of the above colors. This change makes it easier to differentiate the sizes of each.

When you tap on "Manage Storage", you will notice a new option has appeared, "Share With Family"

Family Sharing of iCloud Storage

One of the most requested features for iCloud has been the ability to share storage between family members. Prior to iOS 11, if you wanted users to have more than the default 5GB of storage, each user would have to pay separately for their own iCloud Storage. This meant, that if you had four people in your family and each

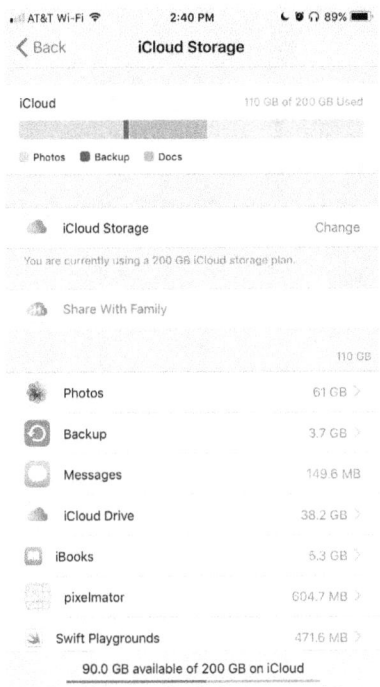

needed 50GB of storage, you would have to buy 50GB for each user, which means the possibility of having four different dates to pay for the storage. Now with iOS 11, you can have the master account purchase the storage and everyone can share in using the storage.

As an example, we take the four person family from earlier, the master account for the family buys the 2TB storage and everyone can share the bigger pool of storage. You are able to notify family members that they now have access to this large storage pool. This is a great feature for many reasons, most notably that there will now only be one bill for the entire family. Secondly, as the storage needs of the family increases, it is not necessary to purchase a larger tier for each family member's own account.

There is an additional benefit to this feature. This feature only needs to be configured from an iOS 11 device, but it applies to iCloud storage across all versions of iOS. What this means is that if you enable Family Sharing of iCloud Storage, a child with an

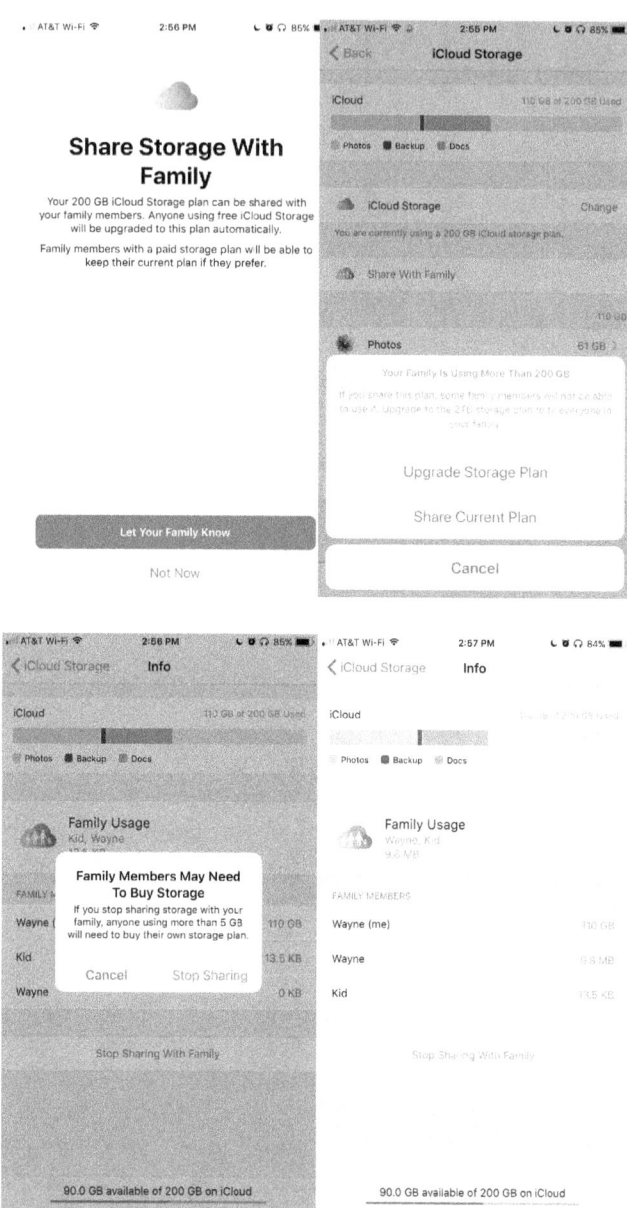

older iOS device that may not be able to run iOS 11 will still be able to take advantage of the cloud storage. This is a significant benefit for anyone who has Family Sharing enabled and does not wish to purchase additional storage for each family member.

One thing to note, family members can decide not to participate and still keep their existing iCloud Storage, should they wish to do so. Depending on your situation, this may be a better solution than just pure family sharing. Let us look at the next changed section of Settings, Cellular.

Cellular

All iPhones are capable of use Cellular, and some models of iPad are as well. When you have a carrier and you have issues it can be a pain to try and find information. Sure, you could use a computer to search for that information, but what if you are no where near a computer and all your have is your device and you are having an issue with your service. It would be handy to be able to get quick access to some information.

With iOS 11 there is a new option under Cellular titled "Carrier Services". Here you can find quick access to information about services provided by your carrier. This could be things like Checking Bill Balance, Paying your bill, or even viewing usage. Anything that your cellular provider offers will be listed in this section. What seems to be missing from the screenshot is how to contact Customer Service for the carrier. For many carriers it is 611, but if you do not normally call them often, it is understandable not to know that information. The next section that has some changes is notifications.

Notifications

With the Notification Center changes in iOS 11, it is inevitable that there would also be some changes around notification settings. Under iOS 10, each application had a series of options for notifications. These options are:

- Allow Notifications
- Show in Notification Center
- Badge App Icon
- Show on Lock Screen

There was also the option for the Alert Style When Unlocked. These options are "None", "Banners", and "Alerts". iOS 11 has adjusted some notification settings.

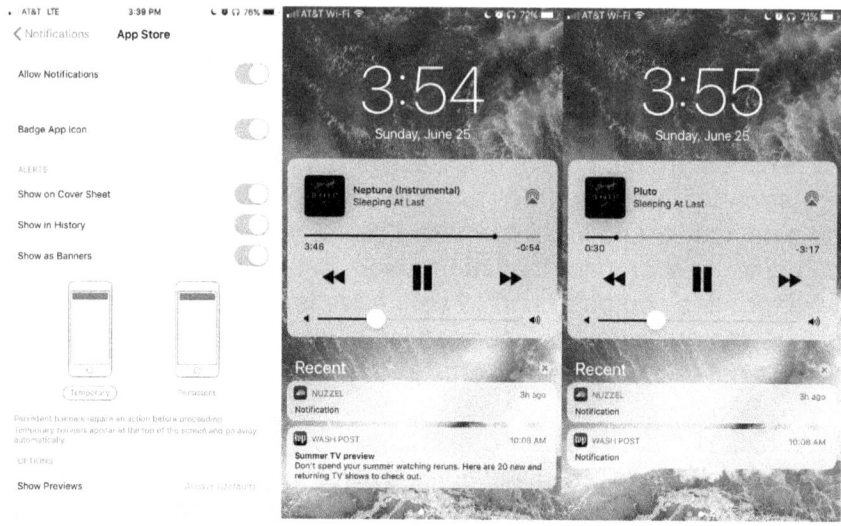

The first change is that there is now a global option for when to show previews. There are three options, "Always", "When Unlocked', and "Never". The default is "Always". This means that previews will be shown on the Lock Screen for all applications. "When Unlocked" will only show notification previews when the phone is unlocked. Where as never will never show previews. You will still see a notification in the Notification History section, but it will only say the word "notification" as the text for the notification and not the preview text.

Under each application that has requested the ability to send notifications, there have also been some slight adjustments. The options "Allow Notifications" and "Badge App Icon" both remain, but the other options have now changed.

You have three new options. The first is whether or not to show the notification for that app on the Cover Sheet. The Cover Sheet, as explained under the Lock Screen and Home Screen section, is a combination of the old Lock Screen and Notification Center. It is now accessible at all times by swiping down from the top of the screen, just like Notification Center was accessible under iOS 10.

The second option whether or not to show the application's notifications under the History. The last option is whether or not to show the notifications as banners.

There are now only two types of "Alert Styles", Temporary and Persistent. If you set an app as having a Temporary Style alert, it will disappear off of the Cover Sheet, but will be shown in your Notification History. If you set an alert style as permanent, it will remain on the screen until you perform an action on that notification.

There is one last option at the bottom, this is an option to override the global "Show Previews". There may be some applications where you do not wish to see previews, this is where you can set this option. Those are all of the changes to notifications. These changes fit nicely into the overall changes to the Cover Sheet and provide even more customization for users than previous versions of iOS allowed.

General Settings

We all have that one location in our homes where just about everything gets thrown. The most common reason for this behavior is because we cannot think of another place where the items should go. It is possible that the "General" section of Settings is that place for iOS. Each iOS version is likely to add another option within this section. iOS 11 is no exception. There have been some additions.

The first change is that "Spotlight Search" is now gone. This is now located under Siri & Search, so this will be covered later. The next section that has some changes is Accessibility.

Accessibility

Accessibility is an important aspect of iOS. It provides those who have different requirements than the majority of users to still be able to use iOS. Apple takes pride in Apple being so accessible. It is not an afterthought, but instead a primary concern for all of Apple. There have some substantial changes to Accessibility in iOS 11.

The first change under Accessibility is under Voice Over. It is a minor location change, but it is necessary to know about. The option for Pitch Change has been moved to under the "Speech" option. This makes sense since the changing of pitch is directly related to speech. A similar item to pitch is how verbose the voice over should be.

Verbosity

One of the settings that is nice to be able to set, for those who need it, is how verbose, or wordy, the speech for Voice Over is. Under iOS 10, Verbosity consisted of only two options, "Speak Hints", and "Emoji Suffix". Under iOS 11, this has been greatly expanded. One could say, the options have become more verbose.

There are still the options for Speak Hints and Emoji Suffix, but there are also now eight additional options. The first new option is how much punctuation should be included in Voice Over. There are three options for this, "All", "Some", and "None". "Some" is the default.

The next option is "Speak Detected Text". This toggle is responsible for whether or not the text that is the focused item is to be spoken. This is on by default.

The next group of options all have the same four choices. The options are "Capital Letters", "Deleting Text", and "Embedded Links". The defaults are "Speak Cap", "Change Pitch", and "Speak", respectively. The choices for these options are, "Speak", "Play Sound", "Change Pitch", and "Do Nothing".

The next group of options is regarding Table Output. These options are toggle buttons. When you navigate tables, you can have the "Table Headers" and the "Row and Column Numbers" spoken out loud. Both of these options are on by default.

The last new option under Verbosity is "Media Descriptions". This option relates to how Closed Captions and Subtitles for the deaf or hard-of-hearing are handled. The choices are "Off", "Speech", "Braille", or "Speech and Braille". By default Media Descriptions are off.

These are all of the new features under Verbosity. These customizations will make the experience for those with difficulties even better under iOS 11 than they were under iOS 10.

Braille

There is one new toggle under the Braille Accessibility settings. That option is Word wrap. It is on by default.

Audio

There has been one slight adjustment to the text under Audio. Under iOS 10, there was an option titled "Use Sound Effects". This option is enabled by default. Under iOS 11, the text has changed to "Mute Sound Effects", and is now off by default. The behavior is no different, there is just a text change. Those are all of the changes for the "Voice Over" section of Accessibility. The next area that has changes is under "Display Accommodations".

Display Accommodations

Under iOS 10, there were two toggle options under the main Accessibility options. These were "Invert Colors" and "Grayscale". These options are still available, but now are under "Display Accommodations" and have been enhanced.

Under Display Accommodations, there are four different options, "Invert Colors", "Color Filters", "Reduce White Point", and "Limit Frame Rate". The "Reduce White Point" option was available under iOS 10, but it was under "Increase Contrast".

Invert Colors has two different toggles, "Smart Invert" and "Classic Invert". These two options differ in slightly subtle ways. Smart Invert will reverse colors, except for images, media and certain applications that use a dark color style. Classic Invert on the other hand will reverse the entire display. As you might expect, only one of the options can be enabled at a time.

Color Filters is an option that was introduced in iOS 10 and has not changed.

The last option, "Limit Frame Rate" is specifically for the 10.5-inch iPad Pro and the second generation 12.9-inch iPad Pro. The screens on these devices have ProMotion, which allows for 120 Hertz refresh rates, some users may not be able to use devices at these frame rates. So this option is available for those users. When this option is enabled the maximum frame rate for the screen will be 60 Hertz.

The next section that has changes is Subtitles and Captioning.

Subtitles and Captioning

Subtitles and Captioning is a crucial setting for those who are hard of hearing. For the Subtitle and Captioning there is one additional style option. "Outline Text". When this option is chosen, the text will be white but it will be outlined. There is one additional, small change. Instead of the name of "default" for the default option, it is not titled "Transparent Background".

Final Thoughts on Accessibility Changes

The Accessibility options for iOS 11 have been greatly expanded and clarified in cases. While most users will not use any of the new features, they will be great additions for those who could really benefit by using the new options. Now let us turn to storage.

Device Storage

If you heavily use your device, there is a very good likelihood that you may eventually run out of space. This could be due to the ever increasing size of applications, or the increase in photos and videos that users are taking. There are some ways that Apple is able to help save space with media, and this will be covered later on. But there are times when you run out space and you want to know what you can do to help offload some of the information. Under iOS 10, this was done under "Storage & iCloud Usage". This has been renamed to iPod Storage, iPhone Storage, or iPad Storage depending on your device.

The idea for this feature is not new, but it is new to iOS. A similar feature was actually introduced in macOS 10.12 Sierra. The overall premise is that there are items that are not really used on your device. Since these are not being used, it is entirely possible to offload these items to iCloud.

When you tap on your device's storage, you will be presented with a whole new screen. The first thing you will see is what is taking up all of your storage. This is similar to the iCloud Storage that was discussed earlier. It is broken down into categories. There are five categories, "Photos", "Apps", "Media', "Mail", and "Other". These are all identified by individual colors. Photos is yellow, Apps is red, Media is a light blue, Mail is a dark blue, and Other is a dark gray. The light gray color shown is is the unused space on your device.

There is a section titled "Recommendations". Recommendations has three options, "Offload Unused Apps", "Auto Delete Old Conversations", and "Review Large Attachments". There is an additional option related to Messages, but this will be covered when Messages is covered.

Offload Unused Apps is designed to automatically remove the least used applications when you begin to get low on storage space. There is an estimate of how much would be saved if this is enabled.

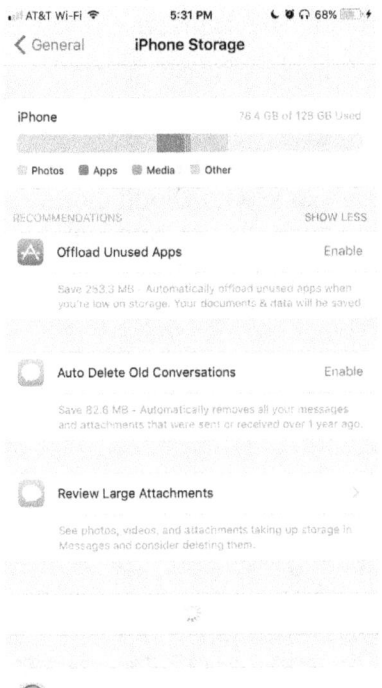

The next recommendation is to "Auto Delete Old Conversations". This will automatically delete messages and attachments that were received more than a year ago. This also has an estimate attached to it.

The last option is "Review Large Attachments". These attachments are ones that are directly into Messages. This option will allow you to look over the largest of the attachments that are on your device and provide you the option of removing them.

The section below recommendations is a list of all of the items that are taking up storage on your device. This is similar to the way that iOS 10 displayed this information, except there is one additional piece of information that may assist in determining whether or not to delete an application or its data. The additional information is the last date used. This is directly below the name of the the application.

Each of the recommendations given is disabled by default, but can be enabled with a single tap. It should also be noted that the enabled recommendations should not be acted upon by iOS until your storage space is beginning to get low. This is just a mechanism for you to indicate to iOS which items it should start deleting items when appropriate.

All of these recommendations are a good start to clearing up data on your iOS device. If you combine this with iPhoto Cloud Library's "Optimize Device Storage", feature, these could go a long way to being able to have enough space on your device so that you do not need to worry about issues arising because you ran out of space.

Background App Refresh

Background App Refresh is a technology that allows applications to be notified that there is up to date information that can be downloaded, while you are doing something else with your device, or while it is not in use. There is a new option for Background App Refresh, and that is whether or not to allow Background App Refresh on Wi-fi & Cellular Data, only on Wi-Fi, or Off. The default is "Wi-Fi & Cellular Data". Adding this option will allow users to choose whether or not they want to use their cellular data for potentially large background downloads. On the topic of restricting when things can be done, there are a couple of new Restrictions available.

Restrictions

Restrictions are great for parents who need to be able to limit what their children are able to do on their iOS devices. It is also a nice feature for those who wish to disable functions but not be tempted by them, or just because they know they will never use them and do not want them cluttering up the screen.

With new options available on iOS there are new Restrictions. The new Restriction options include disabling Screen Recording, and whether or not to allow changes to "Do Not Disturb While Driving". This last option may be a good one for parents to make a requirement of their teenage drivers, by forcing it to always be on.

Dictionary

There are two new dictionary options for iOS 11. These are Portuguese-English and Russian-English.

Shutdown

There is one last additional option in the Settings -> General group. The new option is that there is a button to allow you to Shut Down your device. This button will make it easier for those who may not be able to easily manipulate the power button on their iOS device to be able to shut down the device. Besides this possibility, it will also be useful for anyone who has the need to shut down their device, but their power button may not be responding for some reason. The next area to cover is Search.

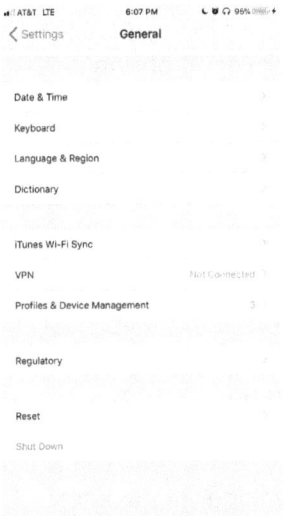

Siri and Search

It was mentioned earlier that the Spotlight Search has moved to under Siri. The options for search are generally the same, with only a slight modification. Now for each application installed on your device, you can toggle whether or not to allow the application to be used in Search and Siri Suggestions. By default all applications are enabled, but they can now be set individually.

Touch ID and Passcode

The idea of a passcode has been around since the iPhone was first released in 2007. As time has progressed, security has improved from a simple four-digit passcode to now being able to use a complex password. With security being a primary focus of iOS, there are settings that have been added to allow you to restrict what is enabled when your iOS device is locked. In iOS 11 there are a couple new options.

The option is a simple location change. The option is whether or not to allow access to Control Center when the device is locked. This was available in iOS 10, but was under "Control Center".

The next option is a new one, and that is "Return Missed Calls". Enabling this option will allow you to return a missed phone call without having to unlock your iPhone and open the Phone application and then return the call. This is a handy feature for many, but can be disabled if you would like. It is enabled by default.

iTunes and App Store

The iTunes and App Store section of Settings has received two new options. These revolve around Reviews and Unused Applications.

The first option is whether or not to allow developers to ask for Ratings and Reviews. It is enabled is by default but can be disabled. This is an on or off setting. It would be nice to be able to have this for each individual application. This is likely not available because you will not receive more than three request per twelve months, so Apple has determined this is a reasonable number of requests.

There is a second new option is one that was discussed earlier under the "Storage" section. There is a toggle whether or not to offload unused applications. Offloading Unused applications will delete the application itself, but keep its data. This option is disabled by default.

Mail

There is a single new option under Mail settings. This option is whether or not to "Collapse Read Messages". This is enabled by default, but you can expand any of the read messages to be able to see the previous messages.

Notes

There are a couple of new options under Notes. The first is Lines & Grids, which was discussed in the updates about Notes. The second option is "Resume Previous Note". This option is how long to resume using the previous note, when access Notes from Control Center when you are on the Lock Screen.

News

There is a new option in News, "Restrict Stories in For You". This option will allow you to limit the "For You" stories to only channels that you follow and not include stories that Apple thinks you might like.

Photos and Camera

There is only a sight change with these. Photos and Camera are now two separate groups, but the options remain the same.

Social Media Accounts

There is an important item that has been removed from iOS 11, Social Media accounts. The social media sites that were supported under iOS 10 were:

- Twitter
- Facebook

- Flickr
- Vimeo

Under iOS 10 you could automatically add these services to your iOS device. iOS applications would then be able to use your account information, provided you gave your permission. This feature has been removed and will require third-party applications that relied upon these services to modify their applications to account for this change. If some of your applications are not functioning properly when you update to iOS 11, this may be the reason.

Final Thoughts on Settings Changes

That covers all of the changes that have been made to Settings. There have been a number of changes. Most notably in the area of Accessibility. The other changes all make sense and will provide easier access for users. All of these changes make sense to be able to more easily organize options and provide users with greater control over their information. There is a relatively new iPad-specific application that has gotten some enhancements. That application is Swift Playgrounds.

Swift Playgrounds

Swift Playgrounds were introduced with the introduction of Swift in 2014. Swift Playgrounds are ways of being able to create programmable environments that allow testing. One of the things that Swift Playgrounds was not able to do is connect to third-party devices and program them. This has changed under Swift Playgrounds 2. Swift Playgrounds 2 will allow you to connect to the following devices:

- LEGO MINDSTORMS EV3
- Sphero SPRK+
- Parrot drones Mambo, Rolling Spider, and Airborne
- MeeBot by Jimu Robots
- Dash by Wonder Workshop
- Skoog musical instrument

If you connect to any of these devices, you will be able to edit and control the robots or drones. There will be Playgrounds that can be downloaded to help you learn all about what the device can do. This will be a huge benefit to not only enthusiasts, but also a great mechanism for teaching kids how to program with real-world demonstrations. There are a couple of large areas of exploration that Apple has brought to iOS 11. Let us look at these now.

Quick Setup

There are many ways that iOS makes life easier, yet when you get a new iPhone, or iPad, there are a number of things that have to be done. Some of these can be rather arduous and tedious. It would be a lot nicer if some of the initial setup were able to be taken care of. This is possible with iOS 11 with the new "Quick Setup".

Quick Setup will occur when you have your iOS 11 device near another macOS High Sierra or iOS 11 device. You will be prompted on whether or not to share the information with the iOS device that you are configuring. Additionally, it can use your Apple ID and automatically transfer the information to your new iOS device. This will make downloading apps, and getting everything setup even faster when you have a new iOS 11 device.x

If you have setup a 4th Generation Apple TV, AirPods, or Beats 3 Solo headphones, you will be familiar with the way it works. Even though it is a relatively small feature, it can significantly improve the on boarding process.

Augmented Reality

In the summer of 2016, there was a phenomena that swept the world, Pokémon Go. Pokémon Go is an app that takes the existing world an provides real-world locations, called Gyms, that allow players to train and ultimately catch Pokémon. This craze was spurred on by one huge factor, it was Pokémon. The concept of finding locations in the real world and doing battle was most definitely not a new idea. It was actually started with a game called Ingress, by Niantic. Niantic actually developed the Pokémon Go game.

There is a big area that Apple has been working on for a few years and will be directly applicable by iOS Users. That area is Augmented Reality. Apple's CEO Tim Cook has made many statements indicating that Augmented Reality, often shortened to AR, is an area of interest for Apple. At their 2017 World Wide Developer Conference, Apple announced a new framework for developers, ARKit. Without going heavily into the developer information, that will come later, ARKit allows developers to place items into the real world.

Apple has not released its own Augmented Reality application, instead it is relying on third-party developers to come up with applications that can use Augmented Reality. There are a variety of areas where Augmented Reality may come in handy. Some of these include, construction sites, landscape designs, games, and even interior designs. The last two genres already have two companies on board. For the game, Pokémon Go will be updated to use ARKit, which will produce even more realistic Pokémon to collect. The interior design company that announced it will have an application is the international giant, Ikea.

With the Ikea app, you will be able to take some of Ikea's iconic furniture and place it in your home. You will be able to see how well it fits into your style and tastes. In particular, it will help with being able to see if a piece of furniture will work in your home. The fit of furniture is not only the physical dimensions but also with the entire aesthetic style and feel of your home.

There are a few limitations with ARKit. First, the surface that uses ARKit must be horizontal. This means that things like walls may not work properly. ARKit will also be limited to devices that have an A9 or later processor. The compatible devices include: the iPhone 6s, iPhone 6s Plus, iPhone 7, iPhone 7 Plus, 12.9-inch iPad Pro, 9.7-inch iPad Pro, and the 10.5-inch iPad Pro are able to support ARKit applications. Augmented reality is not the only big push for Apple with iOS 11, there is another area of exploration, Machine Learning.

Machine Learning

One of the areas of interest for Apple includes Machine Learning. At the highest levels, Machine Learning can be described as the process of teaching a computer how to identify something. There are a couple of different techniques for machine learning. The one that Apple is using is based on "trained models". A trained model, is one that takes information learned with a Machine Learning algorithm and applies that learning to unknown data.

There were many pundits who claimed that Apple was not working on machine learning. In 2016, at their World Wide Developer Conference, Apple unveiled that they were absolutely working on machine learning in many different areas, particularly within Photos. Photos has the capability of detecting over 3,000 different types of objects, along with faces.

There are many machine learning models already in existence. With iOS 11, and macOS High Sierra, Apple has created a tool for converting existing machine learning models into ones that can be ready by Apple's machine learning framework, CoreML. The name of the tools is "coremltools". They are python scripts that will take existing models and convert them into models that are readable by the CoreML framework.

There is a companion framework, which works with CoreML. That framework is the Vision Framework. The Vision Framework is designed to detect faces, features, and identify scenes in both images as well as video.

Final Thoughts on iOS 11 for Users

iOS 11 for users is a huge update, particularly if you use the iPad on a regular basis. The revamped multitasking, which permeates throughout the entire operating system, will be great for iPad users who use the iPad as their primary computer. The ability to drag and drop almost anything will help users be more productive while using their iPad.

Most of the applications that are included with iOS have received improvements. The biggest amongst these has been Notes. The ability to add tables, as well as quickly add handwritten notes will help users be more productive and better organize information within their notes. With Siri analyzing and indexing handwritten notes, users will be able to search their handwritten notes. The new document scanning feature of Notes will let users be able to gather a set of necessary documents together to be able to have them all in one location without needing to manually scan them in, and without needing to take pictures. This will go a long way to helping users.

There are a lot of storage saving features that are in iOS 11, some that you may not even think about. The first being the removal of 32-bit applications. This removal means that applications going forward can be smaller. Alongside this, the operating system itself can be smaller.

The second set of features are actually from the new "Offload Unused Apps", "Auto Delete Old Conversations" and "Review Large Attachments". All of these, in conjunction with the already existing storage saving mechanisms will allow users to have more room for other items like Apps and Games.

On the subject of Apps and Games, the new App Store allows users to easily browse either Games or Apps, with just one tap. Combining this with the new Today tab will provide users with suggestions. The redesigned app store pages will help users find everything that they are looking for, in a much faster manner.

There are a bunch of small, but necessary changes that will help users access information more quickly, provide customization opportunities. iOS is not the only operating system to get some updates. watchOS has also received some worthwhile updates.

watchOS

watchOS is Apple's watch-based operating system. watchOS interacts heavily with iOS. The Apple Watch was originally introduced in September of 2014 and new functionality has been added over time. watchOS is Apple's smallest footprint, in terms of physical device anyway.

watchOS 1 to watchOS 3

When the Apple Watch was introduced, it attempted to become a smaller version of iOS. watchOS 1 included the ability to write applications specifically for the Apple Watch. However, unlike iOS in 2008, the Apple Watch did not become the application powerhouse that might have been intended. Applications on the original Apple Watch were slow and not always responsive. With the reality of slow applications, slow adoption, and overall feedback and Apple honed its focus on the Apple Watch once it became clear that many Apple Watch users were using their Apple Watch for two main purposes, notifications and fitness.

watchOS 2 was not as big of a release as one might expect for a 2.0. Instead it was a major refinement of the existing functions of the Apple Watch. The biggest change actually came for developers where they were now able to build applications that would run natively on the Apple Watch. This was a big improvement for applications. Many pundits indicated that watchOS 2 was likely what Apple wanted to release as watchOS 1, but did not want to wait for the software to be ready before shipping the hardware. watchOS 2.2 released a big update for users who like to have more than one Apple Watch. With watchOS 2.2 it became possible to pair multiple Apple Watches with a single device. This was not only big for users, but particularly helpful for developers.

Apple's watchOS 3 was a big release in terms of the Apple Watch. watchOS 3's primary focus was speed. Not just for applications but for all interactions. Apple had learned that the Apple Watch was all about quick interactions. Nobody was going to be staring at their Apple Watch for minutes on end. watchOS 2 brought some new features to the Apple Watch. watchOS 2 brought the concept of the Dock to the Apple Watch. The Dock, just like the Dock on iOS and macOS provides quick access to applications. The newly included Control Center allowed for quick access to some of the functionality on the Apple Watch. watchOS 3 also took into account the needs of those who were not as mobile as a majority of society by including the new Wheelchair activity. This feature allows those in wheelchairs to get the same activity rings as mobile individual would. watchOS 4 bring even more new features.

watchOS 4

watchOS 4 is Apple's latest version of the software for the Apple Watch. watchOS 4 continues to iterate on the existing Apple Watch software. watchOS 4 adds some new features that will help users be even more productive with their Apple Watch. Let us start with the user interface

User Interface

Since the release of watchOS 1, the Apple Watch has always had a honeycomb shaped layout for the applications that have been installed. One of the downsides with this layout is that is there are too many applications that look too similar, you may have difficulty determining which application is which. This may result in you opening up the wrong application. With watchOS 4, you now get an option of keeping the honeycomb layout or switching to a list view of the applications. To enable the list view, do the following on your watch:

1. Unlock your watch
2. Press the digital crown to bring up the honeycomb view
3. Force Press on the watch. A popup should appear.

Tap on "List View". You applications should now be in a list view. You can still scroll just as before and tap on any application and have it open as it normally would. This may be a small change, but it is a nice change. Another slight change for watchOS 4 is a couple of new watch faces.

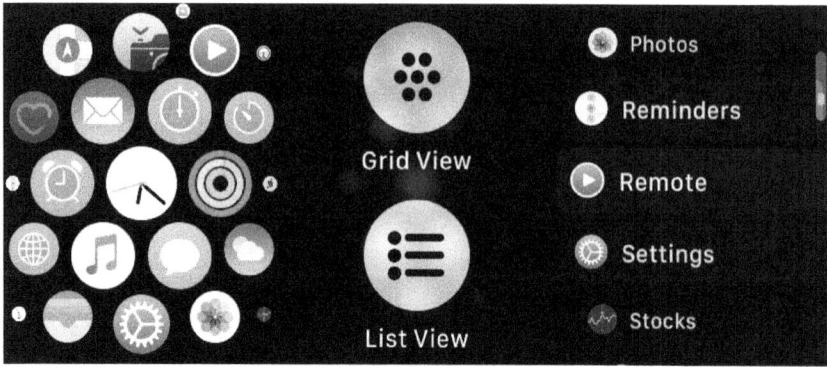

Watch Faces

One of the spots that Apple Watch users can customize is their watch face. The Apple Watch has gained a few watch faces over the past couple of years. The existing Watch Faces include:

- Activity Analog
- Activity Digital
- Astronomy
- Chronograph
- Color
- Mickey Mouse
- Minnie Mouse
- Modular
- Motion
- Numerals
- Photos
- Simple
- Solar
- Timelapse
- Utility
- Xlarge

There are a couple of new Watch Faces. The new watch faces have a couple of new distinct features. The first new Watch face is called Kaleidoscope.

Kaleidoscope

The Kaleidoscope watch face is one that looks as though it is right out the 1960's. An easy way to think of it just like a kaleidoscope that you might have played with as a kid. There are six different photos that you can select from. For each of the six photos, there are also three different styles. These three styles are: Facet, Radial, and Rosette.

The Kaleidoscope watch face allows you to do something a bit different with this watch face. If you spin the digital crown while you have the kaleidoscope face selected, it will mimic the way a kaleidoscope actually functions and it will begin to change shape and color of the watch face. It is a neat effect that adds a bit of pizzaz to the Apple Watch. There is another Watch Face that adds a bit of fun to the Apple Watch.

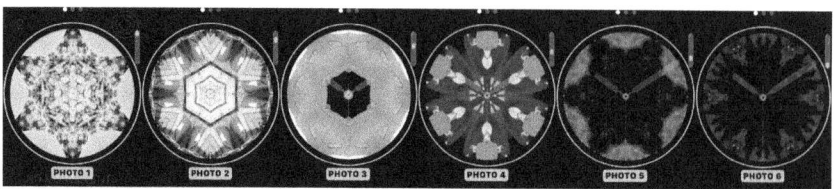

Toy Story

The Apple Watch has already had Mickey Mouse and Minnie Mouse. While Mickey and Minnie are classic Disney characters, there are now some characters that are a bit newer, and may appeal to a certain segment of Apple Watch users; Toy Story Characters.

There are four Toy Story characters that are now available as customizations of the Toy Story face. Those characters are: Toy Box, Buzz Lightyear, Woody and Jessie. You can select any one of the characters and they will do a bit of animation when you look at the watch face. The addition of the Toy Story characters may be a small addition, but for some it will be a welcome one. There is one last new watch face. One that only has two complications, but can be intelligent; Siri.

Siri

The Siri watch face is the last new watch face for watchOS 4. The Siri watch face only has two complications, or areas that can be customized. There is one in the upper left and one in the upper right. The reason there are only two complications is because the entire watch face is taken up by Siri tiles. The Siri watch face is designed to be able to recognition, through machine learning, what you may be interested in seeing.

What is might show could include: Weather, News, Stock tips, Calendar events, news, what's playing now, or anything else that Siri may have access to. What the Siri Watch Face may display varies based on location. This means that you may see something different displayed while you are at home versus when you are at work.

The addition of Apple's proactive assistant, Siri, being able to display things at a glance will absolutely help some individuals. The Siri Watch face will use Machine Learning to be able to determine what you want to see. As with all of Apple's machine learning, this will all be done on device.

The addition of new watch faces is not the end of all of the new features that are included in watchOS 4. There have been some other changes to the Dock.

The Dock

The Dock is probably one of the more important areas of any of Apple's operating system, but particularly on watchOS. The Dock on watchOS is where you are able to close errant applications that may be causing problems, as well as switch applications quickly. The Dock under version of watchOS, prior to watchOS 4, were arranged in a horizontal manner.

Under watchOS 4, they are now in a vertical manner. Changing it to be vertical will allow users to more easily scroll open applications. You still access the Dock by pushing the side button on the Apple Watch. Scrolling through open applications can be done by using the digital crown. You can still close applications by swiping, instead of swiping up to close an application, you now swipe from the right to the left to close an app.

This is a subtle change, but one that makes a bit more sense given the context of the Apple Watch. There are more applications that have been changed, most notably the Workout app.

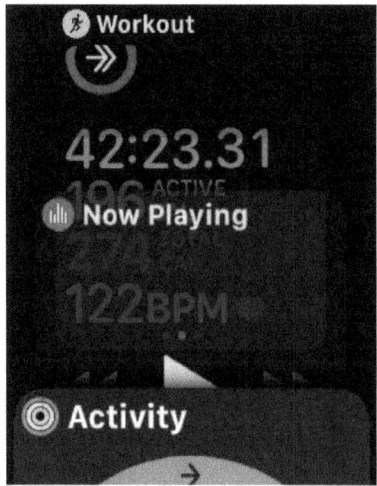

Dock Modes

There are now two modes for the Dock within watchOS 4. The first is "Favorites" mode, which is the behavior that watchOS 3, and prior versions, exhibited. The second option is "Recents" mode.

Recents mode for the Dock works similarly to the Dock on iOS 11. This means that the most recent applications used on watchOS will be at the top. In order to select which view you would like, you can do the following:

1. On your iPhone, open the Watch app
2. Scroll down to "Dock".
3. Tap on "Dock" to bring up the options for the Dock.
4. Tap on whichever option you would prefer.

The ability to allow users to determine which mode to use for the Dock only enhances the new capabilities of watchOS and provides even more customization options for users, which allows their Apple Watch to be even more personal.

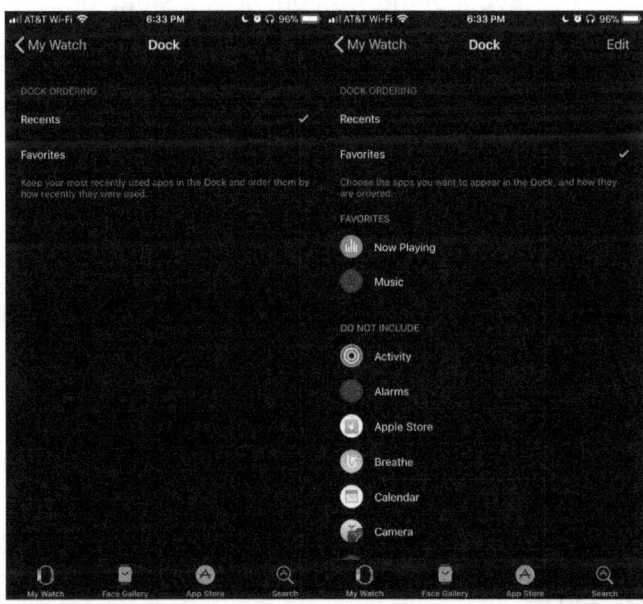

Workouts

One of the primary uses of the Apple Watch is health and fitness. The biggest use is to track workouts. The Workout app has been greatly changed. Under watchOS 3, the workout app presented things in a list view. If you wanted to start a workout, you would have to tap on it, wait for it to load and then decide what type of workout you were going to track. The "type of workout" meant is whether you will be tracking calories, time, or an open workout.

watchOS 4 changes the layout of the workout app. Instead of being a list of a list view, you are now presented with a larger scrolling view. This view is similar to the way that the Dock is now configured. These larger tiles show an icon that represents the type of workout that you are about to start. This will make it easier to easily identify the workout.

watchOS 4 allows you to begin your favorite type of workout and activity with just a tap and uses the goals that you previously set. You can, of course, customize any workout by tapping on the three dots on top of the workout. watchOS 4 will also bubble your favorite workouts to the top. This is intended to allow you to quickly start your favorite workout. One of the limitations with watchOS 3, and previous versions, is that the workout type that you prefer may not have been available. Apple has included a couple of new workouts.

New Workout Type

Being able to get the most accurate health tracking requires the right type of workout. watchOS includes a large number of workouts. However, one very popular workout type was missing. That workout is High Intensity Interval Training. It may be more commonly known as P90X. This is now an option under watchOS 4. There have been a couple of other enhancements within the Workout Interface.

Other Workout Interface Changes

There are many individuals who like to do different workouts during a session. Some of these invidious may be training for something like a triathlon. When they are training, they need to be able to easily add a new workout. Under watchOS 3, this was not an easy task.

With watchOS 3 if you wanted to add an additional workout you would have to end your current workout, locate the next workout type, and the start a workout. While this did work, it was a bit clumsy. watchOS 4 fixes this. Now, if you need to add an additional workout, simply slide over to the left, like you were going to end, or pause, a workout, but instead of ending a workout you simply tap on the "+" button to add a new workout to your session. You can then simply tap on the next workout you want to do and it will begin.

Enhanced Swimming

While it was possible to do an "Open" workout to account for swimming under watchOS 2, it was not an official workout. One of the features added to the Series 2 Apple Watch, which coincided with the release of watchOS 3, was the ability to add a swimming workout. This was made possible because the Series 2 Apple Watch is rated to a water resistance of 50 meters, under the ISO standard 22810:2010.

One of the things that the swimming app did not track easily was laps. Under watchOS 4 this is significantly updated. It will now track sets, as well as when you rest, the pace for each set of swims, and the distance for each type of stroke that you do. The addition of this swim tracking is a major update for those who enjoy swimming as their preferred exercise. The enhanced swimming and workouts are not the end of the enhancements for watchOS 4.

Do Not Disturb

When you are doing a workout and if you are trying to concentrate, such as when you are doing a workout you do not want to be interrupted. With watchOS 4, when you begin a workout, Do Not Disturb will automatically be turned on, just so you do not get interrupted.

Gym Equipment

As much as Apple may try, it cannot track everything. watchOS 4 will allow your Apple Watch to synchronize with capable gym equipment at the beginning of a workout. This enables two way communication. For instance, if you are using a treadmill, your heart rate can be sent to the treadmill while the incline and speed can be sent to the Apple Watch. This two way communication will enable even better tracking of workouts since it will provide even more information. While this seems like a pie in the sky dream, two major gym equipment manufacturers are on board and will be releasing equipment beginning in the fall of 2017. Once your gym updates its equipment, begin to look for this new capability.

Coaching

If you are using a pair of headphones connected to the Apple Watch, while you are working out, you can receive notifications that will indicate when you have begun to fall behind your current pace. This is a great enhancement that will allow you to let you determine if you need to increase your speed to keep pace with your goals.

Goals

As mentioned before, fitness is a primary use case for the Apple Watch. In order to keep people motivated to keep exercising is to use Move, Exercise, and Standing goals. If you attain these goals for a series of days, you create a streak. Maintaining a streak is one of the ways to keep motivating people to continue their exercise routines.

The more difficult part is how to keep the motivation there. Some people are motivated merely by maintaining their streak, while others need a bit more motivation. This is why watchOS will now be a bit more proactive about reminding you that you can accomplish your goal. This is done in a couple of different ways.

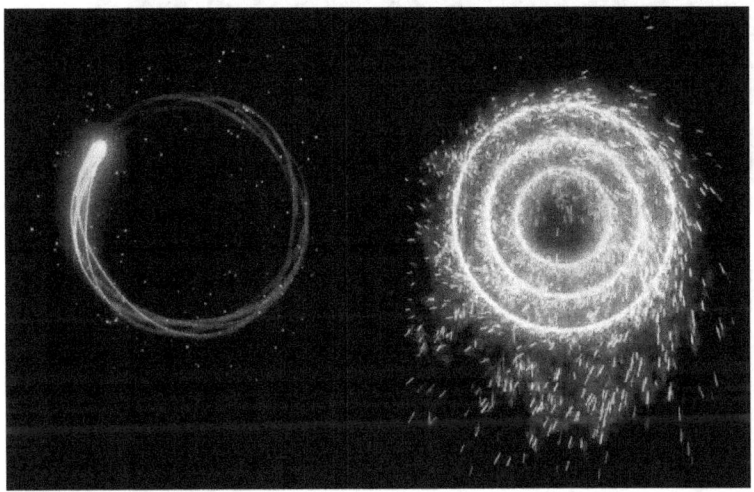

The first is that early in the morning it will remind you that you can keep the streak going, if you have one. It will also remind you throughout the day, particularly for a standing goal, that you only have so much left to do. This is not limited to just days. watchOS 4 will also provide you reminders of how many more days you have left before you get a "perfect week" goal, or even a "perfect month".

While reminders are good, some people like to celebrate their accomplishments. To this end, watchOS 4 will now show an animation, depending on the accomplishment. There is now a spinning wheel of fireworks. How many sparks will depend on what you have accomplished. If you finish only your Move goal, only one ring will be shown. If you finish off two, like the Move ring and Exercise ring, then both of those will be shown. Once you finish off all three goals, all three sparkling rings will be shown.

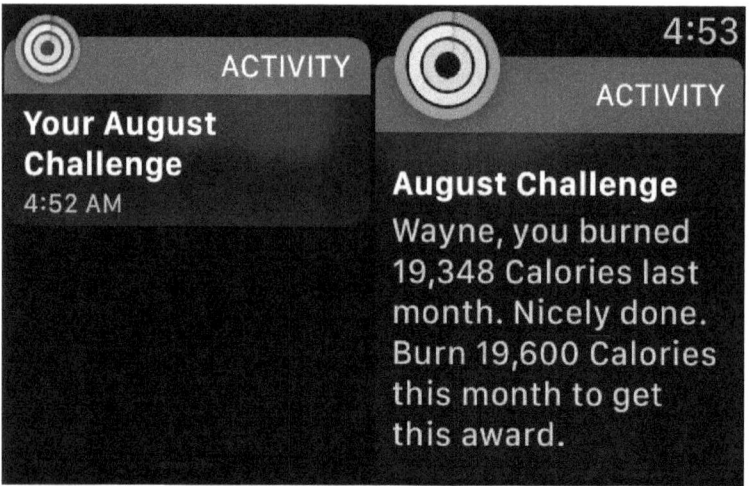

These are all minor tweaks to goals, but they can be significant for those who need just a little bit of an extra push to get them over the finish line to reach their move, exercise, and standing goals.

Final Thoughts on Workouts

Workouts with watchOS 4 have seen great improvements. You will now be able to directly connect your Apple Watch to the gym equipment you use. If you do go to the gym and use a lot of different equipment, you can now easily add a new workout to your session by simply swiping and adding a new workout. If you do not like the gym, but prefer swimming watchOS 4 adds a lot of new features for tracking your swims. When you do a swimming workout, it will now track your sets, stroke length, and even when you rest between sets or laps. The enhancements of workouts under watchOS 4 is a major update. There is one thing that goes well with a workout and that is music. There has been some changes to Music with watchOS 4.

Music

As Apple says, "Music is part of Apple's DNA". Apple was the company that was able to usher in the digital music revolution by making digital music mainstream with its iTunes Store. watchOS 4 has a redesigned the Music app on the Apple Watch.

Before we delve into the app itself, there is a new option. You can now automatically allow music to synchronize to your Apple Watch. You can choose what type of music you would like to synchronize, or you can let the Music app just automatically add music to your Apple Watch. If you do not wish to add music you tap "Not Now". However, if you change your mind in the future, you can add music at any time by doing the following:

1. Open the Watch App on your iPhone
2. Scroll down to Music
3. Tap on Music

From here you can add your favorite playlists or enable the syncing of the "Heavy Rotation" from the "For You" section of the Music app on iOS. Now let us look at the new design of the Music app.

New Music Design

The Music app on watchOS has been completely redesigned. Under watchOS 3, and previous versions, it was a set of tables that would display the music. However, with watchOS 4, you will now be presented with a larger view of any songs that are synchronized to your Apple Watch. You can then scroll through any of your playlists and tap on them.

When you tap on a playlist, it will begin shuffling the songs that are on that playlist. A "Now Playing" screen will appear. This Now Playing screen is very similar to any watchOS Now Playing screen, with one slight difference. There is an icon in the lower left that will allow you to look at the entire playlist.

If you tap on the the Playlist button, it will display all of the songs in that playlist. You can then scroll through and find another song. Tapping on any song will begin playing that song instead of the current one playing. You can always go back to the entire list of Playlists by tapping on the "Back "button in the upper left corner of the screen.

On the main screen of the Music app, on the Apple Watch, you will see two options at the very top. These are: Now Playing and Library. The Now Playing button will bring you to what is currently playing. Whereas the Library button will allow you to see the entire library of what is on your Apple Watch.

Tapping on the library button will display four additional buttons. These buttons are:

- Playlists
- Artists
- Albums
- Songs

Tapping on any of these four buttons will bring up a list of that item. The Playlists button will display the playlists. Artists will display artists, with their corresponding number of albums. Albums will display the Album title, the artist, and a small thumbnail of the album's cover. Finally, songs will show the Song's title and the Artist.

Even though it may appear as a small redesign, the new Music app on watchOS brings a slew of new features. Most notably, the redesign of the scrolling interface. A tangentially related item to the Music app is the Now Playing complication.

Now Playing Complication

The Now Playing complication is a shortcut that can be placed on a watch face that will allow you quick access to the currently playing audio. There has been a couple of changes to this complication. The first is that it can no longer be used in the smallest complications. Under watchOS 3, you could customize

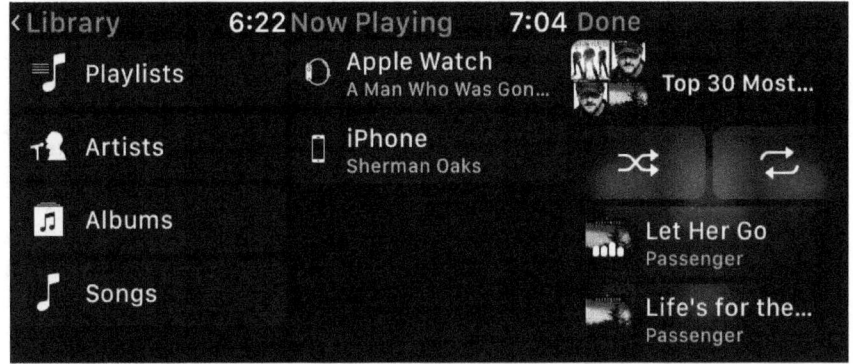

the Modular Watch face to have a "Now Playing" complication in one of the lower three complications. This is no longer the case. Instead the "Now Playing" complication must be in a complication that takes up the entire width of the screen. This could be in the middle section of the Modular Watch face, or in the bottom of the Utility Watch face. This will be a less than ideal setup, but it is still possible to have a Now Playing complication on a Watch face under watchOS 4.

There is one last little change to the Now Play complication. When audio is playing, a simulated wave form will move up and down on your watch face. This will be handy so you can at a glance see if there is any audio is indeed playing. There have been a few other enhancements to watchOS 4, let us look at these now.

Other watchOS Enhancements

Even if the new Workout features and redesigned Music app were all that were added in watchOS 4, that would be a significant update. But there is still a bit more left to discuss. Next we will look at the last bit of enhancements

Apple Pay Cash

Just like on iOS 11, watchOS 4 will also be capable of handling the Apple Pay cash card. This means that if you are out at a store and cannot easily reach your phone, you should still be able to pay with your Apple Pay Cash card since it can be added to your Apple Watch.

News app

One of the features that users enjoy is being notified of the latest news while on the iPhone. However, it is sometimes handy to be able to know the latest news without needing to reach for your phone. This is where the News App can help. With watchOS 4, the News app can now be added to an Apple Watch. When you add the News app you will be able to get news alerts right on your wrist. This means that you do not need to pull out your phone to get the latest information.

File System

Even though you may never interact with it directly, the File System on the Apple Watch is an important factor. Like iOS, the new default operating system on watchOS is the Apple File System (APFS). APFS on the Apple Watch will have a minimal impact, at least that is detectable by users. APFS could however, in the future, allow a snapshot to be taken of the contents of the watch, right before performing an upgrade. Which, could possibly allow for a rollback of an operating system. The ability would need to be created by Apple, but it does leave open the possibility of it occurring in the future.

Final Thoughts on watchOS

Each version of watchOS builds on and further refines the operating system for the Apple Watch. watchOS 4 takes the existing watch faces and adds some iconic new characters, Toy Box, Woody, Jessie, and Buzz, from Toy Story;. The new Siri watch face will allow Siri to proactively inform you of information depending on your location. You can get different information from different sources while at work versus while at home. The Kaleidoscope watch face will allow you to have a more psychedelic view to the time.

Fitness is one of the primary focal points for the Apple Watch. The updates to the Workouts by allowing you to have multiple workouts within the same session will greatly help individuals who like to switch workout types quickly. If you are a swimmer watchOS will allow you to keep track of even more details than you could previously.

On the topic of more details, soon you will be able to pair your Apple Watch with the gym equipment that you use to be able to synchronize data between your Apple Watch and the gym equipment.

The changes to watchOS, even though they may be subtle, are improvements that are well worth the upgrade. iOS and watchOS are not the only iOS-based operating systems to get updates. There have been a few updates to tvOS as well.

tvOS

tvOS is Apple's newest operating system. Its focus is to be the operating system that runs Apple's set top box, the Apple TV. tvOS has received some updates that will be helpful for a larger group of users.

Right-to-Left Language Support

The user faces changes to tvOS are only a couple. The first new feature is for those whose language is right to left. A couple of examples of these types of languages is Hebrew or Arabic. For these users, the tvOS interfaces now fully supports these languages. This means that anything that is on the left for an English-based Apple TV will be on the right, and vice versa. This may not impact that many individuals, but having Right to Left support is crucial to be able to have the Apple TV be available to as many users as possible.

App Sizes

The second change is regarding the size of applications available on the Apple TV. With tvOS 11, applications can be up to 24GB in total. This is the App itself plus any downloadable content. This is up from the 4 gigabyte limit that was available in tvOS 10.2.

There is one new app coming to tvOS. The app is one that has been highly requested; Amazon Prime Video. The Amazon Prime video app will be available on the Apple TV soon. There is an additional change for those times when you do watch your Amazon Prime content on your Apple TV.

Dark Mode Changes

In tvOS 10, a new feature was added, Dark Mode. Under tvOS 10, you were able to switch between Light Mode and Dark Mode. The downside of this was that switching between the two was a manual prospect. This changes in tvOS 11 with the new Automatic mode.

The automatic mode is determined by time of day. If it is after sunrise, but before sunset, your Apple TV should be in "Light Mode". Conversely, if it is after sunset but before sunrise, your Appel TV should be in "Dark Mode". Although it is a small feature, it is one that will help, particularly if you want to watch a movie after dark. There is one last user feature for tvOS.

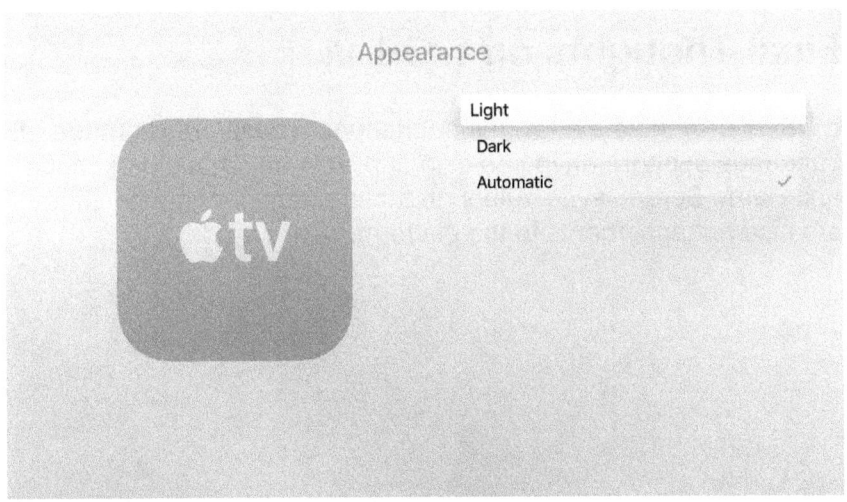

Home Screen

The last new feature for tvOS 11 is one that will be significantly useful for homes with more than one Apple TV. That feature is Home Screen synchronization.

The ability to synchronize the home screen between multiple Apple TVs will allow those who have more than one Apple TV to have everything look the same on all of their Apple TVs. This also means that if you download an app on one Apple TV it will automatically be downloaded on other Apple TVs.

This will be particularly nice for those families with kids. This is because having all of your home screens be the same means that the kids will only need to learn the location of applications, instead of multiple locations. This is particularly nice when a kid may be cranky and want to just use their favorite application or watch their favorite movie or TV show.

Similarly, it will also help organizations whom want to have the same look for all of their Apple TVs.

Those are all of the new user features for tvOS 11. There are not many, but there are plenty for developers. Next we will look at the changes for Developers.

Final Thoughts on tvOS 11

tvOS 11 only makes a few minor changes. These are Right-to-Left Language support, an increase in app size, automatic dark mode and Home Screen sync. Although these are minor changes, they are nice enhancements to the platform.

iOS 11, tvOS 11, and watchOS 4 Developer Changes

When the original iPhone was released many users were hoping to be able to make native applications for the iPhone. However, this was not possible, not officially anyway. At the original iPhone announcement, Apple indicated that web apps were the way to go. This did not please many developers.

The more entrepreneurial developers began to reverse engineer some of apps that were available on the iPhone to see how they were constructed. Ultimately, this lead to unauthorized access to the iPhone and its software. This access lead to the first of the third-party app stores. In 2008, with iPhone OS 2.0, developers got what they wanted, an App Store and an authorized Software Development Kit. A certain subset of developers did not like the restrictions that were being put in place, so they doubled-down on submitting their third-party apps to the "jailbreak" app stores.

In June of 2008, at their World Wide Developer Conference, Apple unveiled that developers would be able to submit their applications to the iPhone App Store. This lead to an influx of developers submitting their applications. Applications written for the iPhone were originally built using Objective-C. This was the case until 2014 when Apple unveiled their all new programming language called Swift. Swift 4 is the latest iteration. Let us look at the changes around Swift

Swift 3.2

Swift 3 was released in 2016 and was a pivotal moment for the young language. Swift 3 was the version that was determined to bring source compatibility. This meant that some developers would need update their source code to be able to compile against iOS

10, or macOS Sierra. Swift 4 does not change this, but there is enough that it might be too much for a developer to change around their code, at the current time. To assist in this, there is Swift 3.2

Swift 3.2 utilizes the same compiler as Swift 4, so the Swift 4 compiler understands Swift 3.2. This is necessary because once a developer is ready to transition from Swift 3 to Swift 4, there is no need to change the compiler.

Swift 3.2 is merely a mode within the Swift 4 compiler that emulates Swift 3. This is being included as a way to be able to undo some of the SDK changes that have occurred with Swift 4. This means that you will be able to keep the same syntax as Swift 3 and are not being forced to adopt the Swift 4 syntax changes, of which there are only a few.

There is one last benefit to Swift 3.2, it can co-exist with Swift 4, but only on a per-target basis. This means that if your main app is built on Swift 3, but you want to build a new extension using Swift 4 you can do just that. You cannot, however, use both Swift 3.2 syntax as well as Swift 4 syntax within the same target.

Swift 3.2 has access to all of the new APIs within iOS 11, and macOS High Sierra. This means that you can get all of the latest and greatest features without needing to adopt Swift 4. When you are ready to move to Swift 4, there is a migration assistant that will help you on your way and provide you with the information that you need to make the transition as smooth as possible.

Swift 4

The entire Swift programming language is a departure for how Apple normally operates. Apple is known as one of the most secretive companies around. Swift, however, while originally built in secret is now entirely open source. This open source nature means that users of Swift can suggest changes to the language, which will only help its adoption. The latest iteration of Swift, is Swift 4.

Swift 4 builds upon the significant changes in Swift 3 to provide more code-level compatibility. Swift 4 brings some big features including:

- Application Binary Compatibility
- Functions with Classes and Protocols
- Rewritten Strings functions
- New Access to memory

Private Extensions to a class

There are those times when you are building a class and wish to be able to use an extension within the class, but you want to make sure that it stays private and it not released to the outer world. When this approach was taken with Swift 3, the compiler would throw up a warning indicating that you attempted to access a private member from a different scope. The workaround for this under Swift 3 was to use the keyword "fileprivate", but this was a bit too broad of a change. This functionality has changed under

Swift 4. With Swift 4, you can now use the private keyword and it will function as expected. However, there is one caveat. This only works within the same file. What this means is that you cannot access private members of other classes, only of the class within the same class.

Functions with Classes and Protocols

One of the hardest things to do is try to create a class that conforms to a set of protocols. Protocol conforming is a straight forward task, but when you are creating a function that can take as a parameter, a subset of of elements this becomes a bit trickier. As an example, let us look at the following code:

```
protocol Dimmable {
        func dim()
}
extension UIButton: Dimmable { /* ... */ }
extension UIStepper: Dimmable { /* ... */ }


func dimControls(controls: [???]) {
        for control in controls where control.state.isEnabled {
                control.dim()

        }
}
```

How would you fill in the ??? Section? You could try UIControl, but not every UIControl is dimmable. In Swift 4, this becomes easier. You can now use classes and protocols as the requirements. The function will then become

```
func dimControls(controls: [UIControl & Dimmable]) {
        for control in controls where control.state.isEnabled {
                control.dim()

        }
}
```

This means that only those objects that are UIControls and conform to the Dimmable protocol will be dimmed when the function "dimControls" is called on an object. This is the exact behavior that Objective-C has had for a long time and will be very helpful for many Swift developers. Let us look at one of the biggest features of Swift 4. And it revolves around Strings.

Rewritten Strings functions

Strings are one of the most fundamental types for any programming language. Strings provide the basis for many of the values shown within a User Interface as well as content that is pulled from a remote server. When using a string within Swift there could be some limitations that may require some custom extensions to be able to do the task you need to accomplish. An example of some of the difficulties with Strings within Swift comes with this example.

Let us say that you want had a variable called "title", that contained the string "Book Title".
Let us say you just wanted to get the first part of the title, say "Book" out of the string. How would one accomplish this? In objective-c, it would be something like this:

```
NSString *title      = @"Book Title";
NSString *firstPart  = [title substringToIndex:3];
```

This is a pretty straight-forward operation. With Swift 3, this is what it would take.

```
var title: String = "Book Title"

public extension String {
    public func substring(_ range: CountableClosedRange<Int>) -> String {
        return String(self.characters[characterRange(range)])
    }
}
```

The "var title" statement is pretty self explanatory. The rest is a function, which is an extension on the String class. This function is called substring. It will then take a closed range and return that substring. In practice it would look like this:

```
//Define a range to get the part we want
let bookRange = 0...3
//create a static text with the part that we want.
```

```
let firstPart     = title.substring(bookRange);
```

firstPart should then be just "Book". It seems a bit excessive to create an extension just to get a substring. In Swift 4, it has a changed a bit. This is the new syntax

```
var str = "Book Title"
let endIndex = str.index(str.startIndex, offsetBy: 3)
var firstPart = str[str.startIndex...endIndex]
```

```
let title = "Book Title"
let space = title.index(of: " ")!
let firstPart = title[..<space]
```

This is a lot less code. Although, it is still an additional line more than in Objective-C, yet it is still less code than requiring an extension. This is made possible because of a new type called Substring. Let us look at this type now.

Substring

Substring is a new type and is very similar to String in many ways. This is because they both conform to the StringProtocol. Substring is a different type because there were three different options for this:

Make the substrings the same type as string, and share storage.
Make the substrings the same type as string, and copy storage when making the substring.
Make substrings a different type, with a storage copy on conversion to string.

The Swift leads determined that the third option was the right one. The reasoning for this is spelled out in the **String Manifesto** page on GitHub.

There are some other new features with Strings, specifically related to Unicode.

Unicode

Swift 4 support Unicode 9. There was one major downside to using Unicode characters under Swift 3. It is not that Swift 3 did not support unicode, it does. However, the issue comes when you try to count characters for a string that contains Unicode characters. Let us see an example.

```
let emoji4      = "😀😃😄😆"
let length      = emoji4.characters.count
print("Character Count: \(length)")
```

In Swift 3, the number of characters would result in 8. This is because an emoji is actually made up of graphemes. There are usually two graphemes for every Unicode code point. Now with Swift 4, it would result in a character count of 4, which is the expected behavior.

Here is an even better example. The character "é" can be represented by the hex code of 0xE9. The same character can also be represented by the hex codes, 0x65 + 0x301 . 0x65 is the hex code for the letter "e", and 0x301 is for the accent mark. These two representations are equivalent, and the second representation would result in a character count of two. This change to Unicode string counting means that you will no longer need to worry about getting a wrong number of characters when you are attempting to count characters.

Getting the proper length of a string is an important aspect for any developer. The most important tool for any developer is Xcode. Let us look at some of the new aspects of Xcode 9.

Xcode 9

Xcode is Apple's integrated development environment, or IDE. Xcode 9 adds some new features that will absolutely help developers. Let us begin with some new source control information.

Source Control

One of the more important functions of Xcode is the ability too maintain a history of the spruce of the applications that you develop. If you are on a team, this becomes even more vitally important. Starting with Xcode 4, Xcode included a built-in version control system, Git. Localized Git works well if you only need to keep version control on your own system. However, many developers work in teams and prefer to use the service, GitHub. With Xcode 9, GitHub support is now built directly into Xcode.

You can add an existing GitHub account by doing the following:

1. Open Xcode 9
2. Go to Xcode -> Preferences
3. Click on the "Accounts" button.
4. Click on the "+" button to add a new account.
5. Click on "GitHub" or "GitHub Enterprise" account, depending on the type of account that you have.
6. Click on the "Continue" button. A new dialog will appear.

7. Enter in your Git user account and password. If you are using GitHub Enterprise, you will also need the URL for your enterprise server.
8. Click on the "Sign In" button. The GitHub account will be added to the "Source Control Accounts" section of the Accounts tab in Xcode 9.

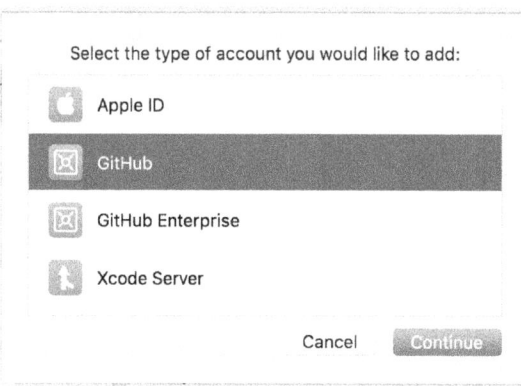

Once you are logged into GitHub in Xcode 9, you can then begin to Clone repositories that you already have defined in GitHub. You can search by going to "Source Control" -> "Clone". A window will popup with all of the GitHub repositories that you are attached to. You can click on any of these and hit the "Clone" button.

Once you hit the "Clone" button a save dialog will appear asking where you want to save the cloned project. Locate the location and hit the "Clone" button on the Save Dialog box. If the project that you are cloning is an Xcode Project it will open up within Xcode. However, if it is not an Xcode Project, it will open up in Finder so you can browse the cloned repository.

While you may want to work on your own projects, there are times that it may be helpful to see what others are doing. There are a couple of different ways to Clone that repository.

The first method is to search the GitHub site via your preferred web browser and click on the "Clone or download" button on the project page. This will bring up a popup which contains the URL for the repository. Copy this URL. Then you can open Xcode and paste it in the GitHub title bar and hit the "enter" or "return" key. Xcode will then ask where you want to save that repository and then begin to download that repository.

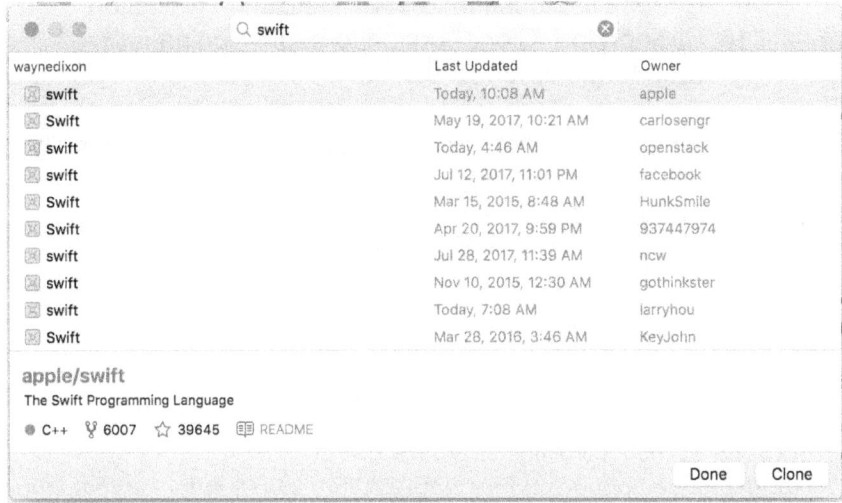

The second method is to do the same as above, but instead of showing "Download Zip", which would download a zip file for that repository, there will be a button called "Open in Xcode". When you click on the "Open in Xcode" button, you will be prompted by Safari to verify that you do indeed want to open the link in Xcode. Once you click on "Allow" it will immediately begin downloading and cloning that repository in Xcode. You will see a save dialog box to determine where you want to download the project.

This is great if you already have the URL for the repository, but what if you want to be able to search GitHub for a specific keyword without leaving Xcode. This is now a possibility. To search, simply do the following:

1. Open Xcode 9
2. Click on the Source Control menu item
3. Click on "Clone. A popup dialog should appear.
4. Type in the keyword that you want to search

5. Hit the "enter" or "return" key to begin searching. Alternatively you can tap on the "search" button to the left of where you typed in your search.
6. The list of projects that meet your keyword.
7. Locate the one that you wish to clone.
8. Tap on the "Clone" button. A Save Dialog will appear.
9. Choose the location to save the cloned repository
10. Click on the "Clone" button to begin cloning and download the repository.

You can now build and run the cloned repository as you normally would. The ability to locate and clone repositories is not the only new feature related to source control. There are some new features once you begin working with the cloned Project.

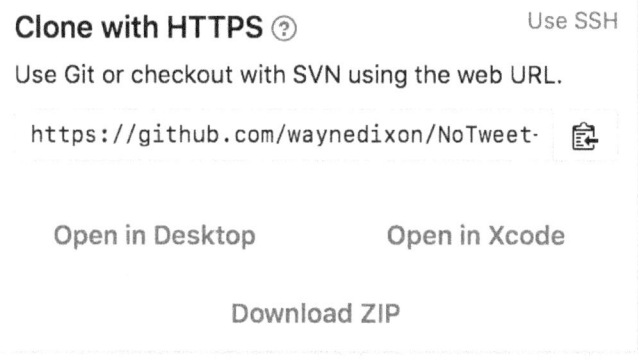

Other Source Control Features

Working with your newly cloned repository provides even more areas to explore. The first of these areas is the new Source Control navigator.

Source Control Navigator

When you clone a repository, you often want to begin looking at the history of the commits for the source code. This is done to begin understanding some of the history of the code. You can navigate the entire source hierarchy by tapping on the "Source Control Navigator" button in the top of the navigator pane.

A set of items will appear in the main window. This is the commit history for that project. The commit history is one of the best ways to see how a project has evolved. At the top of the commit history window, there are a set of predefined filters. These are the filters for setting the timeframe for commits. The options are: "All", "Last 24 Hours", "Last 7 Days", and "Last 30 Days". Tapping on any of these will reduce the commit history to the selected time frame. This can be extremely helpful if you happen to remember when a particular change was made.

If you do not remember when a commit was made, you can also do a bit of free-form filtering. This is done by entering in text in the search bar. You can search for any text that you wish. There is a bit more advanced filtering that can occur within the search box. When you begin typing in a search term, you will get three additional filtering options. You can filter by Message, Revision, or Author. If you know which area contains your query, you can select any one of these options and it will search just that specific area.

Each of the commits should be displayed in the main window. You can perform a couple of different actions with each commit. You can double-click on the commit. Doing this will provide a source code comparison between the previous revision and the selected revision. Something to note is that not all elements of an Xcode project are able to be compared.

You have a few operations that you can be performed on any commit. You can access these by either right mouse-clicking or control clicking on the commit. Once you do this, a popup will appear next to the commit that you have selected. The available actions are:

- Copy
- Copy Identifier
- Email Author
- Tag
- New Branch from

- View on GitHub
- Checkout

Selecting "Copy"" will copy the commit text. "Copy identifier" will copy the commit identifier. "Email Author" will open an email where you can email the author. This will be helpful should you need to contact the commit's author to get some additional information. "Tag" will allow you to add tags to a commit. "New Branch from" will create a new branch based off a single commit. The "View on GitHub" command will view that specific commit on GitHub. Finally, "Checkout" will checkout that specific commit.

Once you tap on the "Source Control Navigation" pane there will be three folders that appear. These folders are:

- Branches
- Tags
- Remotes

Let us look at each of these in-turn, starting with branching.

Branching

The branches folder is the logical structure of the different branches, of the code that you are looking at. There should be at least one branch for each project. This should be the "master" branch. The "master" branch, in the parlance of source control is the primary branch of code. In the structure of a tree, you could think of it as the trunk.

When you are looking to test a feature to see if it would make sense in the app, you can create a branch. To create a branch of code, perform the following:

Select the branch from which you would like to create a secondary branch. Typically, when this is done, you want to select the "master" branch.
Right mouse-click, or control click, on the branch. A popup menu should appear.

Left mouse-click on "New branch from "master"", where "master" is the name of the branch. A second popup menu should appear. Enter in the branch name you want to create.
Click the "Create" button to create the branch. The new branch will be created locally.

Once you have begin making your modifications and are ready to commit. You can click on "Source Control" -> "Commit", to commit the changes that you have made. Once you push those changes to GitHub, they will be reflected on the GitHub site. Next, let us look at Tags.

Tags

Tags can be a useful tool for being able to add contextual information to a commit without needing to put it into the commit message. You can utilize tags for any purpose you want. Some examples include:

- Beta Version
- Bug Tracking Number
- Internal references

You can use a tag in just about manner you can imagine. To add a tag to a commit, simply locate the commit, and right-mouse click, or control click, on the tag and select "Tag". A dialog will appear.

You can enter in your tag, and an optional message for that tag. Once you click on the "Create" button that commit will be tagged with the tag that you just created. You can have multiple tags, but you will need to apply each tag individually. There is something else to keep in mind about tags. For any tag, there cannot be any spaces. You can use a dash if you would like, but you cannot use a space.

If you accidentally added a tag and you want to remove it you can do so. To delete a tag simply open up the Tag folder in the "Source Control Navigator", right mouse, or control, click on the tag, and select "Delete". A confirmation dialog will appear asking you to confirm that you want to delete the selected tag. Clicking on "Delete" will immediately delete the tag.

Let us look at the last folder, Remotes.

Remotes

Remotes are the Remote repositories that contain your code. The Remote folder contains an object called "origin". This is the source of where all of the current code. The "origin" object contains each branch as well as the master. You can use any of the branches or master to view the commit history for that branch of the code.

Final Thoughts on GitHub Integration

The integration of GitHub and GitHub Enterprise will allow all developers to be able to easily locate, search and otherwise maintain the code that they working on. With GitHub being the largest online repository of projects makes it an ideal candidate for integration into Xcode. One thing that GitHub does not offer is continuous integration. If you want continuous integration for your code, you will need Xcode Server.

Xcode Server

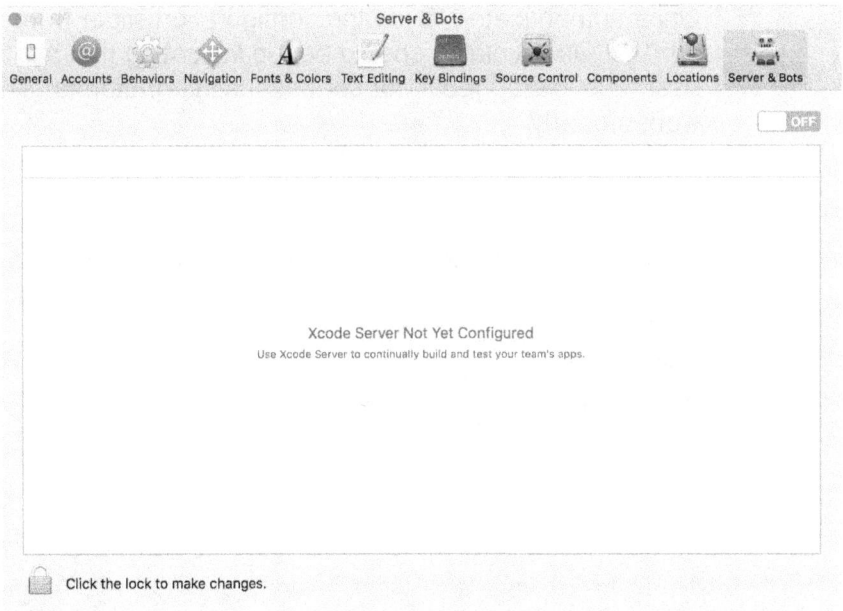

Xcode Server was introduced in 2014 with the addition of the Xcode Server to OS X 10.10 Yosemite Server. Xcode server allowed developers to be able to not only be a git repository but also allowed continuous integration. Continuous integration, in case you are not aware, is the idea of being able to continuously test your applications to make sure that they continue to pasts the tests that you have included. This is necessary to ensure that all aspects continue to work with each new build that you submit. There have been some changes to Xcode Server, most notably that you no longer need the macOS Server application to run an Xcode Server.

Xcode Server still provides the same functionality as the previous versions have, however Xcode Server is now a built-in aspect to Xcode 9. To configure Xcode Server perform the following:

1. Open Xcode 9
2. Go to Xcode -> Preferences

3. Click on "Server and Bots"
4. Authenticate by clicking on the lock icon in the lower corner.
5. Once authenticated, Slide the configuration slider from "Off" to "On". A dialog should popup indicating that a user must be logged in for continuous integration to work properly.
6. Select a user, or create a new account. It is recommended that this user is a standard user account.
7. Enter in the user account's password, if selecting a user.
8. Click on the "Login" button.
9. Fast user switching will be enabled and you will be prompted to enter in the user's password.
10. The integration will then finish running.

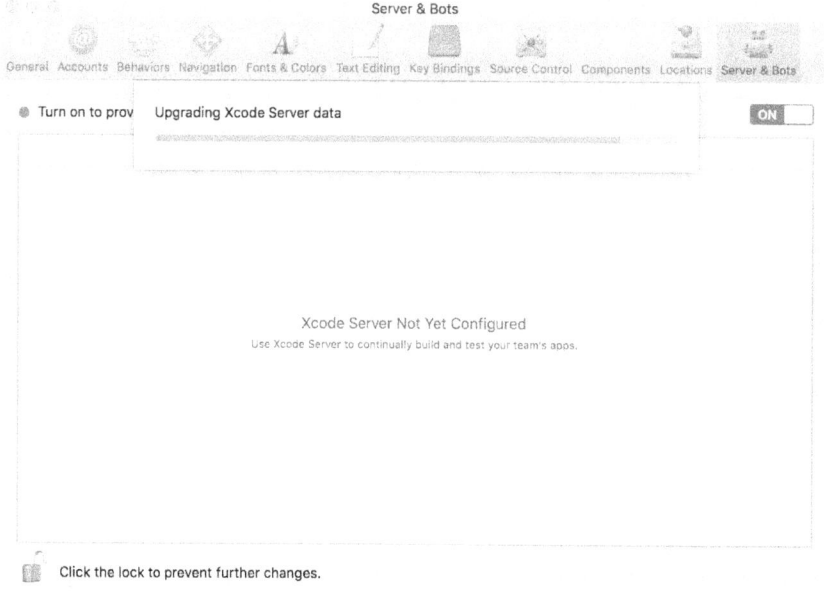

Xcode Server recommends that the user selected for the Xcode Server is a standard user account. This is counter to previous versions where the recommendation was that the user account was an administrator. The new recommendation is a standard user account because it is best to not leave administrators logged into a computer. This is particularly true if the computer is intended to be used remotely.

You are now able to use any other client to connect to the newly configured Xcode Server. There is an additional feature for Xcode Server. Xcode Server can automatically run the tests on any device that is connected to the Xcode Server. This means that if you have some development devices around and they are connected to the Mac running Xcode Server, the applications will be tested on actual devices.

The changes to Xcode Server will allow anyone the freedom to run an Xcode Server without the need for the macOS Server app. There are still other changes around Xcode 9.

Other Xcode 9 Changes

Xcode is full of a variety of tools to assist developers in the building of their applications. One of these is development profiles.

Downloading Profiles

One of the more tedious tasks of being a developer is managing profiles. There are many different profiles that you encounter as a developer. The primary one is the development profile. If you are setting up a new computer, you may not have all of the necessary profiles for a project. It can be a tedious task to try and locate the proper profiles that you need for your project. Similarly, one of the possible downsides of working in a development team is that you may not always have access to all of the profiles that have been created. This is possibly because you are new to the team and you may not have all of the profiles. Again, you could search through the developer portal to try and locate the profiles that you need. With Xcode 9, you may no have to.

If you click on your Developer ID In the "Accounts" section of the Xcode 9 Accounts tab, you will be able to download all of the existing profiles in your developer account by simply tapping on "Download Profiles" button.

Team	Role
Wayne Dixon	Agent

Download All Profiles   Manage Certificates...

When you click on this button all of the profiles that match exactly to your account will be downloaded. There are some certificates that cannot be downloaded automatically. These are the distribution certificates. Instead, these must be exported from another machine and then imported into your machine. There are possibly others who have generated some profiles that you also need access to, these will be listed and you can go ahead and email that user to have them share the information that you need. There is another tool that iOS developers need and it has seen some major improvements. That tool is the iOS Simulator.

Simulator Changes

One of the most necessary tools within Xcode is the iOS Simulator. The iOS Simulator allows developers to build their applications without needing to build and run the app on their device every single time. It is still highly recommended that applications be built and tested on device since the Simulator cannot always accurately reflect what will happen on device, but it is a great start. There have been a couple of changes to the Simulator in Xcode 9. The first of these changes is with the Simulator itself.

The iOS simulator is always updated to support the latest version of iOS. Yet with previous versions of Xcode you were limited to the types of simulators that could run. The limitation was that only one simulator could be running at a time. This limitation makes it quite difficult to be able to test synchronization between devices, local game play, along with many other possible scenarios. Xcode 9 will now allow you to run multiple simulators simultaneously. This will make debugging synchronization issues a lot easier.

Along the same lines, when you are doing some debugging of an iPad, it can be difficult to see everything all at once. To accommodate this Xcode has had the ability to scale devices at 25%, 33%, 50%, 75%, or 100%. While these percentages work a majority of the time, they are not always the most ideal. To help with those situations where a fixed percentage is not enough, the iOS simulator can now be any arbitrary size. You can now scale the simulator to whatever size fits your need. There are still some

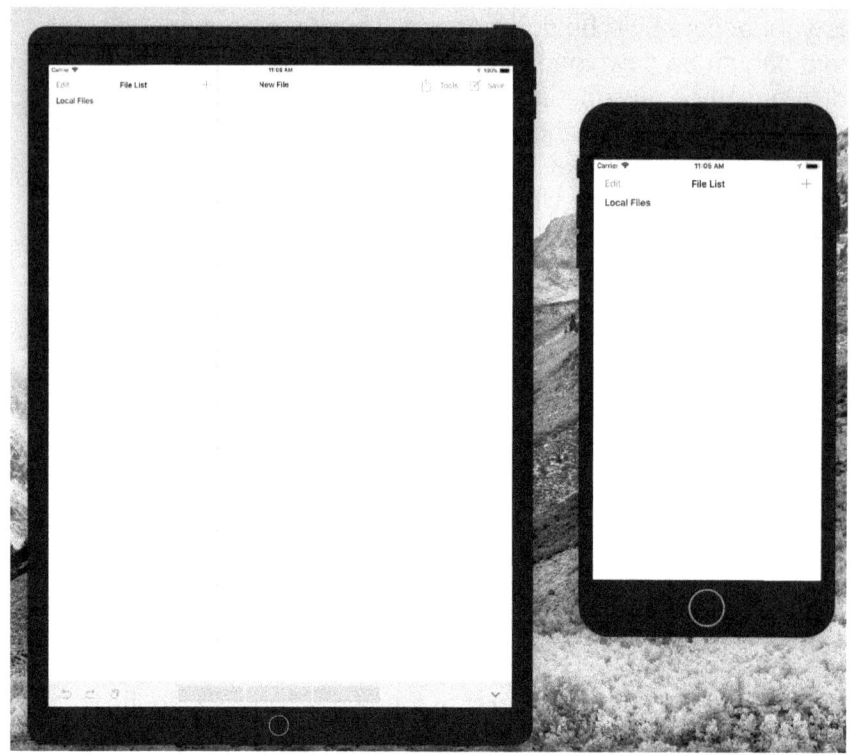

predefined sizes, but they are not the same as what was in Xcode 8. The new pre-defined sizes are 50%, 100%, and 200%.

There is also another new option available. You can now decide whether or not you want your simulator to have a bezel around it. This is enabled by default but can be removed by going to Window -> Device Bezels.

The rationale for having the bezels is to allow you as a developer to better picture how your application will look when on a user's screen. This can help determine if the layout, graphics, and colors will work with a device. The only thing that be a nice feature to have, is the ability to switch the front face. The only option is black, but there are more devices with white fronts than with black fronts. It is definitely not a crucial thing, but would be a nice touch. Let us look at the biggest interaction that developers have with Xcode, the Code Editor window.

Code Editor Window

The Code Editor window has been completely rewritten. It is now written using Swift. What this means is that it should be, according to Apple fifty times faster. The Code Editor Window will now allow you to smoothly scroll even with projects that thousands upon thousands of lines of code. The smooth scrolling window is not the only new feature of Xcode 9's Code Editing Window. There is another new feature, Markdown support.

Markdown Support

If there is one thing that developers cannot agree on it is code formatting. There are many different ways to format code. Some people use tabs, others use spaces. In some cases it merely due to personal preference. In other cases it is due to the language itself treating a character in a particular way. Even with all of the different opinions, there is one type of syntax formatting that is quite common. That syntax is known as Markdown.

Markdown was created in 2004 by John Gruber, of daringfireball.net. Markdown began its life as a text to HTML conversion tool for the web. To quote the site:

"Markdown is a text-to-HTML conversion tool for web writers. Markdown allows you to write using an easy-to-read, easy-to-write plain text format, then convert it to structurally valid XHTML (or HTML).

Thus, "Markdown" is two things: (1) a plain text formatting syntax; and (2) a software tool, written in Perl, that converts the plain text formatting to HTML."

Xcode 9 adds support for Markdown files. Markdown is typically used within Readme files, and end with a .md file extension. To create a Markdown file, perform the following steps:

1. Open Xcode
2. Open the Project that you wish to add a Readme file to.
3. Click on the File menu
4. Click on "New" -> "File"
5. Scroll down to the "Other" section.
6. Click on "Markdown file"
7. Click on the "Next" button. A Save dialog will appear.
8. Choose the location to save the file
9. Click on the "Create" button. The file should be created.

The Code window will then show your newly created file. Here you can go ahead and create your readme file, using Markdown.

The reason that Markdown is included within the Code Editor is more than just that it is used by so many developers, because it is. But it is also supported by GitHub and given the tight integration that Xcode 9 has with GitHub, it makes it easier for developers to use Markdown for their readme files. Besides markdown support, the Code editor has a few more tricks up its sleeves. Next up is another new feature, refactoring support.

Refactoring Swift

One of the tasks that ever developer faces, from time to time, is having to refactor code. Refactoring is the idea of changing around your code to make it even more efficient. This could be removing code that is no longer needed or even just renaming variables so that they are a bit more clear. While there were a myriad of ways to refactor your code. However, the built-in methods do not always work as well as you might like. This is where Xcode 9 will help.

Xcode 9 supports the ability to refactor Swift code. This is huge for Swift developers. Alongside this ability, you will be able to submit your own refactoring code and you will be able to download the refactoring code of others. You can then integrate these with the Xcode Toolchain and you will be able to improve your code that much more. There is even more with Xcode 9.

Some of the capabilities of the Swift refactoring engine in Xcode 9 are:

- Add missing protocol requirements
- Generate missing implementation stubs
- Add missing overrides for abstract methods
- Extract to local variable
- Extract method / expression
- Expand default in switch statements to generate all applicable cases
- Convert if/else to / from switch statement
- Wrap string in NSLocalizedString macro

One of the many items that are included in any Swift project, are assets. There have been some changes to Assets with Xcode 9 as well.

Assets

Every application that is released requires assets of some sort, even for the most basic application. Every application needs icons, and in some cases, a splash screen. Regardless of the number of graphical assets, it is always a good idea to give a user the best experience possible. One of the newest features on Apple displays, whether on a Mac or on an iOS device, is the P3 Color Gamut.

P3 Color Gamut

For a vast majority of the time that computers have been around, back to the original Macintosh, and even before that. The standard color space used is RGB. RGB standards for Red Green Blue. Given the variations in different screens, it became necessary to create a standard, so the representation of the colors could be consistent between manufacturers. This is where the Standard RGB, or sRGB, color space comes into play. Each of the colors is represented by 8-bits, from 0 to 255. This leads to a possible 16,777,216 colors.

The P3 Color Gamut provides an even wider range of color. There are some devices that support the P3 Color Gamut. These devices include the 2015 27-inch iMac 5k iMac, the 2015 21.5-inch 4K iMac, the 2017 21.5-inch 4K iMac, as well as the 2017 27-inch 5K iMac. Besides the iMacs, the Late-2016 and Mid-2017 MacBook Pro, both 13-inch and 15-inch models, all support the Wider Color Gamut.

Similarly, on the iOS side, the 9.7-inch iPad Pro, the 10.5-inch iPad Pro, and 2nd Generation 12.9-inch iPad Pro all support the P3 Color Gamut. The iPhone 7 and iPhone 7 Plus also support the wider color gamut. All of this adds up to a significant number of devices supporting the P3 Color Gamut.

In order to provide the best experience for your users, your assets should also support the P3 Color gamut. Xcode 9 allows this to occur. In fact, you can have up to 16-bit source content. This means 16-bits per channel, for a total of 281,474,976,710,656 colors; or 281.47 Trillion colors. There are no Apple products that support this many colors, but the 2017 27-inch can support 10-bit colors per channel, through dithering. This comes to 1.07 Billion colors that can be represented on the 5K iMac Screen.

One of the requirements for supporting the Wide Color Gamut within your assets is to use Asset Catalogs. To support P3 graphics, perform the following in Xcode 9:

1. Open Up your Asset Catalog
2. Click on "App Icon", or another image set
3. Open up the Inspector.
4. Click on the "Show Attribute Inspector" icon on the far right
5. Under "Gamut", select sRGB and Display P3. A second set of icons slots will appear, and will be labeled "Display P3"

If you do not specify Display P3 colors, any Display P3 device will automatically use the sRGB graphics. Alternatively, if you only use P3 graphics, sRGB versions will automatically be generated. Additionally, if you do choose to include Display P3 graphics, the correct color will be chosen via App Thinning. This means that devices that cannot support the P3 color gamut will not get those assets, which will reduce the size of the application download for those devices. This also works for devices that do support Display P3. Those devices will not get the sRGB assets; again reducing the download size for those devices as well. There is a similar item to asset catalogs, and that is colors.

Colors

Many User Interfaces are chock full of a variety of colors. Whether it is in an icon, or just an accent color. These too should be in Display P3 colors as well. Typically when a color is specified, it is specified using Hex, an example is #FFFFFF, which is pure White. Each of these translates to 255. It is recommended that you use P3 Colors wherever possible.

This is possible to do with Xcode 9, and in code. This can be done using

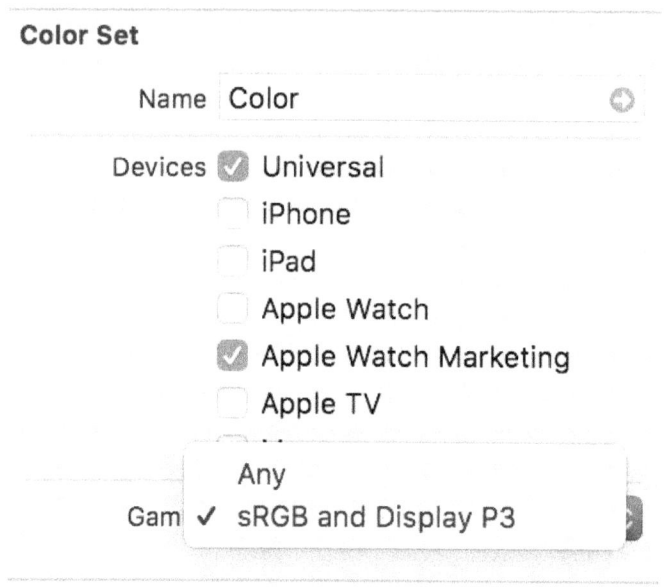

UIColor(displayP3Red: 1.0, green: 0.5, blue: 0.0, alpha: 1.0)

This line should produce this color:

Red: 1.074
Green: 0.463
Blue: -0.21
Alpha: 1.0

The sRGB equivalent is:

UIColor(red: 1.0, green: 0.5, blue: 0.0, alpha: 1.0)

	Red:	1.0
	Green:	0.5
	Blue:	0.0
	Alpha:	1.0

If you compare that to the sRGB color, you may be able to see a slight difference. Creating colors programmatically can become quite repetitive. Besides being repetitive, it can be difficult to really get the exact color you are looking for. Specifying different colors for both sRGB and Display P3 could quickly become overwhelming, particularly if you have a variety of different colors. Combine this with the different color spaces, and it can quickly become an even larger number of variables to keep track of. What would be convenient would be the ability to define specific colors, in each color space. This is actually possible with a new feature called Color Sets.

Color Sets

Color sets, as one might guess, are a set of colors. What you can do is define your specific color for both sRGB and Display P3. To create a color set perform the following in Xcode 9:

1. Open the project you want to add a color set to
2. Click on the "Assets.xcassets" folder
3. Right-mouse click, or control-click, in an empty area to bring up the pop-up menu.
4. Click on "New Color Set". A new blank color will appear in the Asset Catalog.
5. Click on the newly created color.
6. Click on the "Attributes Inspector" icon in the right pane.
7. Click the drop-down under "Gamut".

8. Click on "sRGB and Display P3". The "Universal" Color should switch to two colors, one for sRGB and one for Display P3.

sRGB

Display P3

Universal

You can now define your colors for each. The are specified in floating point, for each color, Red, Green, Blue, as well as the Alpha channel. Given the fact that the Display P3 color gamut is wider, if you enter in the same values for both sRGB and Display P3, you will notice a color difference. You can also specify specific colors for each type of device. iPhone, iPad, Apple Watch, Apple TV, and Mac. There is also a "universal" color, option, which is the default that you modify.

You can then name your color. You do this by double-clicking on the word "Color" in the left pane of the asset catalog.

If you want to have the exact same color, for a particular color, you can use the application "Color Sync Utility". It is available under the Utilities folder in the Applications folder. The Color Sync Utility app can allow you to convert between sRGB and Display P3. This can help you determine the exact color that you want to create. The creation of colors for both sRGB and Display P3 is very helpful, but how would you use your newly defined color?

Using a Named Color

There is a new method on NSColor that can be used to assign your color to a variable, or constant. The method is init?(named: String). The code to use this method in Swift would be something akin to:

let myColor: UIColor = UIColor.init(named: "myColor")!

You can then use the constant, in this case, "myColor" and assign it to any element that you where you want to use that color. When you use a named color, the proper color for the device will be used. Thus, if the device being used has a P3 compatible Display, the P3 color will be used, whereas other devices will use the sRGB color.

P3 Colors on the Web

One of the areas that most would think that different colors would not make a difference is on the web. This thinking can be somewhat rationalized because there is the concept of "Web Safe Colors". Web Safe Colors are a range of colors that will be represented the same on all devices. These colors are within the sRGB color space.

You can specify colors that are outside of of the standard color space by using numbers that are above 100% or negative numbers. This should allow for proper color on Display P3 compatible devices. If the device is only sRGB compatible, it should use anything above 100% as 100%, and anything below zero as 0%. Now that we have finished with colors, let us take a look at some aspects of developing on iOS with Xcode 9.

Developing on iOS

The original iPhone was released 10 years ago, For the first four versions of iOS, if you wanted to sync your iPhone, or iPod Touch, you would have to connect it to your Mac, and then wait for the sync to occur. Starting in iOS 5, you were able to synchronize your iPhone and iPod Touch wirelessly. This changed the way that users were able to do things. This also brought the ability to wirelessly backup your device. Even though users could do just about everything without needing to plug in their device, short of charging, There is one group who has not had that luxury, developers.

If you have been an iOS developer for any length of time, one of the things that you quickly become aware of is that the iOS device that you are testing on, is tied to your computer. That is, until now. With iOS 11, and Xcode 9, you can now do wireless development on an iOS device.

Setting up Wireless Development

Setting up Wireless Development is quite easy. You can perform the following steps:

1. Connect the device you wish to enable Wireless development on to your Mac
2. Open Xcode 9.
3. Click on the Window menu.
4. Click on "Devices and Simulators", or hold down Shift, Command, and hit the number 2, to open Devices and Simulator
5. Click on the Device that you want to enable Wireless development
6. Click on the checkbox titled "Connect via network". It will take a few seconds, but the device will be configured for wireless development.

There is an easy way to determine if a device is configured for Wireless development. In the "Devices And Simulator" window. Any devices that are configured for Wireless Development will

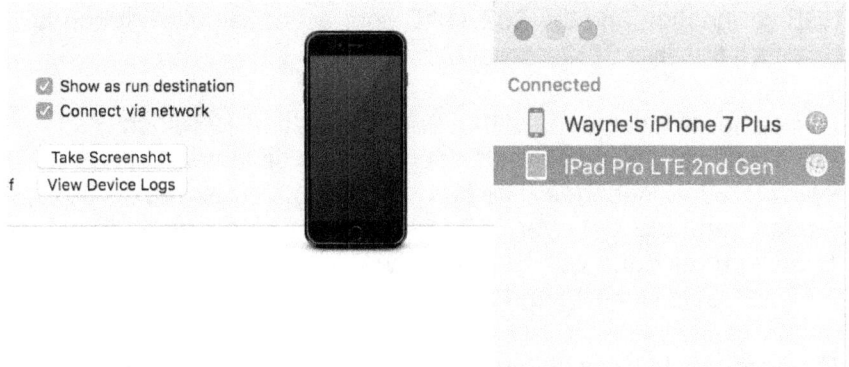

show a globe icon that will indicate that it will connect over the network. You can always decide to disable Wireless Development by unchecking the "Connect via network" box. You will then need to connect the device via a USB cable in order to do any development.

One of the downsides of wireless debugging is that it may be a bit slower. Even though in theory the maximum speed of 802.11AC is 1.3 gigabits per second, which is nearly three times faster than the 480 megabits per second that is USB 2.0. However, in practice networks are never as fast as their theoretical maximums. I ran some tests to see how fast these were. The devices used were a 2015 Dual Core 2.7 GHz Core i5 MacBook Pro and an iPhone 7 Plus. Each test was done by deleting the app from the iOS device and starting from a clean build in Xcode.

The first test was run using a USB to lightning cable connected direct from the MacBook Pro to the iPhone 7 Plus. The time from start to finish was 14.26 seconds. This includes the compile, build, and install phases. This is not too shabby.

The second test was done on an 802.11N network, again with deleting the app, and cleaning the build. This run as 1:01.78. Over four times as long. The router used was a 5th Generation AirPort Extreme.

The last test was done on an 802.11AC connection, with both devices connected to a sixth generation AirPort Extreme. The run time for this was 22.40 seconds. The overall time between the USB connection and the 802.11AC connection is only 7 seconds. Granted, this is a 57% increase in time.

The same test was done with a 2nd Generation 12.9-inch iPad Pro. The times for those tests seem to be a bit faster. The USB 2.0 test was 20.26 seconds. The test over the 802.11N was 43.06 seconds and the test over 802.11AC was 21.55 seconds. Again, these were all done with the same two devices, in this case the 2015 2.7 GHz Core i5, and the iPad Pro.

The same tests were also performed using a 2017 4.2GHz 27-inch iMac and the same iPhone 7 Plus and 2nd Generation iPad Pro. The results were as follows. Via USB to the iPhone 7 Plus, it took 15.00 seconds, start to finish. For the iPad Pro via USB it took 8.70 seconds from start to finish. When building and then installing over wireless, the iPhone 7 Plus took 14.88 seconds, and the iPad Pro took 12.68 seconds. These tests were done on an 802.11AC network with all of the devices running at 802.11AC.

Now there are many different factors that go into the speed of a network. This includes the maximum physical speed that a device can connect to the network, as well as what the speed of the network connection itself. As you can see, the speed of the computer will significantly determine how quickly projects can be built, as well as the network determining how fast the apps will be installed on the device.

Even though the wireless development may be a bit slower, it is a lot more convenient. The ability to develop without the need of wires will help not only those who need to test with multiple devices, but may not have enough ports, as with the MacBook, or a 13-inch MacBook Pro which only has two ports. Even if your Mac has plenty of ports, the ability to use wireless development will prove to be a benefit to all developers.

Final Thought on Xcode Changes

The changes to Xcode 9 are quite substantial. You can now run Xcode server from any Mac with Xcode 9 installed to be able to do your testing. There is no longer a need for macOS Server to be installed. While running your tests, if you have devices directly connected your continuous integration bots can run all of your tests directly on the connected devices.

The new ability to download development profiles that you may not already have will be a boon to productivity for those users who need to be able to get to work quickly. The ability to use one set of images for sRGB and another for Display P3 will allow you, as a developer, to provide the best experience to your users.

Additionally, the new Color sets feature will allow you to specify exact colors for each type of display, again providing the best experience to your users. Another method of providing the best experience is to make sure your apps are running at their best.

For you the developers, Xcode Server is now build directly into Xcode 9 allowing you to run bots on your Mac directly, and if you work in a team, you can setup any Mac to be an Xcode server, without needing to setup Server.app. Similarly, if you have iOS devices connected to an Xcode Server, the tests that you have will run on the iOS devices automatically.

Development can be a pain sometimes. Particularly if you only have This is where wireless development can help. The ability to fully run, debug, and test applications wirelessly, on iOS devices, is one of the most convenient changes to Xcode that has occurred in quite some time. If you are not testing on a device, and only testing in the simulator, the ability to run multiple simulators simultaneously will allow even better debugging and testing between devices than before.

The changes to Xcode 9 will provide a significant benefit to developers of all levels. Whether you are new to Xcode development, or a season professional, and whether you work alone, or in a team, the changes to Xcode 9 will help everyone.

APFS Changes

One of the things announced at Apple's World Wide Developer Conference was a new file system called Apple File System (APFS). At that time Apple said it would be the default file system for all of Apple's operating systems sometime in 2017. Unbeknownst to many the first operating system to get APFS was actually iOS. This came with iOS 10.3. Beginning with iOS 10, Apple began running test conversions when updates were done. These tests were conducted to allow Apple to look at any errors that would occur and take those into consideration. One of the aspects that was not accounted for with APFS on iOS 10.3 was normalization.

If you are unaware, normalization, is the process of taking a file's name and making it consistent with other files. This is normally done to be able to quickly locate and if necessary open files. An example of the process occurred with iOS 10.3:

File Name (Unicode code point)	iOS 10.3 Name
file01.txt	file01.txt
File01.txt	File01.txt
Résumé.pages (é = 0x39)	Résumé.pages
Résumé.pages (é = 0x65 + 0x301)	Résumé.pages

Hmm.. something does not seem right. How can two different files have the same name? This case should not occur. This is what some would call a collision. A collision, as you might expect, is where the same items occupy the same space. In iOS 10.3, files names were stored in non-normalized form. This meant that there were possibilities of collisions. iOS 11 helps address this with some normalization schemes. Before we delve into normalization schemes, it is important to know about the different Unicode variants.

Unicode Variants

Unicode consists of code points. A code point is a representation of a grapheme. A grapheme could be the accent above an é, or even the letter "a". Each possible letter or accent mark has its own code point. A unicode character can be composed of one or more code points. There are primarily two different types of Unicode character variants; pre-composed and decomposed.

Precomposed characters only have one code point, where as a decomposed unicode character has more than one code point. A good place to understand how these are composed is with emoji. Let us look at some examples.

The "police" emoji, 👮 has a code point of U+1F46E. Yet, this "police" 👮 emoji is comprised of two code points; U+1F46E and U+1F3FB. This is because the second code point, U+1F3FB, is used to describe the skin tone. Yet, when you see the emoji displayed, it is only one image. The first emoji is considered a pre-composed emoji since it only has one code point. Whereas the second emoji is considered a decomposed one, since there are two code points.

Another example is the letter e, with an accent, é. This can actually be represented in two different ways. The first is with é, which is U+00C9 and it can also be represented by two code points, U+0045 and U+00B4, yet when you look at either one, it is the same symbol, é. How a unicode character is represented is typically transparent to the user. However, this can lead to some issues.

Normalization Schemes

To quote the Unicode site:

"Unicode Normalization Forms are formally defined normalizations of Unicode strings which make it possible to determine whether any two Unicode strings are equivalent to each other. Depending on the particular Unicode Normalization Form, that equivalence can either be a canonical equivalence or a compatibility equivalence.

Essentially, the Unicode Normalization Algorithm puts all combining marks in a specified order, and uses rules for decomposition and composition to transform each string into one of the Unicode Normalization Forms. A binary comparison of the transformed strings will then determine equivalence."

With this in mind, let us look at some of the Normalization schemes that apple is employing. In iOS 11 there are a couple of normalization schemes available. The scheme that are available are: Native and Runtime. Let us look at each of these.

The Native Normalization scheme will take any unicode characters and make sure that they are composed of all code points. This is the Normalization Form D. The Native normalization scheme is available on macOS High Sierra for Case Sensitive volumes only. It will be available for iOS 11 devices, but only if you do an erase-restore. All iOS devices will be converted at a future date. That date is not yet known.

The second normalization scheme is at Runtime. This scheme will take any pre-composed unicode characters and convert them to their constituent code points. This is available on iOS 10.3.3 and later.

The normalization of Unicode characters will make it possible to avoid any collisions in the future which means that there will not be any lost data.

AirPlay 2

One of the features of macOS, and iOS, is the ability to send audio and video from your Mac, or iOS device, to an Apple TV. The protocol that does this is called AirPlay. AirPlay originally began as an audio-only protocol named AirTunes. AirTunes allowed people to play their iTunes songs on their AirPort Express base stations that were connected to set of speakers. AirPlay then expanded to include the ability to send both audio and video to devices. This came with iOS 4.2 and beginning in Mac OS X 10.8 Mountain Lion, Macs were able to AirPlay their screens to any AirPlay compatible receiver, such as the Apple TV.

AirPlay 2 builds upon the existing protocol to provide some additional features. The biggest is the ability to play to multiple speakers simultaneously. When this is done, the synchronization between the devices is very close. This is necessary not only for Apple's own HomePod, but for the ability to have third-party speakers that support AirPlay 2.

AirPlay was designed in an era where Audio was dominant. One where the primary audio consumed was a song. Similarly, it was also an era where wireless connectivity was just beginning to emerge in the mainstream. Airplay was originally released in 2004, and 802.11G was only certified in 2003 and did not emerge into the mainstream until 2004. In order to ensure smooth functionality, even on slower networks, the buffer sizes for AirPlay were only a few seconds. This lead to needing constant communication between the AiPlay sender and the AirPlay receiver.

AirPlay 2 changes this. Buffers with AirPlay 2 are now minutes long, not seconds. This takes into account the changing habits of individuals, going from song listening to more long-form content, like podcasts. Having the ability to buffer longer times also means that it will be easier for multiple speakers to keep the sound consistent and synchronized. This buffer is available because AirPlay 2 is doing faster than real-time streaming to devices. The larger buffer allows smooth playback, even if there is a network glitch of some sort. This is because the speakers should already have the data, so they should be able to continue to play without any issue. And even if they do not have the data, having a majority of the audio already should allow the network glitch to be rectified before any additional data is needed.

AirPlay 2 works best when you adopt one of the following classes:

- AVPlayer
- AVQueuePlayer
- AVSampleBufferAudioRenderer
- AVSampleBufferRenderSynchronizer

If you adopt one of the latter two classes, your app will be responsible for sourcing and parsing the content. This is particularly useful if you want to do some adjustments, which means that you will have to parse and feed raw audio to player.

AirPlay 2 focuses on enabling long-form audio playing from iOS devices. This will allow multiple speakers to play the same thing throughout multiple rooms, with little or no latency. Implementing AirPlay 2 should be something to consider, particularly if your application is designed to play long-form audio.

MusicKit

One of the features requested by developers is the ability to access a user's music library. This has been requested so that you can suggest music to users. This is where the new MusicKit framework comes into play.

MusicKit is a new framework for iOS 11 and provides developers access to a user's music library. The reason a developer may want to integrate MusicKit could be for a couple of reasons. The first is to be able to suggest songs, artists, or albums to a user. The second reason is that a developer may want to integrate a music player directly into their application.

MusicKit is an HTTPS web-based API that allows developers access to the entire music catalog. Since Apple Music is a web-based API, you need to know the format that a request takes.

https://api.music.apple.com/{version}/catalog/{storefront}/{api}?params

Let us look at each part in turn. All requests for the Apple Music API require an HTTPS connection. There is no HTTP option. The base URL is api.music.apple.com.

The Apple Music API is versioned, as of now there is only version 1, so v1. The "catalog" is the basis for all music requests for a specific version of the API. There is another option available for requesting user-specific information, that path is "me".

Storefront is the language code for the logged in iTunes Store. Developers should not guess at this based upon geo-location. This should be requested via the API.

The last section is the requested API and its associated parameters. There are a few different APIs that can be called. These include:

- Albums
- Songs
- Artists
- music-videos
- playlists
- stations
- curators
- activities
- apple-curators
- Charts
- Genres
- Search

Each of these API expect an ID. This ID is a unique identifier for that particular type. Some of the APIs can be associated with others. For instance, Albums are associated with songs, and an artist.

The user specific APIs include:

/me/history/heavy-rotation
/me/recent/played
/me/recent/radio-stations

All requests for the Apple Music API are done via a Javascript Web Token (JWT).
In order to use the Apple Music API, there are a few steps that you need to conduct. The first is that you need to create Music ID. This is done via the Developer Portal, under Certificates, Identifiers, and Profiles.

Once you have an Apple Music ID configured, You then need to create a private key to be able to sign your Javascript Web Token. This is done in the Apple Developer Account page. The Javascript Web Token will need to be sent with all requests made the Apple Music API.

The key must be signed with an Elliptic Curve Digital Signature Algorithm, specifically P-256 curve and the SHA-256 hash algorithm. This will result in the ES256 Algorithm, which must be specified in the headers of the JWT file.

There are a variety of libraries available for creating a Javascript Token. You can go to jwt.io and locate one that will work.

After you have signed and encrypted the token, you will then be able to make a call to the endpoint that you would like to request information from. The results will be in an JSON encoded object. This object will need to be decoded and then you can proceed to act upon the received data.

If you need to request user-specific information, you will need to request a Music User Token. This token will be required to be sent with every request.

The Apple Music API will allow developers to create experiences for users that will work not just on their iOS devices, but also via the web. The capabilities of the Apple Music API are significant and can allow experiences that users will enjoy.

ARKit

One of the areas that Apple's CEO Tim Cook has stated is of interest for Apple is Augmented Reality. Augmented Reality is the idea of taking the existing world and placing virtual objects within it. When it comes to Augmented Reality there are a significant number of factors that must be taken into account. Things like plane detection, object recognition, object tracking, depth perception, and much much more. If you were to try and create a framework that encompasses all of this, ti would take a significant effort. Be glad, because Apple has created a framework called ARKit that makes it easier for developers to create Augmented Reality applications.

ARKit is a set of high-level APIs that has specific requirements in order to be used. Any iOS device that is going to use ARKit has to be one that contains an A9 processor, or higher. This is because of the requirements needed to be able to perform all of the necessary tasks at one time.

ARKit is comprised of three main areas, Tracking, Scene Understanding, and Rendering.

By combining camera images and motion data ARKit is ARKit is capable of tracking an iOS device's location in the current environment. The best thing about this capability is that there is no setup required. This means that there is no knowledge needed of the environment and no additional sensors are required.

The tracking of ARKit is needed for Scene understanding. Scene understanding is the task of being able to look at the environment and understand different aspects. This includes plane detection, hit-detection, which is the real world topology, and light estimation. Light estimation is the ability to correctly determine the light in a virtual environment. Light estimation includes the ability to render and/or correctly light the virtual environment to match the real world.

The last section is rendering. Rendering is the actual creation of the virtual environment. ARKit can use SceneKit or SpriteKit. ARKit can also use other rendering engines, like Unreal and Unity. Both Unity and Unreal will be supporting ARKit, so you can use those rendering engines if you are more comfortable with those.

ARKit is a session-based API. The procedure for creating an ARKit session are as follows:

1. Create the ARKit Session
2. Determine what type of tracking
3. Configure the session, using ARSessionConfiguration
    - Determine what tracking to run
    - Enabling and disabling properties
4. Run the session using ARSession.run().

The ARSession is an AVCaptureSession which will provide you all of the information needed. The ARSession will output an ARFrame, which will contain all of the elements that are needed to be able to render the Augmented Reality scene.

ARKit will allow developers to create various worlds, in reality anything that they can imagine. Augmented Reality is not a new concept, it has been around for a long time, and became mainstream with the game Pokémon Go for a while. Often when Apple releases a new framework they have implemented it within an application already. However, that is not the case with ARKit. Apple is leaving all of the ideas for developers to come up with and implement.

A similar framework to ARKit is the Metal framework. Let us look at that one next.

Metal 2

Metal is Apple's framework for performing computationally intensive tasks. When these tasks are needed they can often be parallelized. Parallelizing on a general Central Processing Unit, or CPU, is not ideal because CPUs are designed to do things in serial, not parallel. Serial being one thing at a time. There is a processor that is quite efficient for parallelized tasks, the Graphical Processing Unit, or GPU. This is where Metal really shines.

Metal 2 brings some new features with it. The biggest benefit being Argument Buffers. Argument Buffers are a new way of being able to aggregate all of the objects that you wish to generate and then put them into a single argument. Once you have this argument buffer, you can then send that entire buffer to the GPU to then draw the elements in the buffer. Ultimately, what this will do is reduce the number of calls that are needed in order to render a scene using Metal 2. Let us take this as an example.

Previously with Metal, you would put all of the states for your object into a Metal Buffer (MTBuffer), then you could set all of your textures and sampler and then actually draw your elements. These steps are required for each element you need to draw and all of this needs to be for reach frame. With Metal 2, argument buffers makes this disappear, in many cases.

By utilizing argument buffers, you are able to build a buffer of all of these elements and then you can sent the entire buffer to be drawn, but the buffer is not limited to constant items, they can be dynamically generated items as well. Argument buffers can be absolutely anything. This could be texture states, samplers and also pointers to more buffers into the argument buffer. This means that you can put more objects onto the screen in each frame. By putting everything into a large buffer, you will reduce the amount of time needed for each call. With Apple's testing, they found a 7x reduction in time for a simple buffer with 2 resources, with eight textures or buffers you get an 18x performance improvement. If you have sixteen resources the performance increase is almost 32x faster. This is due to only needing two API calls, set buffer and draw. Argument buffers will help simplify the rendering needed for any elements.

Argument buffers are available with all Metal-supported devices. This means that if they have an A7 Chip or newer, the device can use argument buffers. Significant improvements should be possible on even the oldest devices. This also means that the 4th Generation Apple TV should also support Argument Buffers, which could lead to even better game experiences on the Apple TV.

iOS devices, since their inception have all had a screen refresh rate of 60 frames per second. The 60 frames per second refresh rate is a pretty constant one for most displays, even non-Apple displays. With the release of the the 10.5-inch iPad Pro, and the 2nd Generation 12.9-inch iPad Pros, this has changed a bit. These devices now have a new feature called ProMotion. ProMotion is a concept that allows the output of the display to be up to 120 frames per second. These iPad Pros are the first devices to use ProMotion. To coincide with this new display, there are some things that developers must do to support ProMotion. To illustrate what happens, let us look at this example

60fps

		Frame		
GPU	1	2	3	
Display		1	2	3
Frame Time		16.6ms	16.6ms	16.6ms

120fps

	Frame		
GPU	1	2	3
Display		1	2	3
Frame Time		8.3ms	8.3ms	8.3ms

This means that you do not have nearly as much time to render a frame, however you now have more control over when the image is swapped. So, instead of having to refresh the image every frame, you can do ever other frame and get a frame rate closer to 60 frames per second. But what if you cannot achieve 60 frames per second, ProMotion can help here too. It can do a consistent output of a variety of refresh rates. This means that you can maximize your application's output and the display might be able to match.

If you want to opt-in to ProMotion, you will need to add a new key to the info.plist. That key is CADisableMinimumFrameDuration and is a boolean value. If you set it to yes, then ProMotion will be enabled.

When it comes to presenting images on a ProMotion display, There are three different presentation APIs available within Metal. "Present", "PresentWithMinimumDuration", and "PresentAtSpecificTime".

"Present" will indicate that you want your image to be displayed at the next refresh cycle. For non-ProMotion devices, this would be 16.6ms, but for ProMotion devices, this is 4ms. This is a straightforward call with no arguments.

"PresentWithMinimumDuration" will indicate that you want the image to be displayed for a specific duration. If the start time changes, so does the start time of the image being displayed. This means that you will get a consistent frame rate.

The last item, "PresentAtSpecificTime" does just as it indicates, it will display at a specific time. What this means is that the GPU is finished with its cycle before the specified time, the display will wait to show the request information. However, if the GPU rending is taking longer, then it will be displayed at the next possible refresh time, after the GPU has finished its previous task.

There is another new feature of Metal 2 on iOS, called Direct to Display. Direct to Display is a concept of being able to skip the compositing of UI elements. There is no key or info.plist item that immediately enables this. Instead, there are some application requirements that will allow the system to automatically determine when this is appropriate. The requirements are:

- Opaque Layers
- No Masking or rounded corner
- Full Screen, or a window with an opaque black background color
- Dimensions that match the display's native resolution, or smaller.
- Color Space and pixel format that is compatible with the display.

The last two are a bit tricky because iOS and macOS both have support for resolutions that allow the user to selectively scale the resolution. The last one is really difficult given the variety of displays available on iOS and macOS.

Metal 2 provides a number of improvements over the previous version. Argument buffers will allow your rendering times to be reduced by allowing you to pre-allocate buffers, in cases where it makes sense, and then sending that entire buffer to be drawn. The addition of ProMotion capabilities will allow you as a developer to optimize your application for the display. If you are capable of rendering 120 frames per second, then do so. However, if you cannot then creating a consistent frame rate is best, which ProMotion can assist with. Lastly, Direct to Display can help reduce the overall GPU time by providing you with the option of being able to skip the GPU and just go directly to the display to allow an even better user experience. Metal 2 is a a great improvement for those who need it. There is another new framework that is geared towards Machine Learning.

CoreML

One of the larger areas of investigation is the area of Machine Learning. Machine Learning is the idea of being able to train a computer to recognize particular objects. There are a variety of different approaches to machine learning. Apple has been using Machine Learning in some of its applications for a couple of years. The primary application that uses machine learning has been Photos.

Photos has the capability of processing your entire photo library and identifies items within the photos. This process allows users to search for an item and the search will reveal the results. This is all done via Machine Learning. Apple is extending the capability of Machine Learning to developers through a new framework called CoreML.

CoreML is designed to take pre-existing trained models and apply those models to other items. Through the trained model, if there is a match, it should be able to identify it. The training of these models occurs outside of the device. These models require thousands of lines of code to be able to function correctly. This is beyond the scope of what CoreML is capable of doing.

There are a couple of domain-specific areas that work with CoreML to assist with certain areas. These frameworks are Vision, Foundation, for Natural Language Processing, and GamePlayKit for evaluating learned decision trees.

The Vision framework is designed to be able to perform all of the tasks related to identifying objects, faces, Barcode Detection, Image Alignment Analysis, text detection, horizon detection, and Object Detection and Tracking.

These three frameworks are designed to be high-level and easy to use. However, if these do not meet your needs you can always drop down to use CoreML itself, along with the Accelerate, Basic Neural Network Subroutines, and Metal Performance shaders to do the computations for you.

If you do want to use Vision, the natural language processing, or GamePlayKit, you will need a model to do so. Apple supplies a tool to be able to convert existing models into CoreML compatible files.

Converting Models

The ability to use existing models within your iOS or macOS applications requires that existing trained models to be converted. This is done via a python toolset called coremltools. coremltools is designed to take existing models and covert them. The following table contains the model type, the support models, and which tools are supported for conversion using coremltools.

Model type	Supported models	Supported tools
Neural networks	Feedforward, convolutional, recurrent	Caffe Keras 1.2.2+
Tree ensembles	Random forests, boosted trees, decision trees	scikit-learn 0.18 XGBoost 0.6
Support vector machines	Scalar regression, multiclass classification	scikit-learn 0.18 LIBSVM 3.22

Model type	Supported models	Supported tools
Generalized linear models	Linear regression, logistic regression	scikit-learn 0.18
Feature engineering	Sparse vectorization, dense vectorization, categorical processing	scikit-learn 0.18
Pipeline models	Sequentially chained models	scikit-learn 0.18

Coremltools is hosted on the Python Package Index (PyPi). Converting the trained model is quite straightforward. You can do the following commands:

> import coremltools
> coreml_model = coremltools.converters.caffe.convert('my_caffe_model.caffemodel')

You then save the model with this command:

> coreml_model.save('my_model.mlmodel')

That is all that it takes to convert a pre-trained model to a model that can be used with CoreML.

CoreML will allow for all sorts of applications from developers. Some of these may include the ability to detect objects, or even processing language. CoreML will help usher in a new wave of different applications. One of the big areas for iOS 11 is Drag and Drop, that is what will be covered next.

Drag and Drop

Drag and Drop is one of the biggest changes to iOS 11, particularly for the iPad. Users will be expecting that the applications that they use on a regular basis support Drag and Drop. Even if your application uses only standard UI Elements, like TableViews, TextViews and TextFields, there may still be some work that needs to be done.

They key item to remember about Drag and Drop is that you, as the developer, do not get the actual data that is being dragged until after the user lifts up their finger to confirm that they intend to drop the data onto your application. This is by design to maintain the user's privacy, because the user could decide to not drop the data onto your application, at any point.

There are three primary concepts to understand about Drag and Drop. These concepts are:

- Drag Interaction
- Drop Proposals
- Performing the Drop

Each of these concepts has their own usage within the Drag and Drop Timeline. Let us look at the timeline now.

Time				
Touch	Begins	Stays Down	Moves	Ends

Time					
Drag and Drop	Lift	Drag	Perform	Drop Animations	
				Data Transfer	
			Cancel		

Drag Interaction

The Drag interaction is the beginning of an actual drag. A Drag interaction is attached to a view and it is very similar to a UIGestureRecognizer. The drag interaction's delegate provides the items that will be part of the drag. But these items are only provided when the view lifts, as in the user's interaction begins the drag.

The items that are included in a drag are called Drag Items. A drag item contains a drag preview and an item provider object. The Item provider is essentially a promise by the source application to deliver the items when it is requested to do so.

Enabling a drop is very straight forward. You can use a UIPasteConfiguration object. UIPasteConfiguration is a method of announcing to the system what types of files that your User Interface can either accept as a drop or when they are pasted in.

When the items are dragged over an app, the drag interaction's delegate is queried to see if the application is interested in the items. If it is, when the drop is performed, the source application will send representations of the source objects to the destination application. The information is then asynchronously transferred. In fact, for large files, APFS cloning is used to be able to instantly provide the data to the destination application. Once the data begins to be modified by the destination application, a copy of the file will actually be made and the space will be allocated.

The Drag Interaction delegate method is the only required method to be implemented for the drag interaction. The method returns an array of UIDragItems. UIDragItems need to be NSItemProviders, which must be objects. This means that you cannot use a Swift struct in a Drag item. It must be cast to another type that is an object. That covers the Drag portion, now let us look at the Drop portion

Dropping Items

Dropping Items is what occurs when a Touch Up action occurs, while a set of DragItems is hovering over a UIView.

There is a function that must be implemented on the "Drop" portion of Drag and Drop. This is the dropInteraction:SessionDidUpdate method. This method returns a UIDropProposal, with an operation that is a UIDropOperation. This method is called both when a set of DragItems is initially dragged over a UIView, but also when it they are dragged within a UIView.

A UIDropOperation is an enum struct with four possible values:

- Cancel
- Copy
- Move
- Forbidden

Cancel is indicating that you do not want that data, and the action should be cancelled.

Copy indicates that you will copy the data that is dropped. Copy is the most common action when it comes to acting up on the data that is being dragged. This is the default action for drop operations.

Move means that the data that you will receive will be moved from its source. Move is an interesting one. Since the information is meant to be moved, the developer needs to indicate to the user that the data is supposed to moved. UIKit is not capable of doing this for the developer. There are a few restrictions on this. First, this is only available within a single application. This cannot be used between applications. Secondly, your Drag delegate must allow the option to move data. If it does not, the move will not succeed.

Forbidden is the same as cancel, however an additional badge will be added to the Drag Items to indicate to the user that the drop operation cannot occur here.

Performing the Actual Drop

The last step in the Drag and Drop operation is the actual copy or move operation. This does not occur until the Drop has occurred.

The method to implement is the dropInteraction(interaction:performDrop) method. This method is the only location where the data itself can be loaded. There are two different approaches for loading the objects from the session.

The first is using a method on the session object; session.loadObjects(ofClass: [ClassType]). This method provides a closure that will be called when the objects are available. This will allow you to iterate over the objects with that class, and then perform an action on them. Since this is done on the main queue, you will be able to update the user interface as necessary.

The second method is a bit more complex. You start by iterating over the items in the session. You can then use the UIItemProvider to load the object. This method is done on a background queue, meaning that you must dispatch back to the main queue if you want to update the user interface. This method is great if you have additional processing to do on the objects you can do it using this method.

That should cover the basics of drag an drop. There a variety of other methods that will help enhance each of the steps of the Drag and Drop. Some of these include:

- Item Previews
- Animation of the User interface when a Drag, or Drop, occurs
- Cancel animation

There is one last item that is sent to you Drop Delegate. That item is the progress of the data transfer. With this information you can either retrieve the progress for individual items, or the progress for the entire session. You can then provide a progress bar to let the user know how the transfer is progressing.

Final Thoughts on Drag and Drop

Drag and Drop is a core concept within iOS 11. It is the basis for many of the interactions that occur on the platform. This includes the moving of applications within Springboard. Drag and Drop will allow you, as the developer, to create an interactive experience for users where they will not realize that they are performing a standard task, like importing files.

Drag and drop is a crucial aspect to implement if your application deals with files. Drag and Drop functionality is something that iOS 11 users will quickly begin to expect from their applications. To create the best experience possible, it is ideal to animate both the drag interactions as well as the drop animations. This will allow your users to understand what the end result will be once they let go of the data that they are dragging.

Networking Changes

One of the areas where developers do not generally concern themselves with is changes in Networking. If you use any sort of web-based activity in your application then any changes to networking should be something that you should be cognizant about.

If you were around when the World Wide Web really began taking off during the mid 1990s, you only needed to know about one type of IP address, IPv4. IPv4 is a 32-bit address that is capable of providing 4.2 billion addresses. When IPv4 was first developed in 1980, the idea of having four billion devices on a single network was outlandish. However, when the web exploded during the 1990s it became apparent that IPv4's successor would need to be formalized. The result was IPv6.

IPv6 allows for 128-bit addressing. This means that there are exactly 340,282,366,920,938,463,463,374,607,431,768,211,456 possible addresses. For the time being, 340 undecillion, and change, addresses should suffice. What this means for iOS developers is that they should make sure that their applications work on iPv6 networks. This can be done in a few different ways.

The first way is to use Apple's built-in higher-level frameworks when connecting to a URL. These frameworks are URLSession and CFNetwork. Both of these frameworks have native IPv6 addressing support.

Secondly, avoid IPv4-only frameworks. If you are using a framework that does not support IPv6, it is highly advised that you adopt a framework that does support IPv6. There are a few reasons why this is the case.

The first is that excluding connectivity to IPv6 will result in excluding a large segment of your population. This is because there are large areas of the world where the default networking is IPv6. This includes:

- Belgium at 49%

- United States at 32%
- United Kingdom at 17%
- India at 23%
- Japan at 18%

And these are just some of the areas that have IPv6 only networks.

The second reason is that all updates and new submissions to the app store must now support IPv6. Apple tests all updates for this and if your application, or update, does not support IPv6, it will not be allowed in the store.

It is highly advised that you support IPv6 in your applications. If you use either NSURLSession or CFNetwork, then you do not have to do anything differently. There are some other changes regarding Networking.

Network Stack Changes

The Network Stack is comprised of seven different layers, if you are using the OSI model for networks. These layers are:

Layer 7	Application
Layer 6	Presentation
Layer 5	Session
Layer 4	Transport
Layer 3	Network
Layer 2	Datagram
Layer 1	Physical

Most developers never need to deal with anything below layer 3. When a developer does interact with a particular layer, there is one thing that they are usually not aware of. That is whether that layer is located within the Kernel Space of memory or the User Space of memory. This is because the operating system will handle any need to enter into Kernel Memory space, on behalf of the user. However, when a switch is needed to get information from the Kernel memory space when the application is in the User memory space, this does take some time to occur. It may only be microseconds, but the act of context switching does have some cost to it. With iOS 10, and previous versions of iOS, this is how the model looked.

	Layer	Memory Space
HTTP/TLS	Application Layer	User
TCP/IP	Transport Layer	Kernel
Wi-Fi	Network(Interface) Layer	Kernel

Under iOS 11, if you are using URLSession on tvOS, iOS, or watchOS, this is how the model will look.

	Layer	Memory Space
HTTP/TLS	Application Layer	User
TCP/IP	Transport Layer	User
Wi-Fi	Network(Interface) Layer	Kernel

The TCP/IP transport layer has moved into User Space. It should be noted that this will only be implemented provided you are not using BSD Sockets. If you are utilizing BSD sockets, then the old model is still in effect. This change does have some ramifications.

The first thing is that the Protocol stack is now unified within an application. This means that there will be less switching between User Memory and Kernel Memory when going to between the Application and Transport Layer.

The second ramification is that Network Kernel extensions will be going away in the future. This should only affect macOS, but it is still something to be cognizant about.

These changes should allow for a more secure set of applications because any issues that may arise within the Application or

Transport layers will be confined to User Memory space, which cannot affect the system. There are a few other additions for networking, in the form of extensions.

New Network Extensions

There are a couple of new additions for Network Extensions. They are NEHotspotConfiguration and NEDNSProxyProvider.

The first is a new option is NEHotspotConfiguration. NEHotspotConfiguration is designed to allow you to simply connecting to a Wi-Fi Hotspot. This could be something like passing networking information between two devices. The connections you make can be temporary or persistent. NEHotspotConfiguration supports a variety of authentication schemes including:

- Open
- WEP
- WPA
- EAP
- Hotspot 2.0

NEHotspotConfiguration can be particularly helpful when connecting to Smart Devices from an iOS app, or if you need to be able to connect to a device in order to do some configuration.

The second new extension, the NEDNSProxyProvider is an extension that allows you to intercept the system's DNS queries. Once you begin a DNS Proxy you can do what you would like with the requests. This could something like sending the queries over TLS, or even over HTTP. The possibilities are endless. One possible application is for secure web-browsing.

These two network extensions will allow devices to be configured much easier and NEDNSProxyProvider will allow applications to intercept DNS queries so they can be handled as the application deems necessary.

Final Thoughts on Networking Changes

Even though networking is used all of the time, without really being aware of it, it is an important aspect to any operating system. The changes made within iOS 11 will allow better security with moving the Transport layer to User memory space, and supporting IPv6 will allow applications to reach the greatest number of users, given that there are some networks that are IPv6 only.

The new network extension NEHotspotConfiguration will allow simplified connections to devices where the NEDNSProxyProvider extension will allow DNS queries to be intercepted to provide an even better application experience for users.

Final Thoughts on iOS 11 for Developers

iOS 11 brings a ton of new features for not just users, but also developers. Developers can now support big features like Drag and Drop within their applications. Drag and Drop will allow developers to move information between applications on an iPad, or within the same application on an iPhone or iPod Touch. Enabling Drag and Drop will allow developers to create experiences for their users that provide a natural interaction within the application.

The addition of Augmented Reality with ARKit will allow developers to create applications that can help users be more productive, or to create alternative worlds that will allow users to interact with a developer's vision.

The area of Machine learning is still a nascent and upcoming sector of technology that allows developers to take trained models, convert them to a model that CoreML can understand, and the use those models within their applications. The addition of somewhat easily implemented machine learning to iOS applications provides developers with more possibilities for features within applications.

Swift 4 brings a few new features to the language. Most notably the entirely re-written functions with Strings. The new string functions allow developers to more easily get parts of strings. This is a significant improvement since getting parts of string is a consistent task done by developers. The new substring type is not the only new feature revolving around strings. Unicode characters will now be properly counted as a single character, even when there is more than one unicode point within the character.

On the topic of Unicode characters, there are also some changes to the Apple File System that may affect some aspects of developer's applications. This only comes into affect when Unicode characters within files names.

The changes to Xcode 9 will allow developers to more easily collaborate with users with the integration of GitHub to Xcode. The ability to search commits, projects and metadata right from within Xcode will make developers even more productive. Similarly, being able to open a GitHub repository directly from the web will also help developers be able to quickly get started.

The new MusicKit API will allow developers to provide better experiences for users. This includes the ability to pull information about albums, artists, playlists and more. Additionally developers can change ratings on a user's behalf, provide recommendations, and just about anything else that a developer can come up with regarding music.

The ability to use images that work on both Display P3 as well as being able to use Colors sets for both sRGB and Display P3 will make providing the best color for the different types of devices. The added ability to use the named colors, and have the color automatically be display the proper color will make development for so many developers that much easier. This is particularly necessary more so today, since there are even more devices that support the Display P3 color gamut.

Every release of iOS brings with it even more features than can be covered for developers. Apple's developer resources will help developers learn about the new APIs, along with some sample code.

watchOS 4 for Developers

watchOS 4 builds on the already existing watchOS platform to provide developers additional capabilities to improve their watchOS applications. There are a few new capabilities within watchOS specifically for developers. Let us start with Groups

Groups

Everything with watchOS is typically done via a group. A "group" is a collection of user interface elements that are used in conjunction. watchOS 3 had two options, "vertical" and "horizontal" groupings.

If you used a "vertical" group, each element would be aligned vertically in the interface. Similarly, the "horizontal" grouping would align each element horizontally. There is a new group option, "overlay".

The "overlay" group will allow elements to be overplayed on one top of the other. There are some limitations with this. The "overlap" selection does not compute offsets for each element, as would happen with vertical or horizontal groupings. This means that each element is laid out according to its individual settings of "top", "bottom", "left" and "right". This provides a more absolute layouts within the group.

Additionally, groups can be nested inside others, which will provide more complex layouts. When nesting groups, you can determine z-order by setting it. This means that you, as the developer, will have more control over the order that the groups appear, which allows you to provide the desired output that you are hoping to achieve. There is another new feature, water lock.

Water Lock

The Series 2 Apple Watch is water resistant up to 50 meters, this means that if you want to go for a swim, or jump in the pool, you absolutely can without fearing of damaging your Apple Watch.

This is counter to what many have come to understand about electronics. One of the downsides to having a water resistant electronic device that incorporates a screen is that there is the potential for errant taps on the screen. Luckily, Apple thought of this with the original Apple Watch and incorporated a Water Lock feature.

Water Lock will allow Apple Watch users to disable all input to the Apple Watch, to avoid any accidentally taps whilst in the water. The downside to the way that it has been done for watchOS 1 to watchOS 3 is that the user had to go back to the home screen, slide their finger up from the bottom of the screen to bring up Control Center and then tap on the "Water Lock" button. While this worked in a decent enough manner, but is indeed a long way to perform a simple task. This changes a bit with watchOS 4.

With watchOS 4, developers can now include a Water Lock button within their application and it will perform the same action as the Control Center Water Lock. There are a couple of things to be aware of regarding Water Lock. Developers can trigger Water to be enabled, but cannot disable it.. The Water Lock must be explicitly removed by the user. This is to allow the user to determine when to disable Water Lock. The second thing to know is that Water Lock can only be enabled while the app is in the foreground, if a developer attempts to call Water Lock while in the background, the call will fail.

Water Lock is simple to enable there is only one line of code needed.

> WKExtension.shared().enableWaterLock().

That is the entire code necessary for enabling Water Lock within an app. Providing a Water Lock button within your app, particularly if it is a workout app, will go a long way to providing a good user experience. There is another new feature which may be helpful for some.

Autorotate

One of the features that iOS has had for a long time is the ability to rotate the device and have the screen rotate as well. This is not possible on watchOS 3. However, with watchOS 4, it is now possible to enable within your app.

To enable rotation you need to do the following.

> WKExtension.shared().isAutorotating().

Again that is all of the code that is necessary. When you enable this, the entire screen will automatically rotate when your users rotate their wrist. There is another new feature for watchOS 4 for developers to use, if they need it.

Paging Views

Traditionally when using watchOS, many of the ways to scroll have been horizontal. There have been situations where scrolling vertically would make a bit more sense. For these times the use of Scroll View would be work. Yet, there are times that while it would work, it does not make the most logical sense. For the times there is the new Vertical Paging View.

A vertical Paging View is exactly the same as a horizontal Paging View, except the orientation is vertical. This makes the ability to separate content that would work best transitioning vertically feel more realistic and fluid, even on a small screen. A good example might be scrolling through Mail, or browsing a hierarchy of data where going up the hierarchy, or down as the case may be, allows the user to keep track of where they are going.

There is another side benefit of Paging Views.

Setting a Page Index

There are those instances when you as developer would love to be able to display a specific page within your app. This could be because a user requested a specific page, or because you would like to provide the best experience possible when it comes to handing items off from one device to another. This is now a possibility with watchOS 4.

The ability to set an index is done on the reloadRootPageControllers method. Here is an example:

```
func loadPage(variable: String)
{
        wkInterfaceController.reloadRootPageControllers(
            withNames: ["page1", "page2"],
            contexts: nil,
            orientation: .vertical,
            pageIndex: 0
        )
}
```

You can set the page Index to whichever index is appropriate. This is also the location where you would set the orientation to be horizontal or vertical, depending on which orientation makes the most sense for your watchOS app.

Other watchOS Changes

There have been a couple of other changes within watchOS 4.

SceneKit and SpriteKit

watchOS is based on iOS, and iOS has two frameworks SceneKit and SpriteKit. Both of these have been ported to watchOS prior to watchOS 4. When you used either SceneKit or SpriteKit under watchOS 3, you were only given part of the screen to work with. This did not make for the best experience for users. Now with watchOS 4, you are given the option of using the entire screen for your SceneKit or SpriteKit animations. The time will also be displayed in the upper right corner and it will overlay your scene.

Workouts

There have been some changes around workouts as well. The first is that you can now respond to Pause/Resume actions, where the user presses the digital crown and the side of the Apple Watch. This should make it easer for third-party workout applications to work a bit more like the native Workout app.

The second change around workouts routes. Users can already track their workout routes using the official Workout app, but third-party developers can now gain access to this same information, provided that a user gives explicit permission to do so.

CoreBluetooth

There is one last change for developers, watchOS 4 now has a full complement of CoreBluetooth. This new functionality will allow developers to connect to Bluetooth enabled devices directly to the Apple Watch and interact with them via an app on the Apple Watch.

Final Thoughts on watchOS 4 for Developers

Given the limited real estate available on an Apple Watch, the changes that have been made to watchOS 4 only enhance the operating system for the Watch. The new Autorotate feature will allow displaying of an Apple Watch app to others easier, while Water Lock within applications will stop any errant taps from occurring. The new Paging Views will allow data that lends itself to being scrolled in a vertical manner to be displayed a such.

The addition of CoreBluetooth should allow developers to create even better experiences by interacting with hardware that users already have. Even though these are all small feature, they do help the overall experience.

tvOS 11 for Developers

tvOS is Apple's newest operating system, and one of the more specialized operating systems. The new features within tvOS 11 are the smallest, in terms of numbers, but they should help anyone developing a tvOS application. Let us start with changes around On Demand Resources

On Demand Resources

On Demand Resources, or ODR, is a huge boon for tvOS applications. On Demand Resources breaks up tvOS applications into two parts, the App Bundle and the Assets. On Demand Resources live on the iTunes servers, which allows Apple to Under tvOS 10, the limit for the App Bundle was 200 megabytes.

This limit was in place to allow applications to download to the Apple TV fast. With the initial application downloading faster, users would be able to start using the application right away. This did have a downside though.

If you had a game that required game levels, and the game levels were too large to fit into the 200 megabyte limit, the user would have to sit and wait for those to download. To accommodate this, Apple increased the initial limit under tvOS 10.2 to be 4 gigabytes. This is twenty times larger than the previous size. This greatly increased the amount of that could be initially downloaded. It did increase initial download times, but having a better user experience is ultimately the better trade off.

There are a couple of other items related to On Demand Resources. The first is tags. On Demand Resources are identified via tags. There are the Initial Install tags. Install Tags are the resources that would initially be downloaded upon install. These are capped at two gigabytes. The second set of tags are the prefetch tags. These are the resources that will be downloaded after installation, and after the assets that have an "install" tag assigned.

The size of the "install" and "prefetch" tags is a total of four gigabytes. The total size of all of your on demand resources is twenty gigabyte. This means that an application bundle plus all of its on demand resources can be a total of twenty four gigabytes.

Right to Left Language Support

One of the areas that many developers to not think about is the direction that a language is written. This is because a vast majority of languages are written going from left to right, just like the text within this book. However, there are a few languages where this is not the case and instead these languages are written from the right to the left. A couple of examples of this are Hebrew and Arabic. Right to Left language support has been in iOS and macOS for quite a while. It is now coming to tvOS. The way that it is implemented is the same as on iOS and macOS, so if you are already used to supporting Right to Left languages on either of those platforms, it should be easy enough to implement on tvOS as well.

Safe Areas

One of the aspects to modern television is the concept of "overscan". Overscan is when a television does not display all of the possible pixels and instead cuts off some of these pixels. This is a standard practice with many cable providers. Under tvOS 10, the process of compensating for Overscan was a manual one. As the developer, you would have to manually inset your content. While this did indeed work, it was a lot of work for developers and it could cause some issues. To address this tvOS 11 changes the workflow with a new concept called "Safe Areas".

Safe Areas are just that, safe areas. To be more precise, Safe Areas are defined areas that you tell tvOS it is safe to display content. There are a couple of items that are updated automatically.

UIView.safeAreaInsets and UIView.safeAreaLayoutGuide. These are both updated automatically for you. The .safeAreaInsets will change when the view enters and leaves the view hierarchy and the .safeAreaLayoutGuide will update as the safe area insets change.

If you need to add a but more customization there is a method for that as well. UIViewController.additionalSafeAreaInsets. If you specify any additional insets, they will automatically be added into the .safeAreaInsets when those are calculated.

By default, linking against tvOS 11 will have your app use these new methods. However, there are those times when you need to manually handle all of this. There is an option for opting out of the new Safe Area Insets behavior.

Opting Out of Safe Area Insets

If you need to opt out of Safe Area Insets, you can do so with an individual view, or with an entire view controller. For the view, the code is:

view.insetsLayoutMarginsFromSafeArea = false.

Similarly, if you are opting an entire view controller out of the safe area insets, the code is as follows:

viewController.viewRespectsSystemMinimumLayoutMargins = false

By specifying these, tvOS 11 will need to manually handle the insets. There is a specific view controller type that can be set as well, and those are scroll views. The code for opting out of the Safe Area Insets on a scroll view is:

scrollView.contentInsetAdjustmentBehavior = .never

Again, this will allow your Scroll View to manually handle the insets. Using Safe Area Insets will allow your app to specify where the content can be shown. However, if you still need to retain some manual control, this is possible as well. Let us turn to notifications on tvOS 11.

Notifications on tvOS 11

Notifications are an important aspect to any Apple platform. While foreground notifications are more prevalent on iOS than on tvOS, they still have their place on tvOS. With the introduction of tvOS 10, Apple brought the UserNotification Framework over to tvOS from iOS and watchOS. Having the ability to send notifications is an important feature for keeping content up to date on tvOS. Even with this, it did have some downsides.

The biggest downside to Notifications on tvOS 10 was that if multiple notifications came in while an app was in the background, only the last notification would be acted upon when a user started up the application. This did not provide the best user experience, particularly if the notification was providing some data that could have been downloaded in the background. With tvOS 11 this behavior is changing.

Notifications on tvOS 11 will now wake up your tvOS app in the background for every notification that comes in. This means that if there is data that can be downloaded in the background, the data will be downloaded. Additionally, this means that every notification will be delivered to your application, which should ultimately provide a better user experience.

There are two different notification types. The first type is a Silent Notification. Silent Notifications are just that, silent. They are transparent to the user and allow you to download data in the background, update your application's data, or even setup a local notification for once the application has entered into the foreground.

The second type of notification is the "Background Fetch" notification. The Background Fetch notifications will as the name says, they will fetch data in the background. Background Fetch notifications are slightly different than silent notifications. They differ in the fact that when you register for background fetch notifications, tvOS will schedule when to wake up your app to download the data. This will allow tvOS to coalesce the retrieval of information and create a better overall experience, particularly if the user is using the Apple TV at the time.

The ability to use enhanced notifications will provide a better user experience for users.

Wireless Development

One of the more difficult aspects to developing a tvOS application is that the Apple TV must be connected to your Mac in order for development to occur.

There are two different method for configuring your Apple TV for Wireless Development. The first should work, and is quite straight forward and exactly the same as iOS.

1. Connect the Apple TV to your Mac.
2. Open Xcode 9.
3. Click on the Window menu.
4. Click on "Devices and Simulators", or hold down Shift, Command, and hit the number 2, to open Devices and Simulators.
5. Click on the Apple TV on the left.
6. Click on the checkbox titled "Connect via network". It will take a few seconds, but the device will be configured for wireless development.

That should be all it takes to enable an Apple TV as a wireless destination. Just like for iOS devices, a globe icon should appear next to the Apple TV to indicate that Wireless Development is enabled. For some reason if this does not work, as it did not work for me, there is an alternative method. The second procedure is as follows:

1. Open Xcode
2. Click on Window
3. Click on Devices and Simulators to bring up all of the connected devices.
4. On your Apple TV, go to the Settings.
5. Go to Remotes and Devices.
6. Go to Remote App and Devices screen. This screen should show any connected Remote apps, or other devices that are connected to the Apple TV.

7. On your mac, the Apple TV should appear again in the Devices and Simulators Window
8. Select the Apple TV device
9. Enter in the six digit code that is displayed on the Apple TV.

The process to complete should take a couple of minutes. Once complete the Apple TV should be listed in the destinations within Xcode. You should now be able to develop tvOS applications without the need for wires.

The ability to develop a tvOS application without needing to be physically connected should allow developers to more easily create tvOS applications. One of the side benefits of this is that you, as the developer, are able to sit the same distance away as your users will when they are using the app. This means that you should be able to create a better user interface.

The second benefit for tvOS development will be for teams who are developing a tvOS application. This is because all of the interested parties can gather around in a conference room and the Apple TV can be wirelessly connected to, and everyone can discuss the development.

It may be a small feature, but enabling Wireless Development for the Apple TV should boost productivity for everyone. Although there are likely times when a developer accidentally set as an Apple TV as a destination instead of a simulator and it interrupts someone who is currently using the Apple TV.

☑ Show as run destination
☑ Connect via network

Take Screenshot
View Device Logs

Final Thoughts on tvOS 11 for Developers

While tvOS 11 may not bring a bunch of new user features, users should notice some of the changes that developers have access to. In particular the notification updates will allow developers to choose what type of notification to use to best suit their application. The increased size of on-demand resources will allow even more content to be initially bundled with an application, which should allow better first-run experiences for any asset-rich application. The Right to Left language support will be a benefit to those users who want to use their Apple TV with a Right-to-Left language like Hebrew or Arabic. The new safe areas insets will allow developers the ability to specify exactly where content can be shown. While the new wireless development capability of tvOS 11 will not have any direct impact on users, it will allow developers to build a better app by allowing them to sit at the same distances as their users to make sure all interactions are finely tuned. The changes to tvOS 11 should provide an even better base going forward for the Apple TV.

Final Thoughts on iOS 11, tvOS 11, and watchOS 4

The iPhone is celebrating a decade of existence and during that time ti has been a driving force for change not just for phones, but also for technology in general. The iPhone has pushed other technology companies to keep pace with not just the hardware, but also the software. iOS 11 brings even more for Apple's competitors to compete on.

iOS 11 pushes iOS even further, particularly for iPad Users. iOS 11 provides features like Drag and Drop. Drag and Drop will help users on the iPad to not only be more productive, but also to use their iPads more intuitively. iPhone users are not left out of the Drag and Drop, as they can use it within applications; where it makes sense. The redesigned Split View and Dock for the iPad will allow users to customize their experience with iOS.

The redesigned Control Center interface provides users with more control over shortcuts to many of the system functions. Users are also notified when an application is using their location in the background, with a bright blue banner at the top of the screen. The user can then immediately see which application is using the location services. Similarly, on the iPad users are able to determine which applications are to be used together and be even more productive than they were before, because the groupings stay until the user changes them.

The new Dock for iPad on iOS 11 will allow a user to customize which applications are the most important to them, provided there are 15 or fewer applications that a user thinks are super important. The Dock customization is not the end of the ability to customize an iOS device under iOS 11. Users can also customize Control Center to add the features they use the most to ultimately be able to access those functions as quickly as they would like.

iOS 11 brings with it future looking concepts. Some are ones that users will absolutely notice, like ARKit. ARKit will allow developers to include virtual objects that appear in the real world. Even though Apple does not have an Augmented Reality app of its own, there are a couple of companies already on board, Niantic, the creators of Pokémon Go, and the furniture giant, Ikea.

There is another forward-looking feature that uses may notice, but only if their applications need to be updated; that is the removal of 32-bit application support from iOS 11. The removal of 32-bit applications will not only slim down iOS, freeing up more space for users, but it provides a cut-off point for applications that are not being updated. This change provides iOS with a solid base for the future.

iOS 11 also brings some behind the curtains types of features, ones that users may benefit from but may not truly realize they are benefitting from them. One of the is CoreML. CoreML will allow developers to provide new experiences by being able to use existing machine learning within iOS applications.

There are other user-facing features that have been updated includes Notes, with its new tables feature, scanned documents, and even the ability to PIN notes for quick access have all been added. Photos has also seen a couple of improvements, most notably with being able to add some effects to Live Photos as well as tagged face data being synchronized to all of your devices. iOS is not the only operating system to see some improvements.

watchOS has also added some nice features just for users. The new Toy Story watch face will allow some playfulness to be added to your Apple Watch. You can also be a bit more proactive with the Siri Watch face, which will provide a way to giving you notifications based upon your location. The new ability to toggle between the traditional honeycomb layout and the new list view will make it easer for some users to be able to find the applications that they are looking for. The ability to connect to exercise equipment at the gym will mean that users will be able to get even more information to help with their exercise routines. Swimmers will be able to keep track of their laps and rest time, while anyone will be able to add a new workout to their routine with just a swipe and a tap. The updates to watchOS are great, particularly for those on the go or on the move.

The last operating system to get updated is tvOS. tvOS only gains a couple of features, Most notably the ability to have tvOS 11 automatically switch between Light mode and Dark mode depending on the time of day. The most notable other user feature is the ability to synchronize your home screen. This will synchronize to iCloud and means that if you get a new Apple TV all of your existing apps and data will be able to be synchronized to the device.

Users are not the only group to see some improvements, developers have also seen some significant improvements in their tools, with both Swift and Xcode 9. Swift 4 brings some new opportunities with the reworked Strings type and its companion substrings type. Swift 4 also brings the ability to select both controls as well as protocol conformance. This will be big for developers who need this functionality.

Swift 4 also brings the ability to connect to bluetooth devices like Lego Mindstorms to Swift Playgrounds. This will allow students to see the fruits of their labors right in front of their eyes, which should provide even more reinforcement.

Xcode, the primary mechanism for developers, is seeing a significant number of updates, from being able to download their development profiles, to the significant integration of GitHub into Xcode. GitHub integration should improve not only a developer's workflow, but also help them be able to collaborate for more individuals. The ability to open an Xcode Project right from within Safari will be a big boost to productivity.

There are other integrations as well with Xcode Server. Xcode Server being integrated into Xcode 9 means that developers will not need to be server administrators just to configure something that will assist in their work. If you use continuous integration with Xcode 9 and have devices directly connected, the devices will be used to automatically build the application and test it on device, which may find some unforeseen issues with your build.

The new Code editor will help developers not only to be able to scroll through their code, since the window is fifty times faster, but they can also use to create readme files using the Markdown syntax.

Xcode 9 provides access to new frameworks, like Metal 2. Metal 2 provides a huge improvement with Argument buffers. Argument buffers will not work with any Mac, but for those that do support Argument buffers, you should see significant improvement in drawing.

iOS 11, tvOS 11, and watchOS 4 are all fantastic updates. They are available today and they are all free updates. If you use an iPad at all, iOS 11 is a must download.

www.ingramcontent.com/pod-product-compliance
Lightning Source LLC
Chambersburg PA
CBHW050155230526
45470CB00001B/103